COMPUTER SCIENCE, TECHNOLOGY AND APPLICATIONS

ADVANCES IN SECURITY INFORMATION MANAGEMENT

PERCEPTIONS AND OUTCOMES

COMPUTER SCIENCE, TECHNOLOGY AND APPLICATIONS

Additional books in this series can be found on Nova's website
under the Series tab.

Additional e-books in this series can be found on Nova's website
under the e-book tab.

COMPUTER NETWORKS

Additional books in this series can be found on Nova's website
under the Series tab.

Additional e-books in this series can be found on Nova's website
under the e-book tab.

COMPUTER SCIENCE, TECHNOLOGY AND APPLICATIONS

ADVANCES IN SECURITY INFORMATION MANAGEMENT

PERCEPTIONS AND OUTCOMES

GUILLERMO SUÁREZ DE TANGIL

AND

ESTHER PALOMAR

EDITORS

nova publishers

New York

NOTICE TO THE READER

The Publisher has taken reasonable care in the preparation of this book, but makes no expressed or implied warranty of any kind and assumes no responsibility for any errors or omissions. No liability is assumed for incidental or consequential damages in connection with or arising out of information contained in this book. The Publisher shall not be liable for any special, consequential, or exemplary damages resulting, in whole or in part, from the readers' use of, or reliance upon, this material. Any parts of this book based on government reports are so indicated and copyright is claimed for those parts to the extent applicable to compilations of such works.

Independent verification should be sought for any data, advice or recommendations contained in this book. In addition, no responsibility is assumed by the publisher for any injury and/or damage to persons or property arising from any methods, products, instructions, ideas or otherwise contained in this publication.

This publication is designed to provide accurate and authoritative information with regard to the subject matter covered herein. It is sold with the clear understanding that the Publisher is not engaged in rendering legal or any other professional services. If legal or any other expert assistance is required, the services of a competent person should be sought. FROM A DECLARATION OF PARTICIPANTS JOINTLY ADOPTED BY A COMMITTEE OF THE AMERICAN BAR ASSOCIATION AND A COMMITTEE OF PUBLISHERS.

Additional color graphics may be available in the e-book version of this book.

Library of Congress Cataloging-in-Publication Data

ISBN: 978-1-62417-204-5

Published by Nova Science Publishers, Inc. † *New York*

CONTENTS

PREFACE

Network security is still a critical task that involves different disciplines aimed at proactively protecting, preventing, and swiftly responding to attacks. However, the classic management-related flaws still persist, e.g. the analysis of large amounts of reported intrusion alerts, whilst coexisting with novel problematic issues such as the integration of many heterogeneous sensing interfaces.

Security information and event management (SIEM) then appears as the new paradigm to reconcile traditional intrusion detection systems along to recent advanced techniques such as event collection, aggregation, analysis, management and correlation. For instance, research works have recently thrived important advances on SIEM such as those to enhance any task by providing intelligent learning as well as reducing the intervention of operators significantly. However, intrusion techniques are more and more sophisticated to evade detection and this still poses many security challenges in terms of networks threats. Also, critical infrastructure protection is at stake due to the spreading use of interconnected networks.

This book brings together the most novel research findings and the latest advances in security information management as well as compiling deeply settled technologies. The book firstly establishes the fundamentals of SIEM technology in the first part, and finally, new trends are explored in the second part.

More precisely, the first part examines the main sources of information used by SIEMs, the importance of vulnerability assessment and asset inventory for a secure configuration of an organization. Additionally, the complexity of multistage attack detection, importance of cooperation approaches to SIEM and impact of the processing performance is examined as well.

The second part further elaborate on recent approaches to improve correlation especially based on complex event processing, honeypot forensics, and artificial immune systems. Hence, a new generation of SIEM systems is presented for critical infrastructure protection; and a novel adversarial model is studied based on the evasion of SIEM components.

This book will be useful not only for researchers, academics, developers and engineers at Universities, research centers, and in industry, but also for students in the field of security information management and its novel advances.

Guillermo Suárez-Tangil
Carlos III University of Madrid (Spain).
guillermo.suarez.tangil@uc3m.es

Esther Palomar
Carlos III University of Madrid (Spain).
epalomar@inf.uc3m.es

In: Advances in Security Information Management   ISBN: : 978-1-62417-204-5
Editor: G. Suarez-Tangil and E. Palomar   © 2013 Nova Science Publishers, Inc.

Chapter 1

SECURITY INFORMATION AND EVENT MANAGEMENT SYSTEMS ... A NEED IN THE REAL WORLD

Cristian Ruvalcaba*
Mountain View, California, US

Abstract

Security Information Event Management (SIEM) systems are becoming more commonplace in the corporate world. Generally, they are deployed in a plug–n–play fashion and used for fulfilling auditory requirements. Though each organization is different, there are common points and processes that can be followed in order to ensure the proper use and maximum return on investment in the acquired tools, being the SIEM devices central points for the analytical tasks.

Basically, SIEM devices collect logs from a series of the security appliances and applications deployed over the organization's network. Amongst their numerous advantages, SIEM devices have the ability to aggregate the reported logs in correlation with each other in order to assist the analyst in determining which of the security events should take a higher priority. The establishment of this priority is mostly based on the nature, source and severity level of the events. Apart from the logs reported from dedicated security appliances, logs from any other system and application are also sent to SIEM collectors to reach a more complete snapshot of the current state of the environment. The correlation of these logs provides higher reliability and accuracy of the events, and potentially decrease the number of security incidents.

Keywords: **SIEM**: Security Information and Event Management Systems

1. Introduction

On September 11, 2001, two commercial airliners were used as weapon projectiles to bring down the World Trade Center towers in New York City. A third was flown into the Pentagon

---

*E-mail address: cristian_ruvalcaba@intuit.com

and a fourth was brought down by the actions of its passengers, protecting an additional target. This is the single, most significant attack against the United States to date.

Years of investigation and fact gathering produced *The 9-11 Commission Report* which found that threat intelligence had been found by different organizations and some of it was escalated to the proper authorities, but may have been ignored. Each intelligence organization had, up to that point, been working on independently gathering information, but there was no process in place to share the information across these agencies. The lack of resources and proper tools for evaluating threats became evident after this attack. This prompted the creation of the Department of Homeland Security, the goal of which, was centralizing intelligence gathering in order to assess and take action on credible threats.

After almost a decade in information security, I have run across a number of different incidents that were not resolved in their beginning stages, but rather, only after they had brought about some sort of damage to an information system. Individual security tools helped to escalate some events, but failed to address the actual threat. This was the result of effective event correlation.

Security Information Event Management (SIEM) systems are designed to gather event information from security tools and formulate a prioritized collection of incidents for investigation, in real time [Karlzén, 2009]. Had the Department of Homeland Security existed prior to this, and had it gathered the data for proper analysis, there's a strong possibility that the threat may have been stopped before innocent lives were lost. With similar investigative and preventative techniques, the subsequent attacks in Spain and the UK in 2004 and 2005 may have also been avoided.

Although the relationship between network and information system protection and the events that transpired on September 11, 2001 may seem far–fetched, the shift in management of utilities and other public services is growing toward information system and network based management by means of risk assessment [Lewis et al., 2002]. Governments and companies need to protect their assets and information from the growing threats that target them.

This chapter speaks to the need for enterprise security while also exploring some of the related tools commonly used today; tools that are sources of information used by Security Information and Event Managers (SIEMs) for analysis. Some examples and ideas of SIEM deployment practices will be given as well as an exploration of their benefits.

Organization.   The rest of the chapter is organized as follows. Section 3 outlines related work regarding traditional incident handling strategies as well as an overview of how traditional tools are combined to ensure security as an holistic solution is presented in Section 4. Section 5 introduces the main challenges derived from information overload on holistic security solutions, Section 6 describes a number of concerns to accomplish before enjoining a SIEM system, and Section 7 enumerates most important requirements for SIEM deployment. Section 8 discusses expert's cost management in two incident response scenarios, i.e., outsourced security management, and in-house security management. Finally, Section 9 concludes the chapter.

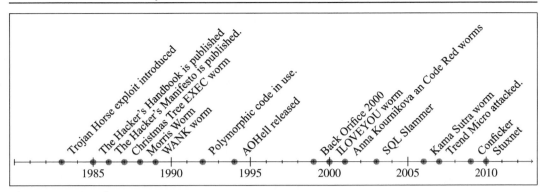

Figure 1. Timeline of advancements in threats.

2. Security Evolution

In the following sections, security attacks, tools and necessities are retrospectively outlined.

2.1. Attack Evolution

Attacks on information systems have been occurring since their inception [Schaefer, 2009]. Once information systems became more prevalent in organizations for the purpose of data storage as well as product and application development, they became interesting targets for attackers [Witten and Nachenberg, 2007]. The most infamous hackers of the 1980's and 1990's had similar practices but different goals; with the use of social engineering, they were able to gather enough information to log in to systems that were available through modems and dial–up numbers as well as some of the world's first available networks.

The first hackers established general technique methodologies for attacks that are still in use today: social engineering for specific information, exploit vulnerabilities, and then find the desired data. These manual interactions between attackers and victims were very involved and often time consuming. This led to the creation of scripts that could, and still can, run a number of these attacks in series or parallel, allowing the hacker to focus on other aspects of the attack.

The use of automated, self–contained, executable software began to find its way to the first networks and eventually the Internet with the intent of spreading to as many end systems as possible, as seen in the timeline depicted in Figure 1. This included those end systems of individuals with a desktop in their homes, allowing for discovery of personal financial details and for the use of available resources on those personal computers. Malware started spreading via websites, email attachments and diskette sharing of bootleg software.

More recent attacks have focused on the use of spam email, trying to mask the true origin of those messages in an attempt to take advantage of the end user's trust. These messages started to look like emails from financial institutions, email providers and other organizations, asking the user to log in to update information, check balances or any other purpose that would make the user access their account immediately. This allowed the attacker to gather credentials to sell or abuse them. These "phishing attacks" evolved into a more focused target specific attack: spear phishing. The targets for spear phishing are typically high value targets such as company executives, individuals that have access to a tremendous amount of data or access to a large amount of funds. In 2007, a spear phishing successfully targeted the United States Office of the Secretary of Defense proving just how dangerous these attacks can be, eventually leading to changes in identity management.

Security has become a topic of great concern in organizations as well as to users. This trend is thriving more complex and time consuming attack methods. Additionally, inside attackers are dedicating many years to leak critical information to avoid detection in a hostile intelligence service (HOIS) environment.

Future attack vectors could include a number of variations on what is already in use, extending the use of social engineering, organization infiltration and technical attacks or simply focusing a major effort into the technological exploitation of specific targets, similar to the concept of an Advanced Persistent Threat (APT). Ensuring that these, and other, attacks become relatively improbable is the main goal of security groups, and ensuring that data is protected as best as possible is the ultimate goal of information security programs.

2.2. Compliance

Over the past few decades, computer crime has increased at an exponential rate. Legislation, though slower, is beginning to emerge with the goal of prosecuting attackers [Von Solms, 2005].

Countries have developed laws for this purpose with jurisdiction within their geographic borders. Beginning in the mid 1980's and continuing to this day, the United States (US) has introduced and updated its own cyber legislative environment as appropriate. The basics of its cyber crime laws include fraud, theft of information and its sale. Penetration testers are often hired by companies in the US to test against the possibility of these sorts of thefts, often mandated by US law and industry compliancy, such as Sarbanes–Oxley (SOX) and Payment Card Industry (PCI) rules. These testers use tools that allow for exploitation of systems during their tests for gap and vulnerability identification, and provide reports used as evidence on which to base corrective action.

Germany, for instance, has its own set of laws, some stricter than those of the US. Notably, the use of computer attack tools is illegal under the anti–hacking law, section 202c of the penal code (Strafgesetzbuch, StGB), essentially making penetration testing within German borders a criminal offense. This may also include foreign penetration testing that uses packets traveling through the country's network infrastructure. In effect, while data packets travel through the Internet from one system to another, they may traverse a number of different geographic borders with more or less restrictive rules.

One example of government regulations directing technology action involves the country of India and Research In Motion Limited, creators of a very common smart phone. Data can travel encrypted to and from these devices, but India's government demanded that encrypted, secure communications' messages be made available to the government in the clear or risk the ban of their use. This was a huge issue in the summer of 2010. Ultimately, protected communications became available to India's government, a clear indication of the control nations have over the use of their own infrastructures.

Data passing through countries would, in effect, come under the jurisdiction of that nation and be subject to its laws and compliance requirements. This plays a major role in the evolution of international laws for electronic communication, namely due to the use of multiple end points in different countries to make a complicated path of travel for packets in an effort to evade law enforcement detection.

3.   Traditional Incident Handling Strategies

"Necessity, who is the mother of invention." —Plato

Over the years a number of different tools have been born out of necessity while others may have been created for different purposes and have evolved for use in the security space [Vigna, 2010]. Though these tools usually have different implementation designs they all come together with a single purpose: to help protect the environment in which they have been deployed. The combined deployment of these tools in conjunction with processes that ensure their proper use by analysts, and strategies to respond to potential incidents is known as "Defense in Depth" [Andress, 2011]. This concept is designed to define acceptable levels of security for highly networked environments. Understanding the tools is important for analysts, who in turn, ensure that their log outputs are correctly addressed.

3.1.   Passive Tools

Passive tools are designed to provide a service without interfering with active traffic and business processes.

3.1.1.   IDS

Intrusion Detection Systems (IDS) are tools designed to do exactly what their name states, detect intrusions [Di Pietro and Mancini, 2008]. When dealing with Network Intrusion Detection Systems (NIDS) and Host Intrusion Detection Systems (HIDS), events are classified as any matches to specific rules flagged for review.

In the case of *NIDS*, the typical deployment model involves either use of an available physical Ethernet port on a hub, or setting one up on a switch along with a span session to send packets to that interface. The span sessions can include mirrored traffic from another interface, from a combination of various interfaces or specific Virtual Local Area Networks (VLANs). The typical physical configuration for these devices includes one networked interface used for management purposes and at least one other used for packet capture.

These systems take the packets and begin to run them through a series of analytical tests to see if they match specific traits to qualify as either malicious or questionable, based on the rule set applied by the responsible parties [Vigna, 2010]. Figure 2 shows a sample NIDS deployment.

In the case of *HIDS*, software is installed on the end system. Whether the system is a user's workstation or a server, the tool is installed and begins to monitor the packets that come into the active network interfaces. This particular type of tool adds additional benefits to the intrusion detection component as it also monitors system internal processes. Anomalous spikes or dips in resource usage on information systems can be signs of rogue processes taking up resources, or, shutting down or halting vital processes, which could lead to a system failure or corruption, and would be detected by HIDS.

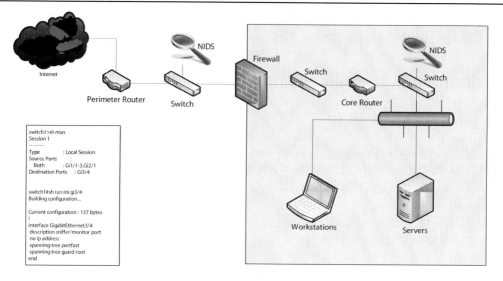

Figure 2. Sample deployment of IDS, including switched and routed network segment and mirrored interface.

3.1.2. Operating System (OS) Detection

When used in conjunction with other tools, OS detection helps in the incident handling processes established within an organization. The main focus of this concept is to allow for quicker identification of high value events. Passive OS detection is designed to monitor network traffic in a similar physical method to an IDS. While monitoring host responses to traffic stimuli, both legitimate and malicious, it determines the OS of the end host with a high level of confidence.

3.1.3. User Identification

User identification tools are designed to provide a similar benefit, but by focusing on the identification of users on a network based on the monitoring and understanding of different user identification protocols. Open protocols like Lightweight Directory Access Protocol (LDAP) may be used to identify users, but when it comes to secure protocols like LDAP over SSL (LDAPS), user identification becomes a service that goes from being a passive effort to a proactive effort.

3.2. Active Tools

Active tools perform similar functions to some of their passive counterparts, running checks to determine appropriate next steps, but in a different physical configuration and with a different outcome.

3.2.1. Firewalls

Network firewalls have evolved over time and now have three main types: packet, stateful and application. Their main purpose is to prevent the communication from beginning be-

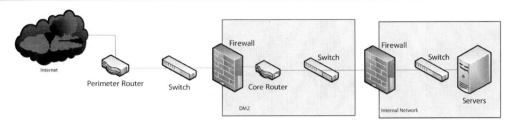

Figure 3. Sample deployment of firewalls used to segregate environments.

tween two hosts, usually between a malicious host on one side and a high value internal system on the other side. This type of deployment is in–line, meaning that traffic must go through the firewall in order to continue on its path. Best practice for firewalls is usually to have a white list, or "deny all" rule, which prevents all traffic from passing, and updated periodically specific rules allowing the necessary traffic [Mitnick and Simon, 2005]. To this regard, Bartal et al [Bartal et al., 1999] demonstrated that managing firewalls configuration is a very challenging task and they show that a promising way to tackle this challenge is by defining an holistic toolkit with global knowledge. Figure 3 shows a sample firewall multi–environment deployment.

Packet firewalls were the first firewalls developed. These would do basic packet filtering, dropping packets when they met specific criteria. The criteria for these types of firewalls is usually field specific, in other words, validating specific fields in the packets match the defined rule sets. Source Internet Protocol (IP) addresses, destination IP addresses, or source or destination ports can be used to prevent or allow traffic to flow.

Stateful firewalls focus on not only preventing malicious traffic from passing through based on port and IP address, but they also bring the advantage of understanding the state of a connection. The disadvantage of the simple packet firewall was that the return traffic, usually sourced at a commonly known port, would return to the source system of the connection via the originating ephemeral port, which if not opened by a rule, would be dropped.

Application firewalls have an additional advantage to the stateful firewalls in that the more commonly used applications and protocols are understood and can be used as rules. An example of where this can help is when a host has been compromised and in order to syphon information out to a malicious recipient, it uses a protocol to transfer the information via a commonly used port. If this port is used for protocol A, and is now being used by protocol B, and the firewall is configured to prevent protocol B from communicating, but to allow protocol A; thus stopping the malicious traffic.

3.2.2.   Intrusion Prevention Systems

Intrusion Prevention Systems (IPS) are devices similar to IDS in the way that they share some configuration methods [Ierace et al., 2005]. In order to prevent malicious traffic from occurring, these devices need to place in–line. If resources are over–used, and then causing devices to slow down or become non–responsive, network latency may cause connectivity problems as well as the established communication to drop out. These are critical concerns and risks for current corporations that rely on their networks for any significant revenue.

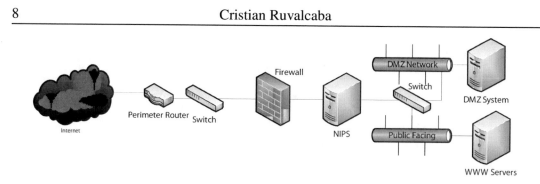

Figure 4. Sample deployment of Network based IPS devices.

The use of IPS can be a political challenge within an organization due to its ability to stop all traffic between hosts, but its benefits can be extremely valuable when deployed correctly. Close monitoring of these is extremely important to ensure that resources are not being over–used and that critical business applications are not being negatively affected. IPS devices have built on concepts of both firewalls and IDS and have successfully combined the two of them in order to provide an extremely useful tool in the efforts to protect network infrastructures. Figure 4 shows a sample deployment of NIPS protecting a network from the threats of the Internet.

3.2.3. Web Content Filtering

Web content filters [Bertino et al., 2006] sometimes cause employees a lot of grief. It may be possible to hear screams down the hall from a frustrated employee who is blocked from accessing a particular website.

At times this seems like a tool used by management to control their employees, but in actuality, there are a lot of benefits to it. The granularity of what gets filtered from within an organization's network can help prevent a potentially serious malware outbreak. The advantage of having this tool be network based is that host resources aren't used, allowing for a user to remain productive. A similarity to IDS is that some deployments of this type of tool also listen to span traffic and focus their preventative efforts based on the web protocol traffic seen.

Network based content filtering can have a number of different configurations, including in–line, monitoring span traffic, and virtually in–line. Figure 5 gives two examples, including a proxy based deployment.

3.2.4. Anti–Virus

Everyone is familiar with anti–virus (AV). AVs are that piece of software that keeps slowing the computer down, which makes everyone say, "what if I didn't have it on? Would it be so bad?" Truth be told, YES! If a developer for a popular locally installed online played game disables AV, there is a potential for the master image of the final to–market release of the game to be infected. If not caught in time, this could mean disaster for the video game manufacturer as brand loyalty may falter, a large number of complaints will occur and the bad press would most certainly cause a huge negative impact on current and future sales.

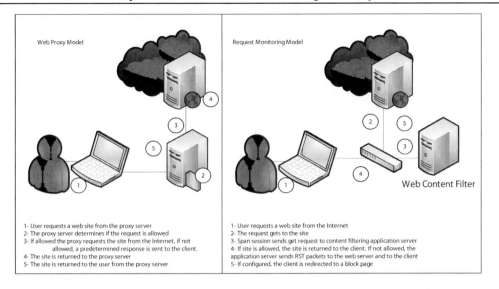

Figure 5. Two types of web content filtering deployments, one using proxy based filtering and the other monitoring traffic similar to how and IDS would monitor traffic.

On the other hand, from the author viewpoint, a myth exists in the believe that Linux/Unix and Apple machines may not be vulnerable to viruses or worms. Apple products are becoming more commonplace in the work environment and more research will be going into compromising those systems. Thus, even Macs need AV, and so does for Linux and Unix systems.

3.2.5. Web Application Firewalls

Web Application Firewalls (WAF) [Becher, 2007] are tools designed to protect web based applications. It's in the name! What makes these firewalls interesting is that they can, as other tools, be hardware or software based. They don't focus on packet details, understanding state or understanding how protocols communicate, but on how a single protocol is used: HyperText Transfer Protocol (HTTP). Specific attributes of traffic and patterns of behavior are checked against rules designed to help prevent traffic of malicious intent from succeeding in its goal.

3.2.6. Data or Information Leakage Prevention

Data Leakage Prevention (DLP) [Hermann, 2008], also referred to as Information Leakage Protection, is used to prevent the unintentional, or intentional, release of data from a secured and secluded network environment. Data can often be emailed out, carried out the door on a thumb drive or even communicated via instant message and other means.

When unintentional, the company involved can suffer a major public embarrassment as well as it may face a number of civil law suits, potentially criminal cases, and also expensive fines from governments or industry compliance organizations. When intentional, the company involved may loose competitive advantage or intellectual property that may end up being reverse engineered by another organization, and at worst, from foreign malicious activities.

As in the case of IDS and IPS, patterns and rules are used to identify and categorize specific streams, so they can be dropped as well as alerts sent out. Other benefits that may be available range from manager notification to allow data to be sent if this is part of a business requirement.

3.3. Proactive Tools

Proactive tools can gather information crucial to event analysis and incident determination, but they need to interact with systems in order to do so. These end–systems can include workstations, servers, network equipment and others [Erickson, 2008, Engebretson, 2011].

3.3.1. Vulnerability Assessment

Vulnerability Assessment (VA) is a process in which stimuli are sent to a host and, based on the host's response, a determination of host exposure is possible via the encountered vulnerabilities. Basically, VA tries to find the cracks in the wall that will allow attackers to get in, or at least to see deeper. Research is currently and constantly being performed to find and release more vulnerability information that is OS specific, application specific and protocol specific.

3.3.2. Exploit Tools and Penetration Testing

There are a number of tools available, some are open source and others are closed source products, which have a single purpose: to exploit a system by any means necessary [Mitnick et al., 2003]. Though both penetration testers and malicious hackers use them, their benefits are undeniable. These tools have the benefit of a software development kit (SDK) to allow for customization, and the potential of taking down an entire network. Often times, these tools are used to verify or defunct results provided by vulnerability scans. If results are combined with other tools' events, they also can be used to help prioritize events within a SIEM.

3.4. Attacking Tools

Security tools get patched on a regular basis once a new attack occurs. This fact is specially critical since it is possible to use several techniques which prevent compromised tools from noticing they are being bypassed.

The example in Figure 6 shows sample packet data and uses the time–to–live (TTL) field of the packet to get to the intended target, but have the IDS see "robot" instead of the username "root", thus allowing for no event to be flagged. Similar to this evasion technique, there are a number of possible ways to evade the tools above. The idea is to not let it happen and to keep an eye out for when it does, by having multiple log sources, each providing a different side of the story.

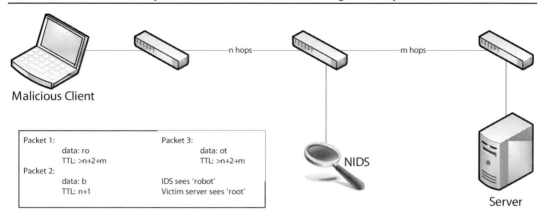

Figure 6. Example of IDS evasion using the IP TTL field. TTL decreases by 1 at each hop. Per RFC, it was designed to measure time, not hops, but network speeds have made it so the two are almost synonymous.

4. Deployment and Use of Security Tools

Tools aforementioned represent a list of common strategies that most analysts may be familiar with, whilst using them to perform their diary duties. However, a proper deployment of the tools appears as an important factor in the ability of analysts at performing their work [Vacca, 2010b].

4.1. Proper Deployment

Ensuring proper deployment of tools can be a time consuming engineering exercise involving a number of engineers, project managers and business units working together to achieve the ultimate goal of providing a more secured working environment for end users [Wool, 2004].

Over the years, the analogy of protecting the crown jewels, and having a castle around them for protection has been used to describe an efficient way of providing better security. The important thing to understand is that there is no one correct way of deployment. The way tools are installed and configured may be different on a case–by–case basis, but often times these are variations on the castle analogy. The concept begins with the model where threats originate from outside the walls of the township with a goal of breaching the walls of the room protecting the jewels themselves.

In terms of networks, this translates to threats originating from the Internet with the goal of breaching the OS and application security of the servers that contain a company's most valuable information. The placement of tools relative to how data is gathered was briefly covered in the previous section.

Figure 7 covers a partial view into possible placement of tools, most networks are not linear diagrams. In fact, most networks have their systems spread both vertically and horizontally; and these systems may be in separate VLANs that need to be secluded from each other. Some systems may contain extremely sensitive data, where others may not have any sensitivity associated with them whatsoever. These systems are at risk, not just from the

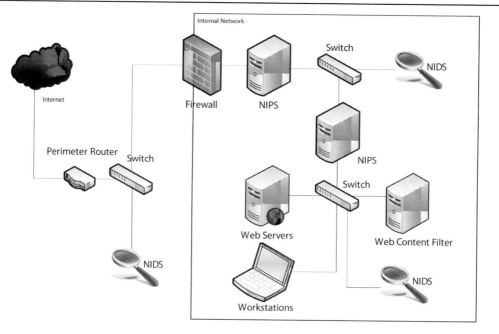

Figure 7. Example of network simplistic network diagram with multiple tools deployed.

outside, but also from within the network. Firewalls, intrusion detection systems, antivirus programs, and two-factor authentication products are just some of the tools available to assist in protecting a network and its data [Vacca, 2010a].

4.1.1. Input for the Tools

The input that these security systems receive can vary. The discussion point here is to determine where in the network they should be placed for monitoring. *Figure 1.6* showed that from the Internet towards the center of the castle, you might find some items in a particular order: firewall followed by IPS then an IDS. This is in order to optimize the use of the resources in the IPS and IDS by first eliminating a large part of the anomalous and potentially malicious traffic at the firewall, and then the next chunk at the IPS. As such, the IDS would see events that need to be monitored that have successfully made it past the first two layers of defense.

This model may work from the outside in, but within a network, the security systems and tools may have to take on a separate design. Highly sensitive networks may need to be completely separate from each other, both logically, and physically. Some may need specific protection from each other using things like IPS or firewalls only while others may require only IDS to be used to accomplish the intended level of security.

At this junction in the engineering efforts, it becomes important to understand which internal environments, or network bubbles, need protection and what kind would be optimal. Business unit leaders are usually involved with the final decision, all while using input from both their engineers and system administrators as well as the input from the groups responsible for security engineering. What will typically end up happening is a number of security tools get deployed spread across different physical areas of a data center, potentially across different geographic locations and perhaps in different network segments.

4.1.2. Network Access Requirements

Because of the potentially dispersed nature of these deployments, a logical design for management needs to be created. Specific protocols, like Secure Shell (SSH), may be used for management of individual devices, or they may even have older protocols, such as Telnet. A shift has been occurring from the SSH connections and thick clients towards a more web–like experience with HTTP and HTTPS interfaces accessed through a regular web browser [Donahue, 2011].

Regardless the access method, centralized management for a group of devices may require additional custom or closed protocols to be available for use. This may require a large number of Access Control List (ACL) changes to occur in order to permit the proper Transmission Control Protocol (TCP) or User Datagram Protocol (UDP) ports to be available for use between systems and the management consoles.

A solution to this issue involves the following alternatives; either by allowing ACL changes across multiple networking devices to ensure its availability or by allowing the management interfaces to reside on a single VLAN, which would also require specific configurations to ensure the IP space is available for use by those interfaces. Both alternatives provide a solution which depends on the organization as well as on the physical configuration of the devices.

Figure 8 shows a sample ACL for specific ports and protocols used for management. These may not relate to a specific tool or vendor, but are protocols and ports commonly used.

```
permit tcp host 10.10.10.10 host 172.16.10.10 eq ssh
permit tcp host 10.10.10.10 host 172.16.10.10 eq www
permit tcp host 10.10.10.10 host 172.16.10.10 eq 443
permit udp host 10.10.10.10 host 172.16.10.10 eq tftp
permit udp host 10.10.10.10 host 172.16.10.10 eq ntp
permit udp host 172.16.10.10 host 10.10.10.10 eq syslog
permit udp host 172.16.10.10 host 10.10.10.10 eq domain
```

Figure 8. Sample router ACL for ports and protocols commonly used for management of different devices.

4.2. Log Analysis

Once the tools have been deployed and are monitoring or actively protecting their intended subjects, or a combination of both monitoring and protecting, it is time to properly analyze their data. This can be a tedious and time consuming activity, but one necessary to ensure maximizing return on investment (ROI) on these tools. Each tool may have its own output format or location. These logs will contain some details that can be useful for investigations, and others may require deeper investigation into systems or network traffic. Individuals or teams involved in the decision on which tool to employ, and ultimately the installation of these tools, should know how to use them and come to the final decision based on an easy deployment, use and manageability.

On the other hand, training is usually involved to ensure proper understanding of what events mean. To conceive a proper analysis is a combination of both this understanding of system use as well as the security mind–set. Analysts and the engineers that test the devices need to be security minded and have a strong understanding of the network environment in which they intend to deploy these tools in order to be able to offer a strong interpretation of what security events mean.

5. Dealing with Information Overload

The manual analysis of the logs reported from any of the tools described above is an extremely tedious task for any individual. Teams of analysts usually perform their functions while transferring responsibilities between shifts. Log forwarders with their log collection capabilities and logic to accomplish tasks when conditions are met, can be seen as metaphorical precursors of SIEM systems. Though SIEMs have a number of additional features, but they share a main goal, namely to correlate logs from different tools to maximize true positive incident investigations and minimize the time spent by running down false positives. The only way these problems can be solved is with effective behavioral technology [Alagna and Chen, 2005].

5.1. Log Correlation Basis

The logic behind correlation use in these tools relies on a number of identifiable data points. These are traits of each packet that's involved in the unidirectional or bidirectional communication: IP addresses, TCP and UDP ports, TCP flags and others. These data points allow for event and incident investigation to happen. Custom data points may also possible depending on requirements. In addition to these data points, the event information is taken into account. Events differ based on the tool and, potentially, vendor.

5.2. Actionable Data

5.2.1. Individual High Value True Positives Pre–SIEM

When dealing with a highly skilled group or individual whose goal is to penetrate a network to take control of or to steal data from it, data can be correlated based on source IP when originating from a single place. Correlation would need to happen to trace logs from the origins of reconnaissance of the external hosts to the final breach and data leakage from the target host or hosts.

Once a breach such as this has been identified, it is important to investigate how it was successful. For breaches of this depth and of this nature, it is often a system administrator that finds the first signs of a potential problem. Once a compromise has been confirmed, a further investigation may occur. Logs may be requested of different system administrators in order to track things down successfully. This would be a highly collaborative effort requiring a number of man–hours to complete.

5.2.2. SIEM Correlated True Positives

Either originated from a single source or from a number of sources, events can be correlated around timestamps, as well as by the type of event. This is especially true when dealing with one–to–many or many–to–one event scenario, that is, one source and many destinations, or vice–versa. This is where SIEMs begin to demonstrate their value, i.e. when dealing with events and incidents. Logs that match a given criteria, such as source IP, would be grouped together, allowing patterns to emerge. These patterns, when analyzed, can indicate any part of a network intrusion's methodology, e.g. scanning for reconnaissance being one of the more common, commonly flooding the Internet and front–end of business networks.

Responses by analysts to these attempts involve anything from identifying false positives. When properly addressed, impact of the damage can be determined quickly. When discovery originates in a properly implemented SIEM, it makes things easier to retrace all steps taken by the attacker in order to address them in a timely manner by system owners [Vacca, 2010a].

5.2.3. Dealing with False Positives

False positives are a non–negligible part with analysts deal diary to improve their analysis processes and their understanding of their network infrastructure. Logs for these events can either flood a network full of unnecessary traffic or flood a SIEM full of logs leading to a number of false incidents that are, but need not be, investigated.

There are options when dealing with some of these issues, including event tuning at the source. This can involve a lot of work when dealing with security tools that have been in place and haven't been properly maintained. A process for review of updates to signature bases should be implemented to ensure a smooth transition between revisions in use and those that will replace them. When too many events are being flagged, the current revision in use can be reviewed as well to remove the least value events. Implementing a process like this can have at least three benefits: resources are saved on the tool, resources are saved on the SIEM, and in the end time is saved for analysts.

Another option is to tune at the SIEM. Initially, it may take more time to tune out everything that would be considered of lesser importance; but this method has its own benefits: seeing all the logs in one central location, allows for centralized tuning, if needed, and other benefits. Three main things can be tuned specifically to reduce incidents for investigation: creating white–lists for systems that are either not affected by specific events or systems with extra privileges, tuning incidents via their event triggers, and active incidents. Analysts will be able to focus on the specific incidents that need to be investigated; true positives.

5.2.4. Evaluating Effectiveness: Results and Stats from SIEM

In addition to, when well tuned, providing a high rate of actionable data, this data can be used to measure workload of analysts. Another possibility from some SIEM tools is to have graphs and charts designed specifically for upper management and can help them better understand the threat landscape, which can vary depending on the industry in which a company operates.

6. Accomplishing SIEM

There exist a number of concerns to accomplish before enjoining a SIEM system, as described next.

6.1. Company Rules

By following industry best practices, organizations have well–established security and privacy policies, and awareness programs for employees. However, to know the policies does not mean employees adhere to them. Generally, it is necessary to deploy a security program and infrastructure designed to accomplish what is laid out in policy on a broad basis.

Standards should be used to specify hardware and software that is considered acceptable, or not acceptable, within network environments. Guidelines can help employees understand proper procedure when conducting business within an organization. If no security requirements are established within an organization, it becomes extremely difficult to justify the procurement of a SIEM, let alone the other tools that SIEMs rely on for their proper functionality.

6.2. Management Buy–In

If a security program is in existence and there is already a collection of deployed tools in the environment, it may prove difficult for non–security minded upper management teams to understand the idea of purchasing more equipment. When SIEM use is not part of the current strategy, examples of other companies in the same industry, or other industries but of similar size, and their security postures can be used to ensure its inclusion [Shon Harris, 2010].

Once management has reviewed the proposal, it becomes a question of both management and the security teams understanding the exact scope of their project or program to achieve the desired security posture. Product vendors can often help in understanding the resource requirements involved in a deployment and can provide resources to help in these efforts, at a cost.

Budgeting for everything can seem like an easy task i.e. capital expenses. This is not true at all. In addition to purchasing the equipment, licensing is often involved for support, on time–based contracts, as well as internal man–hours and the costs associated with it. One of the biggest mistakes an organization can make when trying to achieve a more secure network, is to leave the tools in a 'plug–n–play' configuration, that is to say, they plug it into the network and don't have someone attend to the maintenance and care of the tools. These operational costs need to be taken into account when preparing a budget proposal as well.

6.3. Requirements and Testing

Once the budget is properly approved, it comes time to get a request for proposal (RFP) out there for vendors to bid on. The exception would be when open source tools are used for the enterprise, ensuring that the licensing agreement allows the use in this sort of environment.

Table 1. A sample requirements table for some of the tools discussed. Requirements depend on the environment and direction from management

Sample Requirements		IDS	IPS	AV	VA	WCF	FW
Management	High Availability	✓	R	–	✓	✓	R
	Centralized Management	R	R	R	R	R	✓
	Distributed Architecture	R	R	–	R	✓	R
	CLI Access	✓	✓	–	✓	✓	R
	Thick Client	–	R	R	✓	✓	–
	Web GUI	R	✓	✓	R	R	✓
	Reporting	R	R	R	R	R	✓
	Auto-Updates	R	✓	R	R	R	N
Capabilities	FastE	R	R	–	–	R	R
	1 Gbps	R	R	–	–	R	R
	10 Gbps	R	R	–	–	✓	R
	Fail Open	–	R	–	–	✓	R
	Fail Close	–	–	–	–	R	R
	Customizable Rules and Alerts	R	✓	–	–	R	R
	Auto-Recommendations	✓	✓	✓	✓	✓	–
Vendor Support	24h Support via Phone	R	R	✓	R	R	R
	2h SLA for High Priority Issues	R	R	✓	R	✓	R
	24h SLA for Normal Priority Issues	R	R	✓	R	R	R

Note: R (required), ✓ (nice to have), – (not applicable), N (not preferred)

The RFP should include certain specifications that need to be met, as well as the requirements for product capabilities. This can be a list with a bunch of checkboxes next to it, and internally, it can be decided that meeting 80% of the requirements would suffice, or that all of them need to be met. It's a management and purchasing decision at that point. Cost can also play a huge factor into which product may be chosen for purchase.

Before blindly going on some vendor's word and purchasing the product, it is recommended to test products in–house. Vendors often allow for a product to be demoed in–house for a certain amount of time, that time frame can be anywhere from a week to a few months. This allows the customer to test the devices and to configure them in a way that would mimic what it might be like if it were considered a production deployment. There should be a test plan outlined for evaluating the competing products, this plan should provide a score that can be used to compare the different vendors. Table 1 shows a sample list of requirements for different tools, these requirements would be measured up against each vendor for each tool to ensure the best value. The requirements may vary depending on the environment as well as the desired security stance.

The idea of comparing vendors while evaluating them independently at the same time should apply to all types of tools. Before acquiring security equipment, a decision should be made to determine high value assets and therefore how many and where these tools need to be placed to maximize security posture.

7. SIEM Specific Requirements

Heterogeneous logs and event formulations involve SIEM in a prior configuration of network and data, as follows.

7.1. Dealing with Standard Logs

7.1.1. Logs need to be correctly interpreted by SIEM

Most SIEM vendors will ensure the maximum compatibility with current communication protocols. Backwards compatibility, e.g. to older versions, is standard, as the newest version may not be set up in all production networks. A number of protocols may need to be configured in a certain way in order for the SIEM to accept logs. This is true for newer versions of Simple Network Management Protocol (SNMP), which is a UDP protocol, when used for logs. This is also true for TCP protocols like Checkpoint's OPSEC Log Export API (LEA).

A strong relationship between SIEM manufactures and developers of log sources or sensors of any kind is extremely important. This ensures that communicating with custom vendor designed protocols like OPSEC LEA or Sourcefire's eStreamer™will function properly. Updates to the security tools should not have an adverse affect on SIEM communication capabilities, and the SIEM should continue to be able to properly parse logs.

7.1.2. Support

By contracting support services with SIEM and security tool vendors, customers easily obtain assistance in the proper deployment, understanding interfaces, graphic or command line, and outputs and results. In addition to this, software updates are usually part of a contractual agreement, which allows for the tools to not fall behind. This is important because just like applications and operating systems, these tools can sometimes have vulnerabilities and incorrectly implemented processes and protocols.

Another important benefit of support accounts is the close professional relationship allowing for feature requests to be sent to developers. Depending on the strength of the relationship and the individuals involved on the vendor side, the priority for these feature requests may vary.

These accounts also allow access to a vendor's support site. These sites contain large quantities of information that can help customers troubleshoot issues themselves as well as submit support tickets for issues that could not be found on the support site. Comprehensive Frequently Asked Questions (FAQ) sections can speed up troubleshooting for customers, keeping them happy.

7.2. SIEM Defaults: Rules and Parsers

There are a number of incident triggers that are set by default to alert based on log inputs. These can often be extremely generic events coming together to create an incident. To cover as large a customer base as possible, generic compliance incidents may also be triggered.

These compliancy incidents can be international standards, specific standards that are defined by industries like the Payment Card Industry (PCI) standards, or requirements defined by local and national governments.

These different compliance and triggered incidents may have specific required inputs, and a large amount of effort may be needed to ensure that these inputs are properly configured to send the appropriate logs to the SIEM. This becomes increasingly difficult with larger environments, requiring coordination between system administrators, application owners and network administration teams.

7.3. Customization

7.3.1. Incidents

It is possible to create custom events and incidents from standard inputs. Severity levels should be assigned to these events and incidents to help minimize false positives and false negatives. These incidents should be focused on higher value data stores and sensitive applications and environments. Depending on the sensitivity levels of the target, these incidents should be triggered by a single event, conditions met by a small grouping of events, or a number of event groupings, from most sensitive to least sensitive levels for the targets [Oram and Viega, 2009].

7.3.2. Events

Customized events may be necessary for certain applications or tools that are not currently supported by the specific SIEM software product deployed. However, a possibility exists if these events can be sent via a clear–text protocol to the SIEM, then can be collected and searched. The next step consists of creating customized parsers for these logs. Customized parsing can use regular expressions. These regular expressions pull data and then the data is related to specific fields. As mentioned before, severity levels should be assigned to these custom events to ensure proper priority is assigned to these events. Figure 9 shows a sample custom log and the regular expression used to capture some specific fields for use by SIEM indexing processes and event correlation.

```
Sample log:

13245 Application_xyz on host host_xyz: source_xyz Event
Message Here

Regular Expression used:

[0-9]* [A-Za-z0-9_]* on host [A-Za-z0-9_]*:
[A-Za-z0-9_]* (.)*
```

Figure 9. This is a simplistic example of a regular expression that could be used capturing the fields: *Event ID*, *Application Name*, *Target Host Name*, *Source Host Name* and *Event Message*.

7.3.3. Fixed Hardware and Software Architectures

When the organization already have designed a fixed hardware and software model, customizing a SIEM system involves difficulties. This is another scenario where a close relationship with the vendor can be extremely useful. Either they will work closely with the customer in order to create custom parsers for the customer, or they will grant access to the customer for this purpose and help the customer understand how to do it.

Graphical User Interface (GUI) options may be available to create the custom parsers allowing for the custom events mentioned before to be created. Other times, Command Line Interface (CLI) access may be required, whether remote shell, secure shell or direct access. When using CLI specific file types may define event parsing. Often times, Extensible Markup Language (XML) files are used to define the parsing methods for log sources, other file types may be used. The need to create these files, transfer them to the proper directory and appropriate the necessary privileges to them as well as restarting certain services may be required.

7.4. Physical and Logical Implementation

Deploying these tools may seem like just another installation, but the coordination between teams is just the tip of the iceberg. Proper steps need to be followed to ensure that they are not only implemented properly, but deployed following the internal processes defined by policy, standards and guidelines.

One of the bigger struggles in larger organizations is their ability to successfully apply change and configuration management for their equipment and software. This needs to be taken into consideration when managing projects involving these deployments, including time it takes to get approvals collected as well completing the physical and network changes necessary.

7.5. Training

Once the tools are implemented, next step requires people to know how to use the new available resources for daily function. This can be part of the milestones or can be considered an independent operational task. There are usually a number of options available for training. One of the best options may be to have the vendor provide direct training; this can be expensive and may require travel, adding to the expense. Though this may be justified, as direct training from the vendor usually provides the most comprehensive knowledge transfer and can allow for questions to be directly addressed.

When working with a representative from the vendor, more organization–based questions can be addressed this way and specifics, in regards to sensitive network details, can also be discussed if necessary, as no third parties are involved.

These are some examples of the training possibilities. To decide upon the best option, it would be desirable to talk to the vendor directly, allowing for a mutual understanding of the choices and benefits available for each.

8. Role Specific Importance

Limited resources are often allocated for incident investigations. Time can be wasted on analyzing false positives. An overwhelming amount of false positives can cost the organization a large part of the man–hours available for use. Generally, the analysts can be stretched to 120–150% of their allocated time to attempt investigating as many potential incidents as possible. This fact decreases efficiency and effectiveness of their analysis costing management more in hourly wages and potential data loss. These analysts often spend countless hours tracking down system and application owners to get system information, application information and logs.

8.1. Managed Security Services

8.1.1. Outsourced Security Management

Many organizations employ Managed Security Services (MSS) to handle incident investigations. Generally, outsourced service–providers contact its customers only when an incident is determined to have high priority or to be a true positive. This leverages a considerably reduction of time and effort spent by organizations on burdensome incident response tasks. However, a major limitation of this model can be a weak service–level agreement, i.e. limiting the amount of logs inspected and the amount of escalations allotted a week, month or year. Thus a potential non–coverage time window can be left.

Depending on the service–level agreed, non-negligible extra costs might be charged to the client. Furthermore, the client may require devices' management and log transmission to MSS. In this regard, this environment may contain a SIEM system to avoid manual correlation.

8.1.2. In–House Security Management

When the analysis of the encountered events and incidents are performed by in–house means, a sense of pride may improve their investigation and protection of the environment. This vested interest can be extremely beneficial for both management process and also the analysts. In addition to this benefit, these internal teams have an understanding of the environment in which they work that may not be possible for external teams to achieve. This makes in–house analysts more efficient, an efficiency which is increased when a SIEM is deployed for use in their environment.

Argument of these teams not providing as reliable a coverage as an MSS can be a flawed one in an environment. When trained correctly, analysts can easily be reached out to at any time and called to investigate an incident. On–call rotations can provide a schedule that ensures all team members have an equal opportunity to contribute their skills. The initial investigation to determine if an escalation to these analysts is required can be performed by teams that already have this sort of coverage such as Network Operations Centers (NOCs) or Security Operations Centers (SOCs).

Keeping this service in–house can provide an additional cost savings over the cost of MSS, especially if the tools deployed are purchased and managed by the organization. Keeping the log information internally provides an additional layer of security and lowers

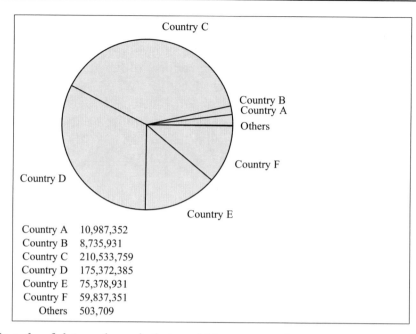

Country A	10,987,352
Country B	8,735,931
Country C	210,533,759
Country D	175,372,385
Country E	75,378,931
Country F	59,837,351
Others	503,709

Figure 10. Sample of data and graph that could be presented to management to show offending countries.

the risk of external exposure. Keeping the brand of the organization within the confidence of their customers is important for continued sales and continued revenue.

8.2. Incident Handlers and Analysts

8.2.1. Tracking and Reporting

A manual handling of the incidents reported requires a manual analysis of timelines, logs, escalations, and so on. System and event logs are collected and organized in time order on SIEM systems, i.e. providing an initial timeline of the incident being investigated. This allows correlation to easily make relationship between the source or several targets of the incident currently being investigated [Young, 2010].

Patterns that emerge from these investigations can provide an incident handler with an understanding of threat vectors that are commonly used to attempt compromising the integrity and confidentiality of the networks they are protecting. This is true for both external and internal threats. This can help network and security operations teams provide better network–based security.

Reporting on these incidents and events provides incident handlers with the most common attack sources and targets. This can help hone in on what analysts need to investigate on their downtime from incident handling. The benefit of reporting on most common events also provides system and application owners a list of specific things to look out for and protect against in their system and application hardening, which improves security stance of the organization's network. Figure 10 shows a pie chart that could be presented to management to get a shared understanding of high value attackers.

Reporting serves another purpose for incident handlers: it is used to show management what is happening on their network, internally and on their front end. Providing these graphs and numbers to management justifies team member headcount, as well as training and security tool purchases. These graphs also provide management with an understanding of high value targets, allowing them to shift resources around for protection appropriately.

8.2.2. Analysts

Analysts using SIEM capabilities minimize the time they use for investigations by having a centralized log collection to search through. This also allows them to escalate to system owners only when truly required. Because of the centralized logging and correlation engine of the SIEM, analysts don't have to sift through countless logs to find a needle in a haystack; instead, they use the compiled results to find signs of a successful breach, or signs of a confirmed unsuccessful breach.

The SIEM provides analysts with what is considered to be actionable data. Tracking these potential incidents that have a higher rate of true positive can ensure that incident tracking numbers are of high fidelity. When tracking incidents and analysts involved with them, SIEMs can provide capabilities that track additional information, including time spent, handler and comments or notes. These additional capabilities provide the possibility to hand–off incidents to the next shift if a handler or analyst is working through the end of his or her shift. This might seem like a small benefit, but can give a huge boost to mental health of an analyst.

8.2.3. Incident Response

The incident response timeline may be shortened dramatically by an automated process for escalating correlated events to the appropriate individuals. When all the correct inputs are configured properly, incidents can be identified and handled with less effort than when they are not and less time is required for system owners to begin their countermeasure efforts [Donahue, 2011].

9. Conclusion

SIEM provides a tremendous benefit no only for alleviating analysts, incident handlers analysis workload but also for improving management tasks. In particular, SIEM optimizes the processes and training to maximize the use of the deployed resources.Vested interests ensure continued efforts to maintain a high level of security.

For a number of governmental and industry regulations, the review of all security logs to find potential incidents is required. SIEM appliances and applications are designed to automatically process millions of logs in order to ensure compliance with these regulations, whilst saving costs in the potential fines for non–compliance, and in post–breach lawsuits. Moreover, SIEM can be used as a checkbox stamp on a list for auditors.

However, SIEM systems do not fit all yet. They need to be customized to ensure that a given organization's security concerns are met. Once these concerns are met with the use of a SIEM system, it needs cares and attention in order to be protected against new threats as well as using intelligent correlation by means of automated intelligent SIEM systems.

Furthermore, cloud and virtual environments are quickly becoming a reference platform for developers and organizations due to its flexible and cost–effective business model. However, this rises some concerns about hardware and hardline protection model —not to mention privacy issues. Future directions could address cloud–based SIEM monitoring by means of hypervisor and guest VMs event correlation.

References

[Alagna and Chen, 2005] Alagna, T. and Chen, E. (2005). *Larstan's The Black Book on Corporate Security: Cutting-Edge Guidance form the World's Leading Experts.* Larstan Publishing, 2nd edition.

[Andress, 2011] Andress, J. (2011). *The Basics of Information Security: Understanding the Fundamentals of InfoSec in Theory and Practice.* Syngress.

[Bartal et al., 1999] Bartal, Y., Mayer, A., Nissim, K., and Wool, A. (1999). Firmato: A novel firewall management toolkit. In *Security and Privacy, 1999. Proceedings of the 1999 IEEE Symposium on*, pages 17–31. IEEE.

[Becher, 2007] Becher, M. (2007). *Web Application Firewalls.* VDM Verlag.

[Bertino et al., 2006] Bertino, E., Ferrari, E., and Perego, A. (2006). Web content filtering. *Web and information security*, pages 112–132.

[Di Pietro and Mancini, 2008] Di Pietro, R. and Mancini, L. (2008). *Intrusion detection systems.* Springer Verlag.

[Donahue, 2011] Donahue, G. A. (2011). *Network Warrior.* O'Reilly Media, Inc., 2nd edition.

[Engebretson, 2011] Engebretson, P. (2011). *The Basics of Hacking and Penetration Testing: Ethical Hacking and Penetration Testing Made Easy.* Syngress.

[Erickson, 2008] Erickson, J. (2008). *Hacking: The Art of Exploitation.* No Starch Press, 2nd edition.

[Hermann, 2008] Hermann, D. (2008). Data leakage prevention.

[Ierace et al., 2005] Ierace, N., Urrutia, C., and Bassett, R. (2005). Intrusion prevention systems. *Ubiquity*, 2005(June):2–2.

[Karlzén, 2009] Karlzén, H. (2009). An analysis of security information and event management systems–the use or siems for log collection, management and analysis.

[Lewis et al., 2002] Lewis, J., for Strategic, C., and International Studies (Washington, D. (2002). *Assessing the risks of cyber terrorism, cyber war and other cyber threats.* Center for Strategic & International Studies.

[Mitnick and Simon, 2005] Mitnick, K. and Simon, W. L. (2005). *The Art of Intrusion: The Real Stories Behind the Exploits of Hackers, Intruders and Deceivers.* Wiley.

[Mitnick et al., 2003] Mitnick, K., Simon, W. L., and Wozniak, S. (2003). *The Art of Deception: Controlling the Human Element of Security*. Wiley.

[Oram and Viega, 2009] Oram, A. and Viega, J., editors (2009). *Beautiful Security: Leading Security Experts Explain How They Think*. O'Reilly Media, Inc.

[Schaefer, 2009] Schaefer, R. (2009). The epistemology of computer security. *SIGSOFT Softw. Eng. Notes*, 34(6):8–10.

[Shon Harris, 2010] Shon Harris, C. (2010). *CISSP All-in-One Exam Guide*. McGraw-Hill Osborne Media, fifth edition edition.

[Vacca, 2010a] Vacca, J. R., editor (2010a). *Managing Information Security*. Syngress.

[Vacca, 2010b] Vacca, J. R., editor (2010b). *Network and System Security*. Syngress.

[Vigna, 2010] Vigna, G. (2010). Network intrusion detection: dead or alive? In *Proceedings of the 26th Annual Computer Security Applications Conference*, ACSAC '10, pages 117–126, New York, NY, USA. ACM.

[Von Solms, 2005] Von Solms, S. (2005). Information security governance–compliance management vs operational management. *Computers & Security*, 24(6):443–447.

[Witten and Nachenberg, 2007] Witten, B. and Nachenberg, C. (2007). Malware evolution: A snapshot of threats and countermeasures in 2005. *Malware Detection*, pages 3–15.

[Wool, 2004] Wool, A. (2004). A quantitative study of firewall configuration errors. *Computer*, 37(6):62–67.

[Young, 2010] Young, C. (2010). *Metrics and Methods for Security Risk Management*. Syngress.

In: Advances in Security Information Management ISBN: 978-1-62417-204-5
Editors: G. Suarez-Tangil and E. Palomar © 2013 Nova Science Publishers, Inc.

Chapter 2

SECURITY INFORMATION AND VULNERABILITY MANAGEMENT

Massoud Kamran[*]
Atos Worldline
Security Architecture & Policies
Brussels, Belgium

Abstract

Security information and event management are related to security risk, whilst security risk is closely related to the existence of vulnerabilities. Generally speaking, we are exposed to a security risk because somewhere we have a specific vulnerability. To discover where the vulnerabilities exist, we need a regular asset inventory, including all packages running on the assets. Moreover, we need a reliable source of information regarding the old and new vulnerabilities related to the packages running on the assets. Whether or not a vulnerability is exploited depends on how the asset with the vulnerability is protected by the security perimeter in place. In this chapter we have considered three main areas: the vulnerability assessment, the asset inventory including the software running on the systems managed by a SIEM, and the configuration and change management of the security perimeter protecting these assets. In most of these cases, the security components managing these three areas are not integrated in a SIEM. Efficient integration of these components can make available valuable information for refining the monitoring and correlation of a SIEM. This integration is one of the key factors for ensuring the full benefits of the SIEM infrastructure are made available.

Keywords: Security Information and Event Management (SIEM), Vulnerability Management, Asset Management

1. Introduction

Giving general ideas about security risk and vulnerability management is not enough for efficient event management. Much information has to be gathered, refined and correlated

---

[*]E-mail address: massoud.kamran@atos.net

before the right action can be taken in order to ensure protection against existing and new vulnerabilities. Risk and vulnerability management are necessary to narrow the scope of monitoring in the area of security incidents and event management. Instead of watching everything, we should pay more attention to where we have vulnerabilities and consequently where we are exposed to different risks. Like a chess player, we can pay attention to a limited area of the chess board where we think some moves may have the greatest consequences. Proper vulnerability management may help us to disregard irrelevant cases and focus our attention on the important areas. The challenge is to avoid being surprised by an important move that we had not considered. In other words, it is better to ignore dangerous attacks that may be carried out on a non-important asset than to ignore an insignificant attack against a very valuable asset.

Log management and compliance reporting are related to Security Information Management (SIM), and real-time monitoring and incident management are related to Security Event Management (SEM) [Nicolett and Kavanagh, 2011]. The main challenge in SIM is refining and improving the quality of available data. In SEM, the main challenge is integrating and building the necessary interfaces among different security components.

Organization.   The remainder of this chapter is organized in the following way. Section 2 describes some elementary notions of risk evaluation and parameters to be taken into account in the case of software vulnerability evaluation. We point out to the reader that recovering from an existing vulnerability is not always straightforward. The difficulties are related to the patch process, the complexity of the security perimeter, necessary integration among different components, and last but not least, in-house and specific knowledge building for better risk evaluation. A global overview of the infrastructure and its main functionalities is given in Section 3 Additionally, Related works in the different areas that can be used to ease the necessary integrations are mainly mentioned here. Section 4 gives a discussion of the building blocks and various challenges to improving the different components of the infrastructure.

2.   Software Vulnerability Evaluation

In order to rate the probability and impact of a risk, it is necessary to take into account different parameters, and to respond to the question 'what is the risk?' we need at least to define a basic approach. An advisory received by a vulnerability management system may be rated with a high probability and a high impact, but knowing your infrastructure, you may consider that the impact in your case will be low. The following is a basic way of carrying out a general risk evaluation.

2.1.   Security Risk Evaluation

The risk can be defined as the (weighted) product of the probability and the impact. Residual Risk can be defined as the product of weighted risk and the impact after deploying a countermeasure. The performance of a countermeasure can be assessed by balancing the weighted residual risk and the cost. The above is a general idea and may be presented in different ways. For example, the risk in Open Source Security Information Management (OSSIM) [Karg, 2004] is defined in Equation 1.

$$Risk = \frac{(Asset \cdot Priority \cdot Reliability)}{10} \tag{1}$$

On one hand, *Asset* defines how valuable the resource is under SIEM monitoring. This value is measured between 0 and 5. The more valuable the asset is, the greater the impact will be. Additionally, *Priority* measures the relative importance of the attack, how important the attack is if it is successful. Its default value is 1. If there is a possibility of bypassing the security of a system and taking complete control of it, the priority may be considered as high. Priority does not take into account how the security perimeter protects the asset. On the other hand, *Reliability* is related to probability, and its default value is 1. Probability should give an indication of the likelihood that the exploitation of a vulnerability in a specific environment will occur. As this evaluation can be difficult to make, the probability in OSSIM is linked to the reliability of information received by an Intrusion Detection System (IDS).

Playing with these notions will help us to evaluate the risk received by an advisory system that does not know anything about the infrastructure hosting our asset. For instance, considering that we rate the probability from 1 to 5 (high to low) and the impact from 1 to 4 (high to low). If we consider that an attack has a high probability (5) and a low impact (1), we can evaluate the risk as: $Risk = 5 \cdot 1$. If a risk of 5 and an impact of 4 (5*4 =20) is scored as 10, a risk of 5 normalized to a score of 10 is 2.5 or our weighted risk is: $Weighted risk = 2.5$

We may consider a countermeasure, and we may evaluate as medium (3) the impact of the countermeasure. In other words the residual risk is: $Residual risk = 2.5 \cdot 3 = 7.5$. If the risk of 10 with a residual risk of 5 is scored as 100, and the residual risk of 7.5 normalized to a score of 100 is 15, the weighted residual risk is: $Weighted Residual Risk = 15$. Considering the cost of our countermeasure, we can measure the performance of each countermeasure as Equation 2.

$$Performance = \frac{Weighted \cdot Residual \cdot Risk}{Cost} \tag{2}$$

Based on this indicator, a countermeasure may be selected. In the following section we will give the parameters used to rate a vulnerability, and will describe the cost and effort that must be considered before deployment of a countermeasure.

2.2. Vulnerability Monitoring

In this section we consider the case of vulnerability in software running on a system that is part of the SIEM infrastructure. SIEM can receive information or regularly fetch new advisories from the vulnerability management system. This system has its own security rating. For example, if the vulnerability is exploitable remotely, leads to the system being compromised, does not normally require any interaction, and there is available code to exploit the vulnerability, we have sufficient reason to rate the probability as high. This information may

Table 1. Vulnerability criticity

Extremely Critical(5 of 5)	For remotely exploitable vulnerabilities that can lead to system compromise. Successful exploitation does not normally require any interaction and exploits are available.
Highly Critical (4 of 5)	For remotely exploitable vulnerabilities that can lead to system compromise. Successful exploitation does not normally require any interaction but there are no known exploits available at the time of disclosure.
Moderately Critical (3 of 5)	For remotely exploitable Denial of Service vulnerabilities against different services.
Less Critical (2 of 5)	For cross-site scripting vulnerabilities and privilege escalation vulnerabilities. This is also used for vulnerabilities allowing exposure of sensitive data to local users.
Not Critical (1 of 5)	For very limited privilege escalation vulnerabilities and locally exploitable Denial of Service vulnerabilities. This is also used for non-sensitive system information disclosure vulnerabilities.

come from a vulnerability management system and could be used for aggregation, correlation and tuning with other available events in the SIEM. Generally speaking, the following criteria may be considered when scoring the risk of vulnerability:

- Exploitable remotely: vulnerabilities where the exploit does not require access to the system or a local network. This covers services that are acceptable to expose to the Internet (e.g. HTTP, HTTPS, SMTP). It also covers client applications used on the Internet.

- Leads to system compromise: Vulnerabilities that can lead to system compromise.

- No necessity for user interaction: Successful exploitation does not normally require any user interaction.

- Availability of code to exploit the vulnerability: Exploits are available.

On the other hand, if one or several of the above conditions are not fulfilled, for example the code to exploit the vulnerability is not yet available, we can rate the criticity as identified in Table 1.

Concerning the evaluation of the impact, it is possible to take other parameters into account. We can ask ourselves what will happen once the vulnerability is exploited, and try to evaluate the impact. The following cases can be considered: *brute force, Cross–Site Scripting* (XSS), *Denial of Service* (DoS), *exposure of sensitive information*, *exposure of system information, hijacking, manipulation of data, privilege escalation, security bypass, spoofing*, and *system access*. By taking the aforementioned factors into account, the vulnerability management system can evaluate the risk and send relevant events to SIEM.

The estimated risk received by the SIEM from the vulnerability management system is independent of the way the infrastructure hosting the asset is protected. In order to refine the risk, the role of the SIEM is to take other information from other sources such as the firewall and IDS. This can refine the risk and start the correct action. For example if the vulnerability can be exploited remotely and the asset is visible from outside to untrusted users, the correct action may be to block the traffic from/to outside via a firewall. In such a case a well-defined interface with a firewall protecting the asset can be used. This will be described in the section related to the security perimeter infrastructure. On the other hand, if the asset is protected from outside and is only accessible to trusted users, the correct action may be to refine the monitoring of traffic from/to the asset. It is possible that the vulnerability of the asset is not directly exposed to the outside but can be exposed via an intermediate vulnerable server. For this reason the system managing and monitoring the security perimeter must be able to give a complete picture of the possible incoming and outgoing traffic as well as its related risks.

2.3.   Perimeter Security Traffic and Risk Monitoring

Firewalls protecting most important infrastructures have a matrix or hierarchical structure and may include a few hundred access rules, objects defining servers, networks and services defining allowed traffic. As a consequence, the refinement of a rule base with many objects defined and changed over the long term will be not possible without the possibility of a regular check of the rule base and without monitoring the existing traffic. To do this we need an efficient tool. Additionally, regularly checking the firewall policy based on a risk profile, and monitoring traffic is needed to clean up the unnecessary rules. Obviously, any misconfiguration leading to holes or introducing risky traffic should be part of the vulnerability management. The results available after the risk and traffic control are valuable data to be taken into account in the SIEM environment to refine the monitoring of the risky rules.

The risk profile is the baseline for rating risky traffic. The evaluation of the risk is based on the predefined risk profile. Some traffic can be considered as risky and can be rated as "High", "Medium", "Low" or "Suspected High". For example, the User Datagram Protocol (UDP) on all ports from outside to the Demilitarized Zone (DMZ) can be rated as "High", while Simple Management Protocol (SNMP) traffic can be rated as "Medium", or a Remote Procedure Call (RPC) from outside to the DMZ may be considered as "Low". Other cases, such as many IP addresses that can be reached by Simple Message Transfer Protocol (SMTP), may be considered as "Suspected High".

The firewall rule base and traffic monitoring can extract the following security information:

- Risky rules based on a risk profile, including source, destination, service and action related to the rules.

- Rules that are a special case in other rules. Removing such a rule will not change the firewall's effective security policy.

- Rules that are covered (hidden) by other rules. Such rules are effectively disabled and can probably be deleted.

- Rule, including source, destination, service and actions related to the rule, number of times the rule is used, last use of the rule, percentage compared to the total traffic.

- Count, last usage and percentage for each, or combination of source, destination, service and action.

- The firewall and the specific rules allowing incoming traffic to the asset.

- The firewall and the specific rules allowing outgoing traffic from the asset.

- Incoming and outgoing of traffic to the asset. The historical baseline of the traffic related to the asset under monitoring can be used to check the traffic rate and trigger the necessary alerts when important deviations from the baseline are encountered.

- Information regarding the criticality of the zone in which the asset is protected by the related firewall. An asset visible from outside is probably more vulnerable than an asset in an internal, segregated LAN. This influences the evaluation of the risk.

The component checking the access control of the security perimeter must be able to send the necessary events to a SIEM infrastructure. In most cases, only the logging of the firewalls is collected by the SIEM. However, an intermediary component is necessary to send more refined events to the SIEM or to react based on the action requested by the SIEM. Actions started by the SIEM may use a specific API to get information from the component checking the access control of the security perimeter.

Infrastructure controlling the security perimeter may be used to evaluate the risk associated with the firewall protecting the zone hosting an asset. Some products also rate the overall security of the firewall protecting the asset.

Equation 3 describes the way Algosec [Algosec-Comapny, 2011] calculates the security of the firewall in general:

$$Risk = 100 \cdot \left(1 - \frac{w_1 \cdot x_1 + w_2 \cdot x_2 + w_3 \cdot x_3 + w_4 \cdot x_4}{w_1 \cdot t_1 + w_2 \cdot t_2 + w_3 \cdot t_3 + w_4 \cdot t_4}\right) \tag{3}$$

where, w_1 is the weight of high risks (10 by default), w_2 is the weight of suspected high risks (4 by default), w_3 is the weight of medium risk (2 by default), and w_4 is the weight of low risks (1 by default). Additionally, x_1 is the number of high risks detected in the current firewall policy, x_2 is the number of suspected high risks detected in the current firewall policy, x_3 is the number of medium risks detected in the current firewall policy, and x_4 is the number of low risks detected in the current firewall policy. Similarly, t_1 is the maximum number of high risks possible for the firewall as determined by the firewall's brand and topology, t_2 is the maximum number of suspected high risks possible for the firewall as determined by the firewall's brand and topology, t_3 is the maximum number of medium risks possible for the firewall, as determined by the firewall's brand and topology, and t_4 is the maximum number of low risks possible for the firewall, as determined by the firewall's brand and topology.

If the asset with a vulnerability is involved in a risky rule and/or is behind a risky firewall, the overall risk of the vulnerability has to be refined.

2.4. Vulnerability Recovery

Once the vulnerability is rated, for any countermeasure we have to take into account the different technical solutions as well as existing processes, such as patch and security incident management, that may influence the time necessary for tuning of the SIEM system.

To configure a SIEM infrastructure the following efforts have to be considered:

◇   The use of software to connect to the source for fetching the necessary data.
◇   The use of software for parsing and normalization of the received data.
◇   On-line monitoring of vulnerable zones.
◇   Finding and tuning correlation rules among events for valuable alerts.
◇   Off–line reporting and related review process.
◇   On–line alert evaluation and development of a procedure to handle the alerts.
◇   Data storage management and archiving capacity.
◇   Historical data manipulation.
◇   Patch management process.
◇   Change and configuration management process.
◇   Security incident management process.

In some cases, deploying a "long term" solution is costly; in other cases the time to implement the solution can be long. Sometimes even the cheapest solution that consists of patching the application may take a long time because of the process of change and patch management. In many cases application of the patches needs preliminary checks in a test and preproduction environment as well as quality assurance tests before applying the patch in a production environment.

In many large infrastructures the mean time for vulnerability recovery may be expressed as defined in Equation 4 [CIS, 2009], and in many infrastructures this can take many days. Alternative solutions can be used when a vulnerability is not efficiently fixed, such as monitoring the traffic from/to vulnerable applications or blocking the traffic in some specific cases.

$$MTTVR = \frac{\sum (date\ of\ vulnerabilty\ discovery - date\ of\ recovery)}{count(vulnerabilities)} \qquad (4)$$

In the case of a new security advisory, the security advisory system can send an event to SIEM. Another solution may be a regular check of the security advisory database by SIEM to fetch new security advisories. When a new security advisory is received, we have to find out which assets are impacted. This can be done by querying the asset inventory. The query is based on the information received in the security advisory event, such as the impacted software package, its version, and other additional information. Based on a correlation rule, SIEM can trigger an external action to carry out a security scan of the related asset.

Integration of the security scanning results is not always part of the existing SIEM. Some tools allow this, such as Cisco Monitoring Analysis and Response System (MARS) [R.Miller et al., 2011]. The security scan result depends on where the security engine is placed in the network topology. In the case of a positive result of the scan an event can be sent to SIEM with information regarding the result of the scan. Based on another correlation rule an external action can be started. This action queries the security perimeter management system. Necessary information such as the possible incoming and outgoing traffic, and rules for accepting such traffic can be gathered. This information will then be used to monitor or block the risky traffic if necessary.

A firewall is still an important protection mechanism in many infrastructures and can protect many applications from hostile connections. Firewalls rely mainly on topology

[Ioannidis et al., 2000]. Topology is all information related to IP addresses, subnets and the ways that they are connected. Firewall interfaces are designated as 'internal', 'external', 'DMZ', etc. giving the possibility to set up the access policy from/to different parts of the network topology. An entity relationship model defining global knowledge of the security policy and the network topology as well as a model definition language is defined by Y. Bartal, A. Mayer, K. Nissim, and A. Wool [Bartal et al., 2000]. The most important aspects of their work can be summarized as follows:

1. Defining an entity-relationship model providing a framework for representing both the (firewall independent) security policy and the network topology.

2. Using a Model Definition Language (MDL) to define an instance of the entity-relationship model as well as a parser for MDL that generates such instances.

3. Building a compiler translating a model instance into specific firewall/router config-uration files that typically include topology and rule-base information.

4. Defining a Rule Illustrator, which transforms the firewall-specific configuration files into a graphical representation of the current policy on the actual topology. This allows evaluation of the security policy.

Many of the above ideas are used in the development of commercial tools like Algosec Firewall Analyzer and Algosec FireFlow products . Few firewalls use the open Appli-cation Programming Interface (API) for their rule base and logging management. Open Platform for Security (OPSEC) API [CheckPoint, 2006] in the case of a security perimeter protected by Checkpoint firewalls can be considered a good example of an integration tool [D.Welch-Abernathy, 2001].

3.   Security Information and Event Management

Efficient interfaces with SIEM and security components such as firewalls, scanning tools, vulnerability assessment and asset inventory are necessary for building valuable correlated security events. For such integration with a monitoring and correlation system in a SIEM infrastructure, we believe that the following factors must be tackled as depicted in Figure 1.

1. The quality of logging information of the different components.

2. Having a reliable source of old and new security advisories.

3. Having a reliable asset inventory, with all software packages hosted by these assets.

4. Having an open API that can pull/push and change information on components such as firewalls, scanning tools, and security advisory and asset management systems.

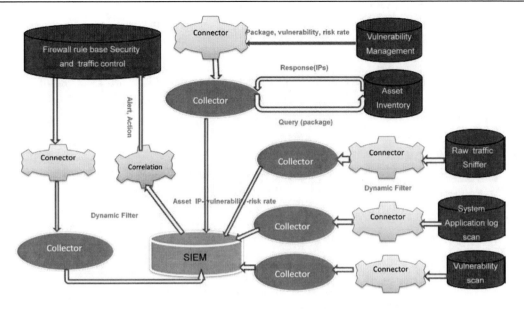

Figure 1. Globalview.

3.1.   Log information quality

One of the major difficulties in the SIEM area is the inconsistency of the layout and semantics of the security events among the different systems, networking components and
applications. In an attempt to resolve this problem, standardization efforts are underway.
Common Event Expression (CEE) [MITRE, 2010] is an attempt to create an open, practical
and industry-accepted event log standard. The Common Event Format (CEF) is an industry
"standard" including subset of CEE objectives, and is used in some commercial products
such as ArcSight and Algosec.

High quality of the collected logs and well defined syntax and semantics of the logs are
essential for any SIEM. Producing relevant and valuable logs is one of the most challenging
aspects of a SIEM implementation. In most cases the logs are missing or they lack critical
information [Chuvakin, 2010] or they do not use a standard layout and semantics. The most
important idea is to know what has to be logged, which data has to be part of the logs and
which data does not need to be included. There are different types of events that must be
logged, which can be summarized as the following:

- Availability issues, such as startups, exhausted resources, connectivity problems.

- Threats such as invalid inputs and usage of specific patterns.

- Authentication, authorization and access.

- Changes to privileges, data changes including creation and destruction of monitored
  objects.

What must be included can be summarized as the following: (i) when an event
happened, (ii) what happened, (iii) why it happened, (iv) where the event happened, and

(v) who was involved, and how it happened. For instance, lets take the following entry of a log as an example:

2011/02/14 10:00:01 AM GMT+2 priority=3 system=gateway module=authentication source=x.x.x.x user=massoud action=login object=database status=failed reason="password incorrect".

We can conclude the following useful information: when the event had happened *2011/02/14 10:00:01 AM GMT+2*, what happened *failed to connect*, why it happened *password incorrect*, where the event happened *in a gateway system with IP: x.x.x.x in authentication module*, who was involved *massoud*, and how it happened *login*. Whereas on the other hand, a useless log could be something like this: *February 11 09:00:00 parameter null gif? exit! call security*.

3.2. Reliable sources of security advisories

It is necessary to have a reliable source of security advisories related to the software running on the assets that are being monitored. An infrastructure must be built to connect to the source of the security advisory. A list of the assets, knowledge of the different types of software running on them and the capacity to link a received security advisory to the related assets is necessary in a SIEM. If the reliable source of the advisories is disconnected from the source of the inventory, linking the vulnerability to a specific asset must be done by the component of the SIEM. On the other hand, in order to have an efficient system, an agent must be built to run on the systems and must be capable of automatically updating the packages installed on the assets. In many cases this update must be carefully checked and is part of a well-defined patch process. Ideally, the advisory will include the vulnerability definition in the language of the available scanner. In such a case a scan can be started to check if the vulnerability exists. The advisory may include the following information: Name and IP address of the asset, criticality based on defined criteria, vulnerability definition and available exploits, references to other sources, information about the operating system and running software.

Defining a vulnerability in a standard way is not commonly done. The question may arise of how, after getting an advisory for a new vulnerability, this can be included in the scanner repository used for checking our systems. Open Vulnerability Assessment Language (OVAL) [Baker et al., 2012] can be considered as an important means of standardizing the state of a system. It includes a language to encode system details and the definition of the different vulnerabilities in a repository held throughout the community.

Appendix 1 describes two example of advisory information reports. On the one hand, Secunia [Kellett, 2011] repository is presented on Appendix A1 and, on the other hand, OVAL repository sample can be found on Appendix A2 It is interesting to see that in the Secunia database a reference to the OVAL repository is also given.

3.3. Accuracy of the asset inventory

Many infrastructures already have their asset inventory before deploying a SIEM infrastructure. The information received by a vulnerability management system needs to be refined by information stored in an inventory management system. The vulnerability management system may have its own asset inventory and receive only vulnerabilities related to the assets already defined in its database and packages installed on it. If the advisories are filtered based on the definition of the assets and packages installed on them, it is very important to keep the inventory up-to-date. If the inventory is not accurate, irrelevant advisories will be received and relevant ones will be lost. The inventory can be part of a vulnerability management database or a SIEM database or a separate database. The inventory must be done regularly or carried out in the case of install or uninstall of a package. A file integrity check client may be used in the SIEM environment to detect changes that may indicate the installation, uninstall or update of a package. Creation of an automatic inventory tool for different operating systems for feeding the inventory database is a challenge that is within the scope of a SIEM infrastructure.

3.4.   Vulnerability assessment

The best starting point is to do a detailed inventory of all packages installed on the different systems, including obtaining detailed information regarding their versions.

Usually, a vulnerability scan tool is used to make a vulnerability assessment. Different types of tools may be used to cover the existence of the different types of vulnerabilities. A network scanner cannot necessarily detect a cross-site scripting vulnerability. In many cases, just an accurate inventory and an advisory with detailed information will be enough to conclude that a vulnerability exists in a specific system.

The vulnerability scan tool must have the definition related to the received security advisory. The information received by a security advisory indicates that a specific package found in a system has a vulnerability. It is possible that the packages found in a system are not used or active. The security scan information may be useful to see how effectively the vulnerability is exposed. The main challenge is to build and run a scan based on the received security advisory information. Information in the received security advisory regarding the existence of the exploit may also be useful for building and running the correct security scan.

In general, the repository of the vulnerabilities assessment must be regularly updated with the new vulnerabilities that are identified during the life of the systems monitored by the SIEM. Each scanner updates its repository of vulnerabilities based on its own language, and the scan engine interprets the vulnerability definitions available on the repository. It is safer in general not to rely on just one specific scanner, but to have other reliable sources of advisories for existing or new vulnerabilities.

Let us suppose that we receive from our reliable source the information that OpenSSL version older than 0.9.8r or 1.0.0d has a vulnerability, and the solution is to upgrade to OpenSSL 0.9.8r/1.0.0d or later. If a correct inventory of software is installed on the different systems, it will be not necessary to define this vulnerability in the language of the scanner. If we trust our inventory and we know that this version is installed on one of our systems, it is better to spend time installing the new version. If the upgrade cannot be carried out soon, we have to find a countermeasure or improve the monitoring to detect any attempt to exploit this vulnerability. If the inventory cannot be trusted, it will be wise to use the scanner to check if it has already been updated with the definition of the vulnerability. Otherwise, the vulnerability must be written into the language of the scanner to carry out the necessary checks on the system under SIEM monitoring. In the following example, an Openssl _1_0_0d.nasl file received from the Nessus [Tenable-Network-Security, 2011] repository contains the definition of this vulnerability written in the Network Attack Scripting Language (NASL) used by the Nessus scanner. In order to check if the system is vulnerable to this, we can imagine that an external action triggered by a correlation rule executes the following command:

nasl.exe -T trace -t x.x.x.x openssl_1_0_0d.nasl

where "nasl.exe" is a version of a "nasal" interpreter and openssl _1_0_0d.nasl is the existing definition in the Nessus repository.

The same vulnerability in the OVAL language is defined in an xml file available in the OVAL repository for checking on an HP-UX 11 system. Running the following command locally on the system can check for the existence of this vulnerability:

ovaldi -m -o oval-2011-08-01.10.02.12.xml

where "ovaldio" is a version of OVAL interpreter, and oval-2011-08-01.10.02.12.xml is the definition of this vulnerability in the OVAL repository.

3.5.   Firewall change management

In order to be able to change automatically the rule base of the firewall, the action related to the correlation rule has to define a rule base, submit this to the system monitoring the firewall rule base, receive a proposed rule base change, and implement this change automatically. This should be part of the integration to be carried out around a SIEM infrastructure, and it can be very complex in a large infrastructure with a large amount of traffic from/to servers. In simple cases the following actions may be started following the occurrence of a specific correlation:

1. Block specific traffic from/to an IP address for a specific period of time.

2. Unblock specific traffic from/to an IP address.

3. Get info on blocked/unblocked IP addresses.

A SAM Server may be used in agent mode or proxy mode. In agent mode, the SAM server inhibits or closes the given connection through its local enforcement module. In proxy mode, the SAM server passes the request to other SAM Servers. Figure 2 illustrates both modes.

Having a historical baseline for traffic related to the asset being monitored can also be useful information. This can be based on the incoming and outgoing traffic rate from/to the asset which has a vulnerability.

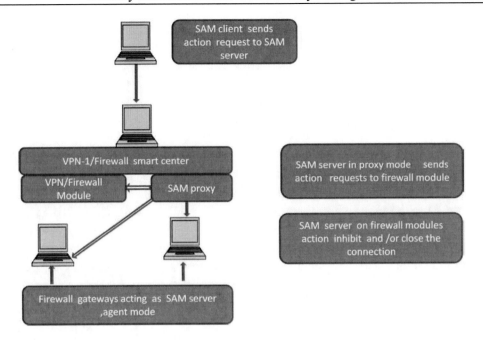

Figure 2. Suspicious Activity Monitoring.

4. Building blocks

Basically, a SIEM environment consists of software components that carry out several processes and functionalities such as: (i), connecting to the source of information for gathering raw data, (ii), collecting, parsing and normalization of the raw data, (iii), data storage handling, (iv), event correlation, (v), on–line monitoring and reporting, (vi), off–line reporting on historical data.

4.1. Building connector

By 'connector' we mean software necessary to hide the details of the connectivity between the source and the SIEM. Connectors can resolve different types of connectivity issues and provide details of their implementation. The connectors may be of different types, such as: a syslog connection, a database connection or another connection based on a specific protocol. OPSEC includes different APIs, namely Log Export API (LEA), Suspicious Activity Monitoring (SAM), and Checkpoint Management Interface (CPMI). These APIs can be used to integrate the necessary actions in a SIEM environment. In many SIEM products, LEA (API) is used to collect Checkpoint firewall logs. The SAM API that plugs into the OPSEC can be used to block suspicious connections.

   Other connectors are necessary to get the necessary information from different databases such as the asset and advisory databases. Specific connectors have to be used to receive events coming from different sources rather than searching the data from the external sources. For example, the scanner, applications, and raw data sniffer can send their data via a specific protocol such as syslog–ng to syslog server listening in the SIEM system.

The sniffer agent may be simply a piece of code to get the "tcpdump" output and send the output via syslog. The sniffer agent may be on a specific system or at a global level, for example in the switches connecting a specific local area network. Necessary integrations must be carried out for connection of such connectors to different types of sources.

4.2.   Building collector

A collector is software that parses the data received by the connector, mapping the different information to the predefined fields of a SIEM database.

Collectors must have the capability to access an external database or take any other actions to refine the input with other metadata before putting them in the SIEM database as depicted in Figure 3. It is possible that the advisory source may indicate a vulnerability regarding a package. In such a case the collector may consult the asset inventory to find all assets running the related package and their location (via their IP addresses for example). In many cases, a collector does not have the capability to refine the data received from a source. This can be done, for example, by accessing the external sources. This needs additional integration, which is not normally one of the functionalities of the predefined collector code in the different SIEM products. The computer language and development environment for developing the collectors must be powerful enough to permit different capabilities.

Naming conventions may help very much to match an asset in an advisory database with an object defined in the rule base of the firewall, a vulnerability scan result, system or application logs. The collectors are used to parse the events and normalize them, and use the same taxonomy when different kinds of tools are used. As an example, each IDS uses its own taxonomy. The normalized form such as Intrusion Detection Exchange Message Format (IDMEF) or CEE may be considered to map different event fields to a normalized one, for example in the case of IDS events.

4.3.   Adaptive filtering and correlation

The connector must be able to filter the incoming information and also change the rate of incoming events when necessary. For greater efficiency we have to be able to dynamically make the necessary changes on the filter and the rate of the incoming events on a connector. The SIEM has to take into account these changes. Still, many SIEM products are not developed in such a way that they can be easily changed and integrated with other components. For example, it is still difficult to use an existing API to stop a connector or a correlation, start a connector or a correlation, change configuration attributes and restart the code governing the connection with the different event sources. A DOS attack on some servers under SIEM monitoring can indirectly produce a DOS attack on the SIEM. Adaptive filtering of data can avoid DOS attacks on the SIEM infrastructure in some cases. It is very useful if a SIEM environment allows a predefined filter to be changed dynamically or a new one to be built and started dynamically. It is also useful to change a predefined correlation rule and to have the ability to build and restart dynamically a new correlation rule.

The above facilities can be used in the following scenario two scenarios. On the one hand, an advisory regarding an asset is received. Our assumption is that there is a vulner-

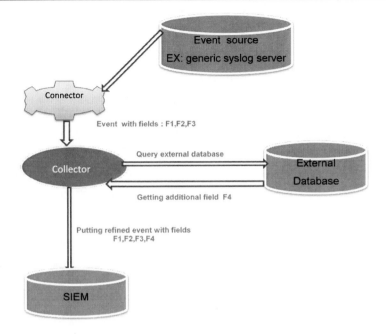

Figure 3. Event Collector.

ability management system receiving on-line advisories regarding all kinds of vulnerabilities. The receiving advisory is checked against an asset inventory including all assets under SIEM monitoring and including all packages running on these assets. If the received advisory is relevant, the vulnerability management system sends an event to the SIEM indicating that asset "A" has a vulnerability.

On the other hand, we assume also that there is a simple correlation rule that is triggered once the above event is received by the SIEM. When the correlation rule is triggered it starts an external action. The external action for example can make a query to the asset inventory to get the IP address of the asset, obtain other information and start a scan. In the case that the scan finds the same vulnerability received by the vulnerability management, the external action sends an event to the SIEM with additional information, for example a field that confirms the existence of the vulnerability on the asset. On the other hand, another simple correlation rule can be triggered if an event with a "confirmed" field is received by the SIEM. Actions related to this second correlation rule may include the definition or refinement of a filter. The refinement can be based, for example, on how a specific pattern can be used to exploit the vulnerability defined in the received advisory.

4.4. Correlation capability

Contrary to what is sometimes supposed, a SIEM is not used to find out correlated events. It is used to give an alert in the case of occurrence of events that are already supposed to be correlated. In order to check if some events are correlated to each other, statistical analysis of representative samples of the events must be used. Generally speaking, if x_i and y_i represent the occurrences of event X and Y, the correlated coefficient can be calculated by

Equation 5. The value of R is between -1 and +1, showing the independency to dependency of the two variables.

$$Corr.\,Coef. = \frac{\sum (x_i - \overline{x}) \cdot (y_i - \overline{y})}{\sqrt{\sum (x_i - \overline{x})^2 \cdot (y_i - \overline{y})^2}} \qquad (5)$$

The above statistical analysis is not normally part of the SIEM functionalities. As we have mentioned, what is called the correlation capability of the SIEM is mainly used to define conditions regarding the occurrence of specific events and to give alerts if the defined conditions are met. These are events that are supposed to be correlated. Let us take the case that a new vulnerability is published and the related exploit uses a specific pattern to be sent to the port on which the application with the vulnerability is listening. Following the disclosure of the vulnerability, attempts to exploit the vulnerability may appear in the traffic of the site monitored by the SIEM, and it is likely that the disclosure of a vulnerability and attempts to exploit it are correlated. The intention in such a case is not to prove that the events are correlated to each other but rather to put in place a filter that will be triggered when the two events occur. Correlation is an important functionality of a SIEM. The better the language used to define the correlation, the greater the chance of sending valuable alerts. In a more general case it must be possible to start any actions, or in other words execute any external program when a correlation occurs. Being able to start an external action gives more possibilities of integration with other components which are part of a SIEM infrastructure. Without going into details we give the main capabilities of a correlation language.

Syntaxes for some general instructions given to a correlation engine to trigger the necessary actions are the following:

Syntax rule 1
Filter (<evaluation expression> [and |or <evaluation expression>...]
<evaluation expression> ::= [not] <meta-tag> <comparison> <value>
Comparison: =,>,<,>=,>=,! =
Value: <regular expression>

Syntax rule 2
Trigger (<threshold count>, <time-window> [,discriminator (<meta-tag> [,meta-tag])])

Syntax rule 3
Window (<evaluation expression>,[<storage filter>,] <storage time window>

Syntax rule 4
Combine (rule 1, rule 2,...<mode>, <time>,<discriminator>)

Syntax rule 5
Combine (rule 1, rule 2,..., <time>,<discriminator>)

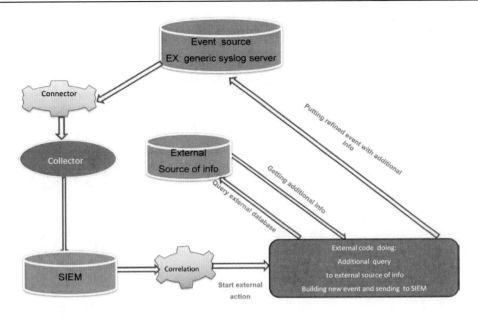

Figure 4. Event Refinement.

The above definition can be more general, with the following capabilities, which indeed gives sufficiently flexible language to express powerful correlation rules:

- Each rule's output may be redirected as input to another rule.

- Output of the rules can be combined by "union" and "intersection" operators.

- The operator in a filter rule can compare the result with the content of a predefined or dynamically created list.

Following the occurrence of a correlation, we can start an external action and pass some information to this external action. The external action can later query any external source of information to build a refined event and send it back to the SIEM, as depicted in Figure 4.

4.5. Correlation scenario

In the following, we give an idea of what the raw messages received by each collector may contain. The collector parses the data, refines them with metadata, and maps data gathered into a generic taxonomy as detailed in Appendix 2. Four scenarios have been considered:

- Asset Security Advisories: Reception of a security advisory for a specific asset defined in the vulnerability management system. The action related to this event is to start a scan on the asset.

- Vulnerability scan: Result of the vulnerability scan on the asset for which an advisory is received. The scan has to be done in such a way that it can bypass the existing

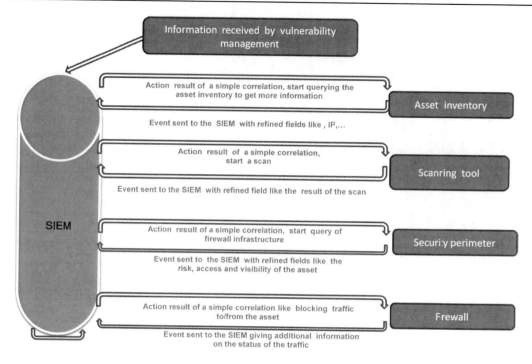

Figure 5. Correlation Actions.

protection such as firewalls, IPS and other protection measures. The result will be sent to the SIEM for confirmation of the existence of the vulnerability. The action related to this event is to start a query on the firewall rule management and monitoring system.

- Firewall rule base & traffic control: Input of a query to identify rules allowing access to the asset, mainly from no trusted zones.

- Application log: Application logs are used to identify the tentative of exploiting a vulnerability. The action related to this event can be the same as that which occurs when receiving a security advisory on the asset.

The results will be used to write the correlation rules and trigger the actions. The actions can block specific traffic or refine a filter at connector level. The above information can be used to refine the scope of monitoring of the vulnerable asset or to block risky traffic to it. Monitoring or blocking the traffic are the countermeasures that should be considered if the vulnerability cannot be fixed by a specific patch. The degree of automation of the different steps such as querying different databases, starting the scan, and monitoring or blocking the traffic depends highly on the availability of the necessary API. If the necessary API is not available manual operation will be required instead. What follows may be a sequence of events and related actions, as shown in Figure 5.

5. Conclusion

The most important functionalities of a SIEM infrastructure are refinement of global risk evaluation, software vulnerability management, accurate asset inventory, monitoring risks on the firewall rule basis, and having the capacity for online monitoring and adaptation of the predefined configuration. Moreover, metadata are necessary to narrow the area of the monitoring, refine the reporting, and for data aggregation and correlation. Efficient and correct interfacing between the SIEM and vulnerability detection are still at a preliminary stage of maturity.

Many steps defined in this chapter need an in–house knowledge building and an important integration of different components of a SIEM. Pending a global standard, mature solutions and flexible integration, organizations must build their own solutions for improving their security, visibility and governance. At the time of this writing there exist various commercial products that can be used as the building blocks for a SIEM infrastructure, as we have described in this paper. However, an important integration effort will be necessary to combine the different functionalities.

For instance, around 22 products are available on the market in 2011. Regarding SIEM systems, we can mention the `Sentinel` product developed in 1999 by a company called `e-security`, which promoted the new ideas around Security Event Management. `E-security` became part of `Novell`, which has now been bought by `Attachmate`. Regarding firewall rule base analyzers, we can mention `Firewall Analyzer` and `Fire-Flow` from a company called `Algosec`. Based on a solid theoretical background, `Algosec` product offers important functionalities. Regarding collecting security advisories and vulnerability management, we can mention a company called `Secunia` and their enterprise vulnerability management product. Concerning vulnerability scans, many are available. For networking scans, the `Nessus` package can be used. For application scans other tools may be used, for example `BackTrack` packaging. Whatever the different components used for integration with the SIEM, the main objective is to remove the possibility of exploiting existing vulnerabilities. This objective can only be achieved by using an efficient and integrated vulnerability management system with the SIEM.

A Advisory Information

A1. Secunia Sample Report

The following appendix gives information available in the `Secunia` Database.

Secunia ID: SA30857
Release Date: 2008-06-26
Last Update: 2008-10-14
Criticality: *Moderately critical*
Impact: *Cross Site Scripting, Security Bypass*
Where: *From remote Software: Microsoft Internet Explorer 6.x*
CVE reference: *CVE-2008-2947, CSS:6.8*
Description: *Ph4nt0m Security Team has discovered a vulnerability in Internet Explorer*

6, which can be exploited by malicious persons to conduct cross-domain scripting attacks. The vulnerability is caused due to an input validation error when handling the "location" or "location.href" property of a window object. This can be exploited by a malicious website, for example, to open a trusted site and execute arbitrary script code in a user's browser session in context of the trusted site. The vulnerability is confirmed in IE6 on Windows XP SP2. Other versions may also be affected.

Solution: *Patch*

Original Advisory: *Ph4nt0m Security Team (Chinese) http://www.ph4nt0m.org-a.googlepages.com/PSTZine_0x02_0x04.txt*

Other references: *US-CERT VU#923508 http://www.kb.cert.org/vuls/id/923508*

Deep Links: *list of references calculated using an advanced search algorithm using* Secunia*'s extensive database of vulnerability information.*

Oval Reference:

http://oval.mitre.org/repository/data/getDef? id=oval:org.mitre.oval:def:5901

CERT-VN reference: 923508

CVE-Reference: 2008-2947

VUPEN References:

http://www.frsirt.com/english/advisories/2008/1940/references
http://www.frsirt.com/english/advisories/2008/2809

Other reference:

http://www.ph4nt0m.org-a.googlepages.com/PSTZine_0x02_0x04.txt
http://blogs.zdnet.com/security/? p=1348

ST reference: 1020382

ISS-X-Force ID reference:

http://xforce.iss.net/xforce/xfdb/45565
http://xforce.iss.net/xforce/xfdb/43366

Bugtraq reference: *http://marc.info/? l=bugtraq&m=122479227205998&w=2*

BIF reference: 29960

CERT reference:

http://www.us-cert.gov/cas/techalerts/TA08-288A.html

Microsoft Security bulletin reference:

http://www.microsoft.com/technet/security/Bulletin/MS08-058.mspx

Provided and/or Discovered by: *Ph4nt0m Security Team*

Changelog: *2008-06-27 added link to US-CERT*

2008-07-09 added CVE reference

2008-10-1' Microsoft issues patches, Updated "Solution" section

A2.   Oval Sample Report

The following shows information available in the OVAL repository.

Title: *Window Location Property Cross-Domain Vulnerability.*

Description: *Cross-domain vulnerability in Microsoft Internet Explorer 5.01 SP4, 6, and 7 allows remote attackers to access restricted information from other domains via JavaScript that uses the object data type for the value of a location or location.href property, related* *to incorrect determination of the origin of a web script, aka "Window Location Property Cross-Domain Vulnerability". NOTE: according to Microsoft, CVE-2008-2948 and CVE-2008-2949 are duplicates of this issue and are probably different attack vectors.*

Family: *Windows*

Status: *Accepted*

Platform(s): *Microsoft Windows 2000, Microsoft Windows XP, Microsoft Windows Server 2003, Microsoft Windows Vista, Microsoft Windows Server 2008*

Class: *Vulnerability*

Reference(s): *CVE-2008-2947*

Product(s): *Microsoft Internet Explorer*

Information given in the above shows that after receiving an advisory, automation of the necessary actions is not straightforward. The following actions may be considered:

◇ Checking the relevance of the advisory.
◇ Finding the impacted systems.
◇ Patching.
◇ Defining closed monitoring.
◇ Defining specific countermeasures.

B Generic Advisory Report Taxonomy

B1. Asset Sample Report

Asset: Gateway-A

Package: BEA WebLogic Express 5.x

Vulnerability Description: BEA has confirmed a problem in WebLogic Server and Express, which potentially can be exploited to conduct cross-site scripting attacks against users. The problem is that WebLogic Server by default responds to HTTP TRACE requests. This fact can be exploited to execute arbitrary HTML and script code in a user's browser session in the context of an affected site when combined with certain browser vulnerabilities

Received date: 01/03/2011

Criticality: Not critical

Impact: Cross-Site Scripting

Where: From remote

Solution Status: vendor patch

CVE References: CVE-2004-2320/CVSS:5.8

IP: x.x.x.x (Metadata to be added by the collector.)

B2. Vulnerability Scan Sample Report

Date: 01/03/2011

IP: x.x.x.x
Plugin ID: 11213
Issue Type: Warning
Risk rating: Medium / CVSS Base Score : 5.0
Short Summary: Test for TRACE / TRACK Methods
Synopsis: Debugging functions are enabled on the remote web server.
Description: The remote webserver supports the TRACE and/or TRACK methods. TRACE and TRACK are HTTP methods which are used to debug web server connections.

B3.   Application Log Sample Report

Server: x.x.x.x (Metadata to be added by the collector)
Last Occurrence date: 04/03/2011 15:28:14
Occurrence: 2
Severity: Critic
Message: Invalid URI in request GET <script>cross_site_scripting.nasl</script> HTTP/1.1
Module: httpd
Client: 10.1.1.1 (IP address of the remote system trying to exploit the vulnerability)

B4.   Firewall Sample Report

Rule: 322
Server as destination: x.x.x.x :
Source: All sources (can be detailed by source)
Service: 80
Action: accept
Count: 1234 (per day)
Last usage: 05/03/2011
Percentage: 1.2%
Baseline count: 1200
Baseline percentage: 1.2%

References

[Algosec-Comapny, 2011] Algosec-Comapny (2011). FireFlow 6.1 Advanced Configuration Guide and Firewall Analyzer 6.1 User Guide.

[Baker et al., 2012] Baker, J., Hansbury, M., and Haynes, D. (2012). The OVAL Language Specification Version 5.10.1.

[Bartal et al., 2000] Bartal, Y., Mayer, A., Nissim, K., and Wool, A. (2000). Firmato: A novel firewall management toolkit.

[CheckPoint, 2006] CheckPoint (2006). *Suspicious Activities Monitoring API Specification*. OPSEC SDK 6.0.

[Chuvakin, 2010] Chuvakin, G. P. (2010). How to do application logging right.

[CIS, 2009] CIS (2009). *The CIS security metrics*. The Security metrics Center for Internet Security.

[D.Welch-Abernathy, 2001] D.Welch-Abernathy, D. (2001). *Essential Check Point Firewall-1 An Installation, Configuration and Troubleshooting Guide* . Addison Wesley, ISBN 0-201-69950-8.

[Ioannidis et al., 2000] Ioannidis, S., D.Kermoytis, A., Steven M.Bellovin, and M.Smith, J. (2000). Implementing a distributed firewall.

[Karg, 2004] Karg, D. (2004). *OSSIM Correlation engine explained*. ossimCorrelation.

[Kellett, 2011] Kellett, A. (2011). *Secunia Vulnerability Intelligence Mangement*. Technology Audit, OVUM Consulting.

[MITRE, 2010] MITRE (2010). *Common Event Expression*. Architecture Overview Version 0.5.

[Nicolett and Kavanagh, 2011] Nicolett, M. and Kavanagh, K. M. (2011). Magic quadrant for security information and event management. Gartner.

[R.Miller et al., 2011] R.Miller, D., Harris, S., Harper, A. A., and Stephen VanDyke, C. B. (2011). *Security Information and Event Management (SIEM) Implementation* . MC Graw Hil ISBN:978-0-07-170108-2l, New York Chicago San Francisco.

[Tenable-Network-Security, 2011] Tenable-Network-Security (2011). Nessus 4.4 Installation and User Guide.

In: Advances in Security Information Management
Editors: G. Suarez-Tangil and E. Palomar

ISBN: 978-1-62417-204-5
© 2013 Nova Science Publishers, Inc.

Chapter 3

TOWARD A MULTISTAGE ATTACK DETECTION FRAMEWORK

*Jules Pagna Disso**
EADS Innovation Works, Quadrant House, UK

Abstract

The current sophistication of cyber attacks has made the task of security protection increasingly difficult. There is a clear and urgent need to enhance such protection especially since recent attacks have targeted the Critical National Infrastructure (CNI). These attacks not only cause damage to the environment and economy, but also have the potential to cause significant losses of human life. In this chapter, we explore three common attack scenarios which take advantage of the weak nature of current security mechanisms. The first scenario identifies weaknesses of current protection mechanisms by utilising virtualisation to bypass these protections. The second scenario concerns a level of attacks that are not addressed by current protection solutions. This prompted us to look at attacks from another angle, where the source of the attack is of primary interest. In the third scenario, we focus on an infected computer which is in the process of registering other computers to a botnet. For each attack scenario, we perform an in-depth step by step analysis of each attack type. Our analysis will show that some attacks can be performed in up to twelve steps. We also discuss the security mechanism options that are available for each of the discussed attacks focusing on SIEM approaches. Finally, we introduce the design of a SIEM system which addresses the four levels of attack visibility identified in our work.

Keywords: Security Information and Event Management (SIEM), Multistage Attack Detection, Critical National Infrastructure (CNI) attacks

1. Introduction

Mitigating today's attacks has become a very serious challenge for Internet based businesses and services. The level of sophistication of cyber attacks has risen considerably and it is becoming more difficult to distinguish normal behaviour from malicious behaviour.

---

*E-mail address: julesferdinand.pagna@eads.com

Recently, hackers have developed systems that allow them to autonomously compromise and infect computers. These infected computers are grouped into an army of computers ready to obey commands from a master computer. These armies are referred to as botnets which are generally used to send SPAM messages or to launch Denial of Service (DoS) attacks. Also, when computers have been compromised they are subject to various attacks, since they are controlled remotely. The malicious user controlling the computers can then decide to perform various actions such as installing key loggers, installing worms, viruses, destroying and copying data.

Like botnets, current malicious programs use common port numbers for their communications. For instance, `Holland C&C` uses port 80 for sending commands to zombies [Choi et al., 2007], [Cremonini and Riccardi, 2009]. This poses a serious challenge for existing network security countermeasures, namely Intrusion Detection Systems (IDSs), Intrusion Prevention Systems (IPSs), firewalls and Security Information and Event Management (SIEM) solutions. For example, regarding firewalls, the traditional strategy of blocking port numbers would not be appropriate as, in that particular case, port 80 is used for Internet browsing. Hence, an in-depth approach would require an exhaustive analysis of the payload. However, most botnet tools encrypt their communications, defeating the objectives of deep packets analysis [Vogt and Aycock, 2006], [Yang and Ting, 2009]. In addition, the intensive volume of data in current communications networks is another important challenge for the security experts. There is evidence to indicate that the higher the speed and volume of data communication, the more data is dropped by IDSs [Alhomoud et al., 2011], [Alserhani F. and J, 2009] and the more likely attacks will go undetected.

An static analysis is still very common in IPS, IDS, and other security countermeasures against malware activities. In fact, Snort [Sourcefire, 2012] still remains the most commonly used IDS in research communities despite its limitations in handling attacks that have been previously analyzed. Over the years, various solutions have been proposed to resolve cyber–attacks. Recent works on firewalls focus on improving the management of rules rather than improving the underlying analysis [Sheth and Thakker, 2011], [Diksha and Shubham, 2006]. As for IDS, recent works deal with improving IDS management processes [Roschke et al., 2009], distribution of sensors, and reorganization of rules [Zaman and Karray, 2009]. There are also other research efforts enhancing the understanding of the attack behaviour, though they are based on static signatures [Zhong, 2010]. Another work presented in [Ormerod et al., 2010] is limited to examining specific attacks rather than looking at the overall picture.

In this chapter, we examine attacks from a different angle. We look at each attack step–by–step to reason about why such attacks are successful. We also scrutinize current security mechanisms to understand the limitations of these systems. Whenever it was possible to use a trace file, we did an in–depth offline analysis. In other cases, due to the nature of the attacks, it was not possible to record related traffic. We then analyze such attacks using a step–by–step methodology. For our offline analysis, we have defined and used a particular methodology enabling consistency in our analysis.

Organization.   The rest of the chapter is organized as follows. We start discussing the analysis methodology that was used in our traffic analysis in Section 2. We then present three attack scenarios organized as scenario `alpha`, `beta` and `charlie`. Scenario alpha looks at how virtualisation has been used to bypass current security protections Scenario beta discusses drive by download attacks, with a focus on the visibility of such attacks. Each level of visibility presents particular challenges that will be discussed. In the final scenario, charlie, we look at 'noisy' network traffic that is generally discarded. We argue that early signs of attack can generally be found in 'noisy' traffic. Finally, after the three attack scenarios, we propose a solution in Section 3. In our solution design, we identify four levels of visibility of attacks. We discuss about incorporating these four levels of attack visibility to significantly improve the success of protection mechanisms. Based on these four levels of visibility of attack, we propose an architecture that requires collaborative efforts from both organisations and communities to fight against malware. Finally, some conclusions and research directions are presented in Section 4.

2. Attack Scenarios

2.1. Analysis Methodology

Analysing captured traffic can be very challenging given the large number of protocols. However, many tools can be used to facilitate such analysis: Wireshark [Foundation, 2012], Network Monitor [Microsoft, 2012], and others will capture traffic and provide a basic analysis. For the purpose of our study, we will analyze a series of scenarios according to the following steps:

- **General statistics**: This step gives us a quick summary of the file contents. We use the Linux command *capinfos*. Additionally, statistics on IPs presence within the network traffic being analysed.

- **Operating systems (OS)** involved: This step will allow us to see what OS are involved in the recorded traffic. Predictions can be made regarding the type of attacks that are taking place once we have identified the OS, combined with other information, such as the port number.

- **Summary of TCP transactions**: TCP transactions can provide a greater understanding of the sort of activity that is occurring. Many studies have analysed TCP transaction for critical path analysis [Barford and Crovella, 2001] and network performance [Walrand, 2000, Spragins, 1996, Ge et al., 2011]. At times, TCP transactions have helped to differentiate the problem of slow traffic. Confusion is often made between attacks and network configuration problems when there is a slower than usual flow of communications between the different nodes.

- **Summary of conversation**: This is a very important step in the analysis since it indicates the IPs and port numbers involved in any exchange of information, along with a summary of packet sizes and durations of communications. Using TCP flag, TCP conversations have been used to analyse botnet traffic [Ma et al., 2010] ; they have also been used for web 2.0 characterisations [Shuai et al., 2008].

```
root@ubuntu:/home/administrator/stuff# capinfos suspicious-time.pcap
File name:              suspicious-time.pcap
File type:              Wireshark/tcpdump/... - libpcap
File encapsulation:     Ethernet
Number of packets:      745
File size:              305902 bytes
Data size:              293958 bytes
Capture duration:       231 seconds
Start time:             Fri Jan  1 00:00:29 2010
End time:               Fri Jan  1 00:04:20 2010
Data byte rate:         1274.94 bytes/sec
Data bit rate:          10199.51 bits/sec
Average packet size:    394.57 bytes
Average packet rate:    3.23 packets/sec
root@ubuntu:/home/administrator/stuff#
```

Figure 1. Trace file information.

- Extract any file present in the **trace file**: Extracting the file will help understand the type of communication and any possible problems to expect. For example, the use of a .*zip* file and .*exe* files could indicate the transfer of a malware.

- **In–depth analysis**: In this step we perform a free style analysis where we look at all possible details of the file.

2.2. Scenario Alpha

The trace file analysed on this first scenario has been used in challenge number 2 of the 2010 forensic challenge called "Browser under attack" [Project, 2010].

2.2.1. General Statistics

Information inferred from this analysis is generally informative and does not always carry attack information. However, information such as the file type, file size, data bit, and data byte rate, can give us preliminary indications on how to process incoming information, i.e., network traffic with flood attack. Figure 1 depicts a summary of the information extracted from the trace. It is shown that the average packet rate results from a network where either normal or low activity was occurring. Generally, SIEM systems have several plugins with the ability to process different input files.

Additionally, indications of the traffic behaviour can be obtained by analysing the the number of message IP addresses, as shown in Table 1. For instance, the presence of closely related IPs could indicate a scan. In this case, most of the communication takes place between less than 10 IPs which represent about 30% of all IPs in the trace file. Note that, at this stage, traffic has been synthesized, and then foreign IPs have been replaced by *192.168.x.x.* In this scenario, IPs *192.168.56.52* and *192.168.56.50* are the two external IPs with the most presence in the communication.

Table 1. List of IPs and rate of participation on the data set

IP address	Number of Occurrences	Rate of Participation (%)
0.0.0.0	8	1.09
255.255.255.255	8	1.09
10.0.2.2	6	0.82
10.0.2.15	96	19.10
10.0.2.255	25	3.41
224.0.0.22	8	1.09
192.168.56.50	113	15.42
192.168.56.52	175	23.87
10.0.3.2	6	0.82
10.0.3.15	236	36.70
10.0.3.255	37	5.05
192.168.1.1	15	2.05
64.236.114.1	130	17.74
74.125.77.101	9	1.23
209.85.227.106	8	1.09
209.85.227.99	18	2.46
209.85.227.100	8	1.09
10.0.4.2	6	0.82
10.0.4.15	317	43.25
10.0.4.255	38	5.18
192.168.56.51	74	10.10
74.125.77.102	18	2.46
10.0.5.2	6	0.82
10.0.5.15	43	5.87
10.0.5.255	25	3.41

2.2.2. Summary of Conversations

After analysing a trace file, 16 Ethernet conversations were found, 29 IPv4 conversations, 25 TCP conversations, and 15 UDP conversations. Looking further into the conversations, it appears that four different systems in the communication had the same netbios name. However, they appear to be in different subnets. This is a typical setting for a virtual machine environment.

```
root@ubuntu:/home/administrator/stuff# tshark  -r  suspicious-time.pcap  |  grep
'NB.*20\>' | sed -e 's/<[^>]*>//g' | awk '{print $3,$4,$9}' | sort -u Running as
user "root" and group "root". This could be dangerous.
10.0.2.15 -> 8FD12EDD2DC1462
10.0.3.15 -> 8FD12EDD2DC1462
10.0.4.15 -> 8FD12EDD2DC1462
10.0.5.15 -> 8FD12EDD2DC1462
```

The setting used by the malicious user here is simple to be successfully launched since IDSs are not able to detect such a conversation. More precisely, current IDS systems are not able to build a map either of the attacking system or the system being attacked. A good understanding of the network architecture would be an advantage for the detection mechanisms. Moreover, Snort uses configuration variables to identify networks which are, however, not capable to provide any dynamic behaviour analysis. For instance, in this case, VMware systems could have been configured after Snort configuration variables have been specified. Snort will interpret these new systems (IPs) as different physical systems (and therefore different PCs). Thus, a more accurate network mapping will improve detection of insider attacks, which still poses a serious challenge [Yang et al., 2011, Kim, 2011].

In this regard, SIEM can give a good representation of the network architecture as well as the topology of triggered alerts. In addition, visual representation of the network and the incidents can be used to efficiently correlate alerts within sub–networks. SIEM systems identify the attacks described in this scenario, in which multiple IP points to the same physical MAC address or the same BIOS name can be correlated.

2.2.3. In–depth Analysis

An in–depth analysis of the trace file is described in this section. First, Snort 2.8.5.1 was used to detect possible threats or attacks in the trace file, not reporting any alert due to the use of obfuscation techniques.

A manual analysis shows that the attacker makes connections to various systems by using the same physical computer but different virtual machine each time. In the local network, the IDS considers each connection as a different and separate node. Even if the IDS was able to detect each separate occurrence of network connection, there will be no link between the different network connections yet they are all from the same attacker. This technique is commonly used as a way to obfuscate attacks, so IDSs should be able to detect it. In fact, only an holistic security solution can infer the fact that different IP address have been registered with the same Netbios name.

The attack scenario is depicted in Figure 2–a. In this scenario, the attacker uses one of the virtual machines to connect to *rapidshare.eyu32.ru/login.php* using Firefox. Snort did not report any alarm as there is nothing visible or apparent that appears illegitimate. The only way for Snort to recognize this action would depend on knowing the URL to be searched.

The page is then returned successfully, but with a non–readable text. Snort does not

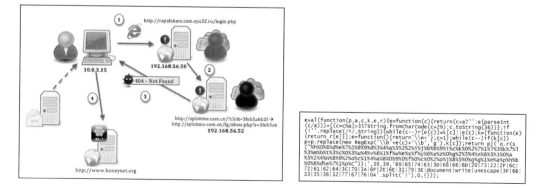

Figure 2. **(a) Attack scenario, and (b) obfuscated function.**

provide any mechanism to read non–trivial text. Any encrypted text is generally ignored by Snort and hence considered as safe. This is a popular way to hide attacks. However, using a popular and free tool that is widely available [Edward, 2010], the obfuscated code can be made clear, readable and returned the function showed on Figure 2–b.

The obfuscated function, even though it is not completely clear, suggests that the malicious user was trying to hide some code that could have been detected by the IDS. A complete de–obfuscation of the code reveals that the attacker was using *iframe* to hide another link with another malicious code.

```
<iframe    src="http://sploitme.com.cn/?click=3feb5a6b2f"width=1    height=1
style="visibility: hidden"></iframe>
```

Additionally, the link, when clicked, redirects the user to another page which returns a code [HTTP 404], which normally would mean that the page was not found. Further analysis will look at the irregular non–readable section of the page.

Snort does not analyse traffic in depth, which limits the ability to actually see the intention behind actions. Snort would have been able to examine this behaviour if the attack tree was defined and Snort supported this. Obfuscating HTML code becomes increasingly attractive since this bypasses most security systems. It is therefore important to have a system that is capable of analysing obfuscated portions of code. Thus, in this scenario, Snort falls short of addressing the following problems: (i) insider attacks, (ii) virtualization of nodes, (iii) obfuscations, and (iv) iframe.

2.3. Scenario Beta: Drive by Download Attacks

In one of their Security Intelligence Reports (SIR), Microsoft describes a typical malware distribution scenario launched by botnets. The attack process starts by a bot sending an SPAM message. This message consists of a link to a malicious web site which will exploits social engineering techniques. More precisely, when innocent users clicks the link, a hidden iframe redirects them to a malicious page which silently downloads the malware to the host computer.

This technique is generally referred to as "drive by download" [Microsoft, 2010]. Drive by download was considered to be one of the most serious threats in 2008, with 1.3% of Google queries redirected to a website labeled as malicious [Hsu et al., 2011]. Furthermore, in 2010, 79.9% of websites hosting malicious software were legitimate, which represents an increase of 3% from 2008 [Naraine, 2011].

There are two main elements that characterize this attack: **spam messages** and **malicious websites**. Unfortunately, the vast majority of current security systems does not integrate intelligent mechanisms into the correlation of the different steps of attacks [Websence, 2010]. Nevertheless, current SIEM systems have proven to be good at correlating the different alerts together. It is critical, however, to enhance security protection mechanisms so that they can dynamically be activated as the need is presented.

A further analysis from Microsoft report identifies the malicious redirection, the vulnerability exploitation on the server and the payload injection as the only features that characterize the attack. However, the 83.4% of email messages in 2010 were SPAM messages whilst the 79.9% of websites hosting malicious files were legitimate websites [Websence, 2010]. In addition, communications between the attacker and the victim are generally encrypted, hence, invisible to most security solutions [Vos, 2010]. A typical example of the "drive by download" attack was used during the 2010 Honeynet Challenge entitled "browser under attack". Snort v2.8 was used to analyze the traffic, but could not identify any use of iframe nor any irregularity. Further analysis revealed that the instructions containing the iframe were obfuscated.

Looking further into the honeynet challenge of 2010, it appears that the malicious users crafted the attacks at the malicious server level, adding another complication for any analytic tool.

2.3.1. Drive–by–download Detection Challenges

The level of sophistication of "drive by download" is demonstrated in the last step of infection. Once the vulnerable system has been infected, it is then prevented from connecting a second time to the malware server [Vos, 2010]. A typical drive by download poses the following problems:

- SPAM message: this can be detected by existing tools, but the end user is generally left to deal with the message to avoid any misinterpretation of the system. As a consequence, sending SPAM messages remains a very high source of contamination. Despite the fact that existing tools can detect some level of SPAM messages, there is no known tool that will link a SPAM message to an attack unless this is done offline in forensic analysis.

- Compromised server: The number of legitimate websites being compromised is increasing. IP blacklisting has sometimes been used as a solution, but given the current popularity of shared hosting, an IP could host more than 50 websites. Blocking one IP address could result in blocking 49 websites that are unaffected by the problem. There are services that offer URL blacklisting, but they operate on a daily update basis. Also, any Internet user can add any website without being monitored. As such, there is an urgent need for a better solution.

- Obfuscation: IDS or antivirus are only able to detect very classic obfuscation such as converting an IP address to its hexadecimal form. However, when dealing with custom obfuscation there is very little that can be done in real time. This remains a serious challenge for security communities. In the best case scenario, obfuscation can be dealt with offline after the traffic has been recorded.

- Error code message: As was the case in the honeynet challenge 2008, malicious users can display a page with an HTML code 404 pretending that the page was not found, yet the actual HTML code in the source is 200. This is usually the case when the victim users have had their credentials stolen. A malicious page will be used to request a username and password. Once the victim has entered these details, the page will then return a fake 404 error message. A similar behaviour has been identified as FraudTool.Win32.Agent.eh [F-Secure, 2009] when installed through Virusresponse

Lab 2009. IDS could be used to detect this protocol misuse. However, the risk of false positives is very high.

- Customized injection of attack: Based on the victim (client) browser, the server will change the way the malicious code is injected. There is very little that can be done by current countermeasures to prevent this malicious action taking place. IDS signature could be created for plain traffic. Any encrypted traffic would overcome the IDS capabilities.

- Blacklisted: Once the exploit has been downloaded on the victim system, a block is then installed preventing the victim system from connecting a second time to the malicious user. This will prevent the malicious code being downloaded for analysis [Vos, 2010].

- The drive by download attack has been around for some time, but still poses serious challenges. Most solutions today are based on URL blacklisting. However, if the database of attacks is not updated, the risk of infection is very high. One of the major limitations of existing solutions is that they are not linked to each other. Most browsers today will display a warning for any known malicious websites. However, the user is rightly given the choice to visit the webpage or not. If the webpage is then visited despite the warning, there is no indicator that the antivirus or firewall has to raise the level of alert. For most existing security tools the alert level is purely informative rather than being active and evoking a dynamic change to defense strategy.

2.3.2. Search Engine Attacks: Invisible Attacks

A number of tools, techniques and commands have been created to take advantage of the information made public through search engines [Oh et al., 2009, Abdelhalim and Traore, 2007]. Social engineering is another powerful tool used to collect valuable information against targets.

Very little has been done in providing countermeasures to protect against reconnaissance attacks and against social networking attacks. Due to poor systems configuration, search engines collect more information than they should when crawling the web. Every single directory of any public IP is subject to being indexed.

Many malicious tools are available online that would allow anyone without any Google search skills to find information at a click. The information collected from such tools can then be used for malicious purposes. SearchDiggity is a tool that was created to take advantage of Google, Bing, Baidu and Shodan search engines whilst respecting the terms and conditions imposed by various search engines [Brown and Ragan, 2011]. The number of vulnerabilities exposed by search engines is continually growing. These vulnerabilities are organized into 14 groups as shown in Table 2.

Search engine hacking poses serious challenges to existing security countermeasures. A simplified and typical attack scenario taking advantage of a search engine result is shown in Figure 3. One of the biggest challenges of attacks presented in Figure 3–a is that the victim system is not aware its credentials are being exploited. A well–crafted query (also available in automated tools) would return the username and the password as shown in

Table 2. Group of vulnerabilities and attack commands

Attack category	Number of commands
Footholds	23
Files containing usernames	15
Sensitive Directories	64
Web Server Detection	72
Vulnerable Files	60
Vulnerable Servers	63
Error Messages	71
Files containing juicy info	251
Files containing passwords	147
Sensitive Online Shopping Info	9
Network or vulnerability data	59
Pages containing login portals	240
Various Online Devices	207
Advisories and Vulnerabilities	1965

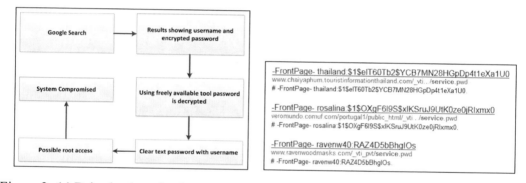

Figure 3. (a) Drive by download, and (b) Google results showing usernames and passwords.

Figure 3–b. Using "John the Ripper" [Openwall, 2012], the password could be decrypted within minutes. The victim system has no way to identify that the credentials used to access the system have been acquired illegitimately. IDS, IPS, and Firewall will not be able to block such attacks unless there is a strict policy on IP addresses that are allowed to access the system. One of the biggest challenges of attacks presented in Figure 3–a is that the victim system is not aware of the exploitation of its credentials. A well–crafted query (also available in automated tools) would return the username and the password as shown in Figure 3–b. Using "John the Ripper" the password could be decrypted within minutes.

The victim system has no way to identify that the credentials used to access the system have been acquired illegitimately. IDS, IPS, and Firewall will not be able to block such attacks unless there is a strict policy on IP addresses that are allowed to access the system. Google is not the only search engine used for malicious purposes. From this scenario, we could conclude that there are attacks that are not visible to the victim security system. The victim system will only see actions that look legitimate. In this scenario, we identified few issues:

1. Search engine attacks are not visible by the victim, hence implementing a local way to prevent it is a very challenging process.

```
[root@fedsecury stuff]# capinfos sick-client.pcap
File name:            sick-client.pcap
File type:            Wireshark/tcpdump/... - libpcap
File encapsulation:   Ethernet
Number of packets:    209
File size:            17860 bytes
Data size:            14492 bytes
Capture duration:     341 seconds
Start time:           Sat Dec 10 20:26:01 2005
End time:             Sat Dec 10 20:31:43 2005
Data byte rate:       42.47 bytes/sec
Data bit rate:        339.74 bits/sec
Average packet size:  69.34 bytes
Average packet rate:  0.61 packets/sec
[root@fedsecury stuff]# █
```

Figure 4. Infected PC trace file information.

2. Attacks use encrypted and/or obfuscated communications.
3. The attacker use fake HTTP 404 messages which can confuse the IDS.

Conducted analysis show that using isolated protection mechanisms, but not connected together, can lead to the so-called evasion techniques. An holistic solution would bring stronger security mechanisms.

2.4. Scenario Charlie

This scenario analyzes the traces of an attack that was trying to recruit computers to its botnet. An analysis similar than the one described in Section 2.2 shows that the network activity during the attack presents an slow rate, as depicted in Figure 4. For instance, the average packet size is rather small. These facts do not give much indication at this stage as to what could be happening.

2.4.1. General Statistics and Summary of the Conversations

Several conclusions from an initial analysis of the trace files are as follows. On one hand, it is shown that there are many IP address, with a high percentage of occurrence as described in Table 3. In addition, there are many connection requests with [Seq = 0, Len = 0] and several "Destination unreachable (Port unreachable)" messages, indicating a flooding or a TCP scan. On the other hand, one of the $IPs 10.129.211.13$, a Windows workstation is involved in every single conversation. Furthermore, we can observe that there were 130 conversations in total observed around port 445 and port 139.

2.4.2. In–depth Analysis

An in–depth analysis of the trace file is described in this section. A total number of six multi–step attacks have been identified and described as follows.

Table 3. Summary of IP presence in network traffic

IP Addresses	Number of occurence	Percentage of occurence
10.129.211.13	268	100
10.129.56.6	6	2.24
216.234.235.165	9	3.36
61.189.243.240	12	4.48
205.188.226.248	3	1.12
10.129.102.0	6	2.24
10.129.102.1	6	2.24
10.129.102.2	6	2.24
10.129.102.3	6	2.24
10.129.102.4	6	2.24
10.129.102.5	6	2.24
10.129.102.6	6	2.24
10.129.102.7	6	2.24
10.129.102.8	6	2.24
10.129.102.9	6	2.24
10.129.102.10	6	2.24

Step 1 of the attack: First, the attacker starts sending a DNS query to a domain name. This type of traffic would be absolutely normal, however in this context the DNS service is used as part of the attack to discover the Command & Control (C&C) bot. The DNS query is shown as:

```
10.129.211.13 10.129.56.6 DNS Standard query A bbjj.househot.com
```

Step 2 of the attack: Second, the compromised IP gets a response back from the DNS query made earlier with the following IP address:

```
2 0.237997 10.129.56.6 10.129.211.13 DNS Standard query response CNAME
ypgw.wallloan.com A 216.234.235.165 A 151.198.6.55 A 216.234.247.191
A 68.112.229.228 A 61.189.243.240 A 218.12.94.58 A 61.145.119.63 A
202.98.223.87 A 218.249.83.118 A 68.186.110.158 A 221.208.154.214
```

A typical DNS query will generate a response with about 5 IPs or less. In this case the answer retrieves 11 IP address.

Step 3 of the attack: In this step, the compromised host tries to establish a connection with the first IP that appeared in the DNS query.

```
3 0.239858 10.129.211.13 216.234.235.165 TCP neod1 > 18067 [SYN] Seq=0
Win=64240 Len=0 MSS=1460
```

Table 4. Connections attempts

Pckt No	Time	SourceIP	DestinationIP	Prot.	Other Info
11	337.761	10.129.211.13	61.189.243.240	TCP	neod2 > 18067 [SYN] Seq=0 Win=64240 Len=0 MSS=1460
12	338.160	61.189.243.240	10.129.211.13	TCP	18067 > neod2 [SYN, ACK] Seq=0 Ack=1 Win=65535 Len=0 MSS=1460
13	338.161	10.129.211.13	61.189.243.240	TCP	neod2 > 18067 [ACK] Seq=1 Ack=1 Win=64240 Len=0
14	338.162	10.129.211.13	61.189.243.240	TCP	neod2 > 18067 [PSH, ACK] Seq=1 Ack=1 Win=64240 Len=13
15	338.719	61.189.243.240	10.129.211.13	TCP	18067 > neod2 [ACK] Seq=1 Ack=14 Win=65522 Len=0
16	338.719	10.129.211.13	61.189.243.240	TCP	neod2 > 18067 [PSH, ACK] Seq=14 Ack=1 Win=64240 Len=17
17	339.122	61.189.243.240	10.129.211.13	TCP	18067 > neod2 [PSH, ACK] Seq=1 Ack=31 Win=65505 Len=23

Step 4 of the attack: Next, an ICMP message is received, indicating that the host is not live or not accepting connection on the port number used. The compromised host does not have any success establishing connection with hosts (IP) from the first DNS query. From the trace, the author notices that the compromised host will start a second DNS query aiming at the canonical name (CNAME) that was in the DNS response on step 2.

```
9   337.528083   10.129.211.13   10.129.56.6   DNS   Standard   query   A
ypgw.wallloan.com
```

From the latest DNS query, stage 4, the DNS response will give another set of IPs.

```
10 337.757036 10.129.56.6 10.129.211.13 DNS Standard query response
A  61.189.243.240  A  61.145.119.63  A  151.198.6.55  A  202.98.223.87  A
218.249.83.118  A  68.186.110.158  A  68.112.229.228  A  218.12.94.58  A
216.234.235.165 A 216.234.247.191 A 221.208.154.214
```

Step 5 of the attack: Again, the DNS query returns 11 IPs, which is also highly unusual. After that, the compromised host attempts another connection with the first host of the DNS response. On this occasion, the connection is successful and the malicious $IP10.126.211.13$ tries to establish the connection with other IPs as depicted in Table 4.

Step 6 of the attack: On packet 13, the three hand shake process is completed. From packet 14, the malicious IP start sending packets using the PUSH flag (this will be referred to as step 6). The PUSH flag indicates that no delay should be observed, whether the receiving system is ready to accept the packet or not.

Tracking down the conversation between the infected host 10.129.211.13 and the target host 61.189.243.240, and inspecting the payload exchanged, one could identify commands

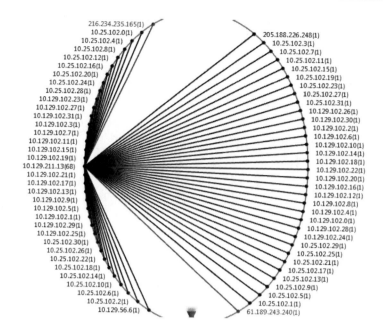

Figure 5. Matrix of communication between attacker and victim PCs.

that botnet use such as join, userhost, nick, and user.The author argues that at least three of the different steps described above could have triggered an alert indicating some sort of irregularity. A further analysis on the DNS servers revealed commands that are commonly used by the IRC–MocBot virus [McAfee, 2005], which communicates through port 18067 to a bot master and awaits command such as scan, DDoS or execute other malicious programs.

Overview of the attack: Going a few steps back into our analysis, the malicious user had tried to establish communication with all IPs that were under the CNAME of the DNS server. Figure 5 shows the matrix of communication between the malicious users and all the targeted computers. Having one IP communicating with multiple IPs does not generally presents a threat, neither necessarily indicates something unusual. However, the nature of the communication between that one IP and all the other IPs will help us to understand and identify any sort of irregularities.

Network communication matrix depicted in Figure 5 shows clearly that the attacker bases all its communications on one central IP. Again this is very unusual and should be flagged by any sensitive IDS. However, almost none packets were actually transmitted between the victim and the attacker.

Analysis of the trace file with Snort: Resulting analysis of the trace file is shown in Figure 6 and described as follows. Snort did not detect any of the different attack steps that were identified as part of this research. Referring to the different attack steps, Snort does not provide a way to detect: (i) a known bad DNS server;, (ii) a way to detect irregularities within the DNS response, (iii) a way to detect botnet communications, (iv) a way to track

```
Snort exiting Run time for packet processing was 0.8000 seconds ======
Snort processed 209 packets. ========
Breakdown by protocol (includes rebuilt packets):
ETH: 209 (100.000%)
ETHdisc: 0 (0.000%)
VLAN: 0 (0.000%)
IPV6: 0 (0.000%)
IP6 EXT: 0 (0.000%)
IP6opts: 0 (0.000%)
IP6disc: 0 (0.000%)
IP4: 209 (100.000%)
IP4disc: 0 (0.000%)
TCP 6: 0 (0.000%)
UDP 6: 0 (0.000%)
ICMP6: 0 (0.000%)
ICMP-IP: 0 (0.000%)
TCP: 144 (68.900%)
UDP: 6 (2.871%)
ICMP: 59 (28.230%)
TCPdisc: 0 (0.000%)
UDPdisc: 0 (0.000%)
...
Action Stats:
ALERTS: 0
LOGGED: 0
PASSED: 0
```

Figure 6. Snort analysis of scenario Charlie.

connections, and (v) does not correlate different alerts.

A modern IDS should be able to cover all the points mentioned above. In the light of events that took place in this scenario, it is difficult to identify each step as a successful attack if considered separately. In *step 1*, the attacker contacted a DNS server which is completely legal and does not violate any law. However, there was an indication that the intention behind this activity was suspicious since the DNS server contacted is known as a bad DNS server [Snort, 2010]. *Step 2* in this scenario is a normal DNS response. Yes, the responses contained more entry than usual, but the response was quite legitimate. The activity of the attacker could have been stopped when the scans were performed. However, unless the scans are of a type that will create a DDOS attack, most systems would consider them as noise. The only step that could have been flagged as a medium step is the last step. Again, this very step is a normal activity of IRC chat servers. There are nine steps that could be interpreted as very legal when taken individually but yet, when put together, form a very powerful attack [Pagna Disso, 2010].

As shown in Figure 7, one would think the system would identify a successful attack if the malicious user starts by scanning one of many computers, with some possible failure in the scans, then moves on to sending botnet commands or IRC commands. The attack presented in this scenario could be made more serious and more difficult to detect. Using similar settings, as was the case in scenario alpha; the attacker could perform the differ-

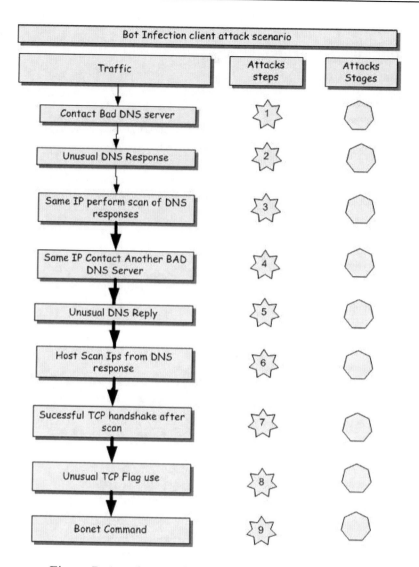

Figure 7. Attack steps from a bot infected computer.

ent steps of the attack using different virtual systems. A simplistic scenario of the attack discussed in this scenario is represented in Figure 8–a.

The attack steps in Figure 8–(a) could be altered by using a proxy server. A malicious user will use a proxy server to perform SCANs. Also, proxy can be used to push data to a victim computer. The new attack steps would be as shown in Figure 8–(b).

Attacks can easily be obfuscated to deceive IDS and other security mechanisms. There is very little correlation between the different elements of the attack or between the different attacks themselves.

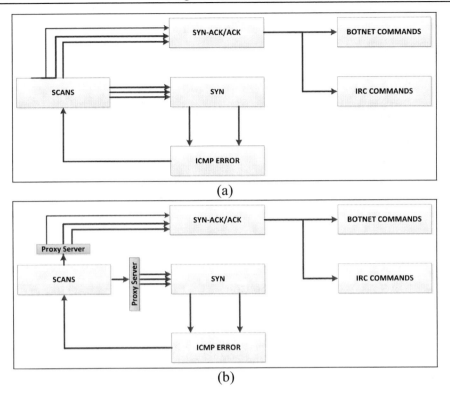

Figure 8. (a) Attack tree 1 —bot infected computer—, and (b) attack tree boot infected with proxy.

3. Solution Design

Modeling the attack behavior presents a big challenge as a single attack can be performed in multiple ways. On one hand, the number of attacks is continually growing with multiple variances towards attack mutation. On the other hand, the level of sophistication of attacks has risen considerably and it is becoming increasingly difficult to distinguish normal behavior from the attack pattern. In some cases, only the intention behind the actions performed during attacks differentiates legitimate from malicious users. One of the difficulties resides in the uniqueness of almost every single attack.

This section introduces a new framework aimed at enhancing the detection of multi–stage attacks based on the case studios described above. Following are presented some assumptions made throughout our model:

- There is very little difference between legitimate traffic and illegal traffic, as shown in scenario alpha.

- Legitimate, but not innocent, steps are taken in favour of the attacks.

- Tracking even legitimate steps is important, but will be resource intensive.

- Predefined actions need to be defined.

- Known attack patterns are predefined in an attack tree.

- An administrator should have a knowledge of the system being protected.

- Interaction with internal event: this will be done by installing an IDS agent on the local system to report events (events that are generally sent to SYSLOG).

3.1. Overview of the Proposed Framework

To successfully detect attacks, the framework proposed in this chapter will consider (i) the activities as performed by the attackers, and (ii) the activities as received by the victim. As demonstrated in the different scenarios, tracking attacker activities could be a tedious task. However, all activities convey to a victim. Hence, keeping track of both attacker and victim activities is important. On the attacker side, tracking the illegal activities as well as the intermediary activities is also crucial.

After analysis of the most common and challenging attacks existing on the Internet, we first present four levels of visibility of attacks. We then move on to suggesting a framework for attack detection and analysis based on these four levels of attack visibility. Intensive research activities have been carried out so far to understand and model attacks in order to build solid detection and mitigation systems [Maggi et al., 2008]. In addition, to these existing research activities, we suggest approaching the attack's detection with a two–fold strategy: identifying first the origin of the attack as a countermeasure, and subsequently analyzing possible strategies for preventing the attacker progressing from one step to the following one.

There are four different categories that emerged from our analysis when looking at vector and multistage attacks and the kind of protection needed against such attacks:

I The first category of attacks is composed of attacks that are visible to network security systems. These attacks can be detected and stopped by well configured detection and mitigation systems. These attacks include, but are not limited to, violation of protocol definition, protocol abuse, and known patterns used by malicious users in order to disrupt, change, or stop any legitimate activity.

II The second category is composed of attacks or at least part of attacks that are generally considered to be legitimate actions and therefore not a subject of concern for security systems. For instance, a computer could be sending information to another computer. This is completely legitimate and is the basis of any communication. However, sending data from one computer to another may not be legitimate if the previous action was a brute force attack on root passwords, for instance.

III The third category is the type of attack that affects a system without any physical contact to the actual system. This is the case for Google hacking or reconnaissance attacks. For instance, the command will return the *username* and *password* of a website that uses Frontpage extension.

Even though passwords returned in the result are encrypted, they can be unencrypted with "John the Ripper", often in a few minutes. Alternatively, there are other programs readily available that could also be used to discover the password by brute force attack, but this technique is likely to be discovered by the victim system. Antivirus, Firewall,

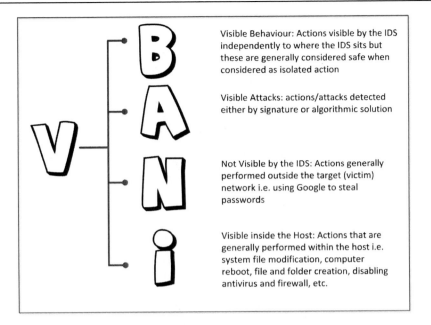

Figure 9. V-BANI Framework.

IDS and IPS are completely blinded to this category of attacks, as they will not be in violation of any rules. Systems have to be configured in a way that access can only be granted from specific IP addresses. Using search engine results would be an excellent starting point for a malicious user. In this case, the victim system would not be aware of any irregularity or violation in their system.

IV In the fourth category, attacks are partially performed inside the local system. Some rootkit or malware require rebooting after installation. Rebooting the system can be visible within the local host, but not on a network level. Also, malware generally performs modifications on system files. In order to have the full picture of the attack, it is important to understand the changes that are made on local systems.

Depending on where IDS are installed in the system, there might not be any direct communication within the protected systems and the IDS. A good security system should consider investigating the critical changes on the protected systems.

3.2. The V-BANI Framework

The V–BANI framework has been previously defined in [Pagna Disso et al., 2011] and is sketched in Figure 9. The proposed framework identifies a classification to identify complex multi–step attacks based on the case studies above described.

The visibility for the "drive by download" actions described in [Vos, 2010] resolves into four levels which would be the case for a good number of attacks. The attack visibility framework would be interpreted as:

Table 5. Visibility of attack level analysis in a typical drive by download attack

Attack action	visibility
Download script	V-B
Generate random key	V-I
decrypt code	V-I
format key as URL parameters	V-I
Read URL parameters	V-B
Vulnerability scan	V-B
Download malware	V-B
Join bot-net	V-A
SPAM relay	V-A
Man in the middle	V-A
Spread worms	V-A
Reboot computers	V-A

- Visible Behaviour: the actions are generally legitimate, especially when each action is considered independent of others. These actions tend to come to light during forensic investigations. Yet, the actions are visible to most IDS and IPS but they are generally considered safe or non–risky.

- Visible Internally: Network IDS are not aware of the changes that occur locally in victim computers. Victim computers need to be equipped with a host IDS or with an anti–virus that reports to a central management node. However, this is not always the case. Solutions exist for this category of attacks but, generally, these solutions are not connected to each other. Creating a full picture of attacks would maximize the protection.

- Visible Attacks: the actions performed under this category of attacks can be identified by most IDS when signatures have been created.

- Invisible Attacks: the second attack scenario, web browser attacks, has leveraged another level of attacks that are not visible to the victim computer. None of the existing security countermeasures incorporate this level into their protection. Current IDS or security systems tend to address a maximum of one or two at a time, yet the level of sophistication of attacks is such that, if any level of visibility of attack is ignored, the attack will go undetected.

Based on this classification, we can identify the steps analyzed on the "drive–by–download" scenario as depicted in Table 5.

3.3. The Architecture

3.3.1. The Problem of Invisible Attacks

This kind of attack presents a challenge for detection frameworks as attackers uses search engine queries to target its victim. McGeehan and Engert suggest implementing a honeynet that will allow the administrator to know which of its network resources are targeted and decide what to do with this information [McGeehan and Engert, 2007]. We look at the

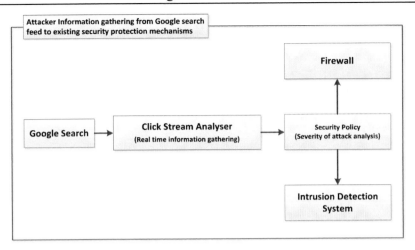

Figure 10. From Web server hacking to firewall architecture.

problem in a different and more efficient way. We use click stream data analysis to feed information directly to the firewall.

Click stream analysis software has been used for a variety of purposes but has not, as yet, been applied to a security context. Click stream is used: (i) in the analysis of revenue trends in advertisement, (ii) to improve product image, (iii) to target new customers, and (iv) for many other commercial applications.

However, looking further into the stream information generated by these kind of attacks, we observed that we are able to obtain the IP of that user as follows. Using the Application Programming Interface (API) of the click stream, the information received from the data stream is then parsed and fed directly to firewalls or IDS, as shown in Figure 10. Using the API, the IP of the potential attack is then extracted and sent to the firewall.

Even though attacks appear to be invisible to the victim security system, a correlation between the "http_referer" field, the type of query from search engines, and data stream analysis, means that victim systems have enough information to update their firewalls or IDS accordingly. The "http_referer" will indicate that a search engine is actively being used to identify vulnerabilities (type of search), whilst the data stream analysis will give the information about the actual IP opening an HTTP session within the victim system.

3.3.2. Enhancing Webserver Protection

Similar concepts can be used to enhance protection of vulnerable webservers. Directory transversal is a vulnerability that allows the attacker to see the structure of a local directory without permission. In our work, we identify an IP attempting to access a restricted directory. The IP is then added to the watch list rather than sending the IP directly to the firewall. This has the effect of reducing false negatives. A threshold of attempt offenses should be set. Once the threshold has reached its limit, the IP is then added and blocked by the firewall.

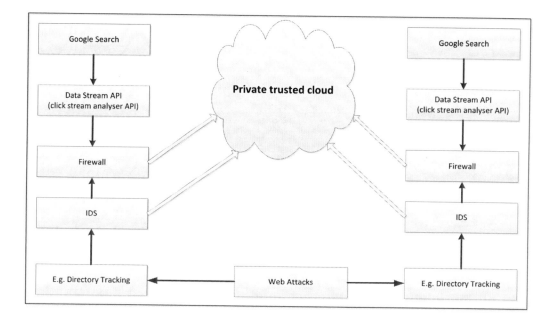

Figure 11. Distributed collaborative framework for attack detection and mitigation.

3.3.3. Google Adwords

Google Adwords is well known for advertisement and benefit related studies [Kodialam et al., 2010]. Google Adwords lets companies specify the keywords by which they need to be identified. However, in the report given by Google, all the keywords that were used to make a target website appear in Google results are presented. This is to indicate that a website_A could appear in a result that is targeting a website_B, but both website A and B could have the same vulnerability. This will give the opportunity to non–targeted websites to update their security before they become a target.

3.3.4. Collaborative Protection

A fundamental element in sharing security information is trust. The work presented in this section assumes that the level of trust required by the parties involved has been met. However, this is not to say that each participant will reveal all of their security mechanisms.

In our detection and mitigation framework shown in Figure 11, each participant (Enterprise) will be responsible for ensuring that its perimeter is safe. However, a number of companies, especially those working in the same business environment, would benefit from sharing in real time information about malicious users. In a nutshell, the framework is devoted to share not only information related to the relative success of attacks, but also the possible source of problems. For instance, a search of Barclays bank usernames and passwords would be of interest to Lloyds TSB bank, as they both operate in the same business sector. This trust–based community approach extends the property framework proposed in [Jones et al., 2009]. Our framework is based on four levels of visibility of attacks aforementioned: the V–BANI framework [Pagna Disso et al., 2011]. One of the

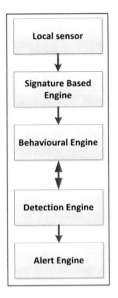

Figure 12. Basic IDS Architecture.

most challenging attacks is those that are not directly visible to the security of the targeted system. However, using data stream analysis, the IP of the attacking user can be identified and firewall or IDS rules can be created accordingly. Information of the attacker can then be shared in real time to a private cloud where all participants are known and work on the trust basis. In fact, other participants will then be able to connect to the shared (but secured) cloud via web services to automatically update their security firewall. However, publicly available blacklisting generally does not validate the input. For any reason, even for fun, one could enter random IP addresses and report them as malicious even when they have not been involved in any malicious activity. The safe browsing initiative by Google should be more integrated into computer security systems, and needs to be connected to both IDS and firewall.

Thus, protecting against websites hosting malicious software is very important, and SPAM messages should not be neglected either. They carry messages which sometimes have well written content to target a particular group of Internet users. However, if a message is targeting a particular bank for example, it would be beneficial for other banks to know the threat a similar organization is facing. A verified intelligent correlation of such messages should be used to update malicious targets. Finally, firewalls can then be automatically updated to systematically block access to any link going to the malicious servers known to facilitate certain attacks.

3.4. Our Intrusion Detection System Architecture

A collaborative approach brings together many systems to fight against malware. However, that collaborative system relies on the efficiency of each local system.

Even though limited, signature based detection is still very useful for baseline security. Here, we outline the main features:

- Local sensors: This feature does not exist in Snort. The local sensors (agents) act as host IDSs. Based on the analysis done previously in this chapter, it is very important to have knowledge of what is happening in the victim system, as well as knowledge of what is happening at the network level. IDS can be installed at various points in a network. Independently of where they sit in the network, each node should be monitored. Many of the recent attacks are performed with such sophistication that most IDS will not alert. It is only the combination of all the actions that would indicate the presence of an attack. The remote agent will be responsible for monitoring local shell i.e. file and directory changes; Monitory CPU usage as a high consumption of resources could also indicate an attack (i.e., a Denial of Service attack).

- Behavioural analysis: This engine should be used to correlate the different information collected on a network. There is a need for flow analysis. However, flow information can easily be by–passed in scenarios such as the use of VMware to perform attacks. This suggests that a stronger control and correlation is needed between the different flows. Using proxy servers, it would be very difficult to link the flow together. However, this can be addressed by keeping an analysis of the different steps that are generally performed by attackers.

- Protocol analysis: most protocol analyses look at anomalies in the protocol message formats and rules, but more should be done to look at irregularities. Even when a protocol is not violated, attackers can stretch the protocol definition to bypass security. The protocol analyser should be part of the behaviour analysis.

- In critical times, it is important to ensure that legitimate users continue to access their service. A scoring algorithm is generally used for this purpose to ensure that regular good users can be identified and given priority when necessary.

Conclusion

Since defeating malicious users remains a challenge, adopting a defensive strategy to fight current attacks has proved to be limited. Attacks need to be tackled from their origin. For instance, using Google, a malicious user can have full rights to a vulnerable system. This invalidates any protection in place as there will be no violation of any rule. Furthermore, isolated solutions have not been very successful.

In this chapter, we have discussed and analyze complex attacks from a novel perspective. We have identified four levels of visibility of attacks. To use a collaborative protection framework where different companies or parties can share intelligence about attacks would be much more efficient than isolated security systems. Companies with a similar profile are likely to be targeted by the same people using similar techniques. Sharing that intelligence will improve security barriers.

Last but not least, IDS usually fail to detect malicious activities because they do not have enough information about the attacks. Many internal activities are generally not reported to the IDS, depending on where the IDS is placed. It is often the case of Snort which is located at different sensors that will report to a central node. However, the work of IDS such as Snort will not detect the majority of internal changes. Every single participant node should analyse local activity and report to a central location. Protecting against current attacks is a real challenge and IDS should be re-designed according to the current level of attacks and their sophistication. Otherwise, patching current IDS may lead to poor processing performance and hence allow attacks to go through.

References

[Abdelhalim and Traore, 2007] Abdelhalim, A. and Traore, I. (2007). The impact of google hacking on identity and application fraud. In *In Proc. IEEE Pacific Rim Conference on Communications, Computers and Signal Processing (PacRim'07)* , pages 240 – 244.

[Alhomoud et al., 2011] Alhomoud, A. M., Munir, R., Pagna Disso, J., Awan, I., and Al-Dhelaan, A. (2011). Performance evaluation study of intrusion detection systems. *Procedia CS*, 5:173–180.

[Alserhani F. and J, 2009] Alserhani F., Akhlaq M., A. I. C. A. and J, M. (2009). Multi-Tier evaluation of network intrusion detection systems. *Journal for Information Assurance and Security (JIAS)*, pages 301–310.

[Barford and Crovella, 2001] Barford, P. and Crovella, M. (2001). Critical path analysis of TCP transactions. *IEEE/ACM Transactions on Networking*, 9(3):238–248.

[Brown and Ragan, 2011] Brown, F. and Ragan, R. (2011). *Pulp Google Hacking: The Next Generation Search Engine Hacking Arsenal* . Published: Black Hat Conference Las Vegas, NV, USA.

[Choi et al., 2007] Choi, H., Lee, H., Lee, H., and Kim, H. (2007). Botnet detection by monitoring group activities in DNS traffic. In *Proceedings of the 7th IEEE International Conference on Computer and Information Technology* , pages 715–720, Washington, DC, USA. IEEE Computer Society.

[Cremonini and Riccardi, 2009] Cremonini, M. and Riccardi, M. (2009). The dorothy project: An open botnet analysis framework for automatic tracking and activity visualization. In *In: EC2ND09 : European Conference On Computer Network Defense*, pages 52–54, Los Alamitos, CA, USA. IEEE Computer Society.

[Diksha and Shubham, 2006] Diksha, N. and Shubham, A. (2006). A novel self configuring dynamic firewall for load reduction of network administrator. In *In Proc. International Conference on Communication Technology, 2006. ICCT '06.* , pages 1 – 4.

[Edward, 2010] Edward, D. (2010). /packer/. http://dean.edwards.name/packer/.

[F-Secure, 2009] F-Secure (2009). *VirusResponse Lab 2009* . Published: F-Secure Weblog : News from the Lab [Accessed: 30-Sep-2011].

[Foundation, 2012] Foundation, W. (Visited on March 2012). Wireshark. http://www.wireshark.org/.

[Ge et al., 2011] Ge, F., Tan, L., Sun, J., and Zukerman, M. (2011). Latency of FAST TCP for HTTP transactions. *IEEE Communications Letters*, 15(11):1259–1261.

[Hsu et al., 2011] Hsu, F., Tso, C., Yeh, Y., Wang, W., and Chen, L. (2011). Browser-Guard: a Behavior-Based solution to Drive-by-Download attacks. In *In IEEE Journal on Selected Areas in Communications*, volume 29, pages 1461 – 1468.

[Jones et al., 2009] Jones, K., Janicke, H., and Cau, A. (2009). A property based framework for trust and reputation in mobile computing. In *In Proc. 23rd International Conference on Advanced Information Networking and Applications Workshops (AINA'09)*, pages 1031 – 1036.

[Kim, 2011] Kim, J. (2011). Development of integrated insider attack detection system using intelligent packet filtering. In *2011 First ACIS/JNU International Conference on Computers, Networks, Systems and Industrial Engineering (CNSI)*, pages 65–69. IEEE.

[Kodialam et al., 2010] Kodialam, M., Lakshman, T. V., Mukherjee, S., and Wang, L. (2010). Online scheduling of targeted advertisements for IPTV. In *Proceedings of the 29th conference on Information communications*, INFOCOM'10, page 1550ï¿½1558, Piscataway, NJ, USA. IEEE Press.

[Ma et al., 2010] Ma, X., Guan, X., Tao, J., Zheng, Q., Guo, Y., Liu, L., and Zhao, S. (2010). A novel IRC botnet detection method based on packet size sequence. In *2010 IEEE International Conference on Communications (ICC)*, pages 1–5. IEEE.

[Maggi et al., 2008] Maggi, P., Pozza, D., and Sisto, R. (2008). Vulnerability modelling for the analysis of network attacks. In *In Proc Third International Conference on Dependability of Computer Systems (DepCos-RELCOMEX ï¿½08).*, pages 15 – 22.

[McAfee, 2005] McAfee (2005). IRC-Mocbot. http://www.mcafee.com/threat-intelligence/malware/default.aspx?id=136637.

[McGeehan and Engert, 2007] McGeehan, R. and Engert, R. (2007). *GHH - The Google Hack Honeypot*. [Accessed: 04-Oct-2011].

[Microsoft, 2010] Microsoft (2010). *Featured Intelligence*. Published: Microsoft Security Inteligence Report Online [Accessed: 14-Nov-2010].

[Microsoft, 2012] Microsoft (Visited on March 2012). Network monitor. http://www.microsoft.com/download/en/details.aspx?id=4865

[Naraine, 2011] Naraine, R. (2011). *Drive-by Downloads: The Web Under Siege*. Published: Securelist Online [Accessed: 09-Sep-2011].

[Oh et al., 2009] Oh, O., Chakraborty, R., Rao, H., and Upadhyaya, S. (2009). An exploration of unintended online private information disclosure in educational institutions across four countries. In *In Proc. eCrime Researchers Summit, eCRIME '09.*, pages 1 – 11.

[Openwall, 2012] Openwall (Visited on March 2012). John the ripper. `http://www.openwall.com/john/`.

[Ormerod et al., 2010] Ormerod, T., Wang, L., Debbabi, M., Youssef, A., Binsalleeh, H., Boukhtouta, A., and Sinha, P. (2010). Defaming botnet toolkits: A Bottom-Up approach to mitigating the threat. In *In Proc Fourth International Conference on Emerging Security Information Systems and Technologies (SECURWARE)* , pages 195–200.

[Pagna Disso, 2010] Pagna Disso, J. F. (2010). *A Novel Intrusion Detection System (IDS) Architecture: Attack Detection Based On Snort For Multistage Attack Scenarios In A Multi-Cores Environment*. PhD thesis, University of Bradford, United Kingdom.

[Pagna Disso et al., 2011] Pagna Disso, J. F., Jones, K., Williams, P., and Steer, A. (2011). A distributed attack detection and mitigation framework. In *Workshop on Collaborative Security Technology (CoSec 2011)*, Bangaluru (Bangalore), India.

[Project, 2010] Project, T. H. (2010). *Challenge 2 Of The Forensic Challenge 2010 - Browsers Under Attack*. Published: Honeynet Project [Accessed: 11-Jul-2010].

[Roschke et al., 2009] Roschke, S., Cheng, F., and Meinel, C. (2009). An extensible and Virtualization-Compatible IDS management architecture. In *In Proc. Fifth International Conference on Information Assurance and Security, 2009. IAS '09.* , pages 130–134.

[Sheth and Thakker, 2011] Sheth, C. and Thakker, R. (2011). Performance evaluation and comparative analysis of network firewalls. In *In Proc. of International Conference on Devices and Communications (ICDeCom 2011)*, pages 519 – 524.

[Shuai et al., 2008] Shuai, L., Xie, G., and Yang, J. (2008). Characterization of HTTP behavior on access networks in web 2.0. In *International Conference on Telecommunications, 2008. ICT 2008*, pages 1–6. IEEE.

[Snort, 2010] Snort (2010). Snort :: Additional downloads. http://www.snort.org/snort-downloads/additional-downloads#zeroshell.

[Sourcefire, 2012] Sourcefire (Visited on March 2012). Snort ids. `http://www.snort.org/`.

[Spragins, 1996] Spragins, J. (1996). TCP/IP illustrated, volume 3: TCP for transactions, HTTP, NNTP and the UNIX domain protocols. *IEEE Network*, 10(5).

[Vogt and Aycock, 2006] Vogt, R. and Aycock, J. (2006). Attack of the 50 foot botnet. Technical Report TR 2006-840-33, Department of Computer Science, University of Calgary.

[Vos, 2010] Vos (2010). Challenge 2 of the forensic challenge 2010 - browsers under attack. http://www.honeynet.org/challenges/2010_2_browsers_under_attack. Published: Honeynet Project [Accessed: 11-Jul-2010].

[Walrand, 2000] Walrand, J. (2000). A transaction-level tool for predicting TCP performance and for network engineering. In *8th International Symposium on Modeling, Analysis and Simulation of Computer and Telecommunication Systems, 2000. Proceedings* , pages 106–112. IEEE.

[Websence, 2010] Websence (2010). Websense 2010 threat report. White paper, Websence. Published: Websense White Paper.

[Yang and Ting, 2009] Yang, C. and Ting, K. (2009). Fast deployment of botnet detection with traffic monitoring. pages 856–860. IEEE.

[Yang et al., 2011] Yang, J., Ray, L., and Zhao, G. (2011). Detect Stepping-Stone insider attacks by network traffic mining and dynamic programming. In *2011 IEEE International Conference on Advanced Information Networking and Applications (AINA)* , pages 151–158. IEEE.

[Zaman and Karray, 2009] Zaman, S. and Karray, F. (2009). Lightweight IDS based on features selection and IDS classification scheme. *In Proc. IEEE International Conference on Computational Science and Engineering,* , 3:365–370.

[Zhong, 2010] Zhong, X.-y. (2010). A model of online attack detection for computer forensics. In *In Proc. International Conference on Computer Application and System Modeling (ICCASM),* , pages 533 – 537.

In: Advances in Security Information Management
Editors: G. Suarez-Tangil and E. Palomar

ISBN: 978-1-62417-204-5
© 2013 Nova Science Publishers, Inc.

Chapter 4

COOPERATIVE APPROACHES TO SIEM AND INTRUSION DETECTION

Mirco Marchetti* and Michele Colajanni[†]
University of Modena and Reggio Emilia, Italy

Abstract

This chapter presents an extensive survey of previous works in the field of cooperative SIEM and cooperative Intrusion Detection. In particular, we focus on all the approaches that leverage cooperation among multiple, (parallel and/or distributed) components in order to analyze and manage security events related to large and complex information systems, typical of modern IT infrastructures. We identify several relevant research prototypes as well as commercial solutions, and classify them according to two different taxonomies: the former is based on the architecture that enables cooperation among multiple components; the latter reflects the different cooperation algorithms, methods and strategies that characterize all the relevant works. Our goal is to give the reader a better understanding of cooperative SIEM and Intrusion Detection Systems, highlighting the issues that have already been solved and the areas that are still wide open for research and innovative approaches.

Keywords: Cooperative Security Information and Event Management (SIEM), Cooperative Intrusion Detection (IDS), Architectural Taxonomy, Cooperation Algorithms

1. Introduction

The original approach to intrusion detection and security event management was based on the deployment of a centralized component that gathers and analyzes events at system or network level. In this chapter we present architectures that leverage multiple components and cooperation techniques for the analysis and management of large numbers of security events generated by complex information systems. Their goal is to enhance the system capability and/or to improve the analysis efficacy by merging and correlating security alerts coming from different sources.

---

*E-mail address: mirco.marchetti@unimore.it
[†]E-mail address: michele.colajanni@unimore.it

Organization. This chapter is organized as follows. Section 2 describes the limitations of traditional IDS and SIEM approaches based on centralized and independent appliances. Section 3 proposes a taxonomy of architectures for intrusion detection and for security events management by distinguishing parallel architectures, described in Section 4, and distributed architectures, presented in Section 5. A different classification based on the co-operation strategies used by parallel and distributed architectures is examined in Section 6. Open issues and research perspectives are presented in Section 7.

2. Limitations of Centralized Architectures

Novel emerging issues are limiting the applicability of centralized SIEM and IDS approaches to existing network-based information systems. The increasing volume of events to be examined and the growing complexity of the analysis algorithms represent a challenge for the computational capacity of any centralized solution. Moreover, the complexity of modern networks, characterized by a crumbling perimeter, mobile connections and virtual private networks spanning across wide areas prevents a centralized IDS to monitor all the security events that are relevant to its analysis algorithm. We identify four main issues that limit the effectiveness of a centralized solution and its applicability to modern and future information systems:

1. the computational capacity of one hardware device is inherently limited and cannot scale;

2. a centralized IDS can only monitor a simple environment, in which all the events are directly measurable;

3. traditional solutions for SIEM and IDS have difficulties in coping with the "crumbling perimeter" of modern networks;

4. not cooperative IDSs and SIEMs are unsuitable to implement the modern in-depth defense principles.

2.1. Computational capacity

A traditional appliance for intrusion detection or security event management, implemented through one physical device, has an inherently limited computational capacity that bounds the number of events that can be gathered and processed. This problem is further exacerbated by computational and memory requirements of modern algorithms for intrusion detection and security event correlation.

As an example, let us focus on a specific scenario of a simple NIDS realized by installing the popular Snort [Snort, 2012] software on standard hardware components. As a case study, we show the performance limitation of a NIDS built with an Intel Xeon 2.4 GHz CPU, 1 GByte RAM, 32 bits and 33 MHz PCI bus and Gbit Ethernet NICs. This NIDS is used to analyze the network traffic generated by a machine with the same hardware configuration. As the experimental testbed, we use the well known IDE-VAL [Lippmann et al., 2000] traffic dumps.

The highest throughput sustainable by the NIDS is shown in Figure 1. The x-axis represents the throughput of the analyzed traffic, while the y-axis measures the packet rate. The three lines represent the packet rate received by the IDS, the dropped packet rate, and the received packet error rate, respectively. As shown by the "Dropped packets" line, this NIDS is able to analyze all the incoming traffic only for bandwidth up to 40 Mbps (corresponding to roughly 25.000 packets per second in the test case). For bandwidths higher than 40 Mbps, the NIDS is unable to analyze all the incoming traffic and starts dropping packets, thus compromising the analysis reliability. When the input traffic reaches 120 Mbps, the CPU of the NIDS saturates. At this point, the analyzer is unable to handle all the incoming packets, hence the dropped packet rate saturates and the received error rate increases. As a result, even a Fast-Ethernet link is sufficient to overwhelm a NIDS built with standard hardware components. IDS solutions leveraging custom hardware, such as *Network Processors* (NP) [Clark et al., 2004, Liu et al., 2004], *Application Specific Integrated Circuit* (ASIC) [Cho and Mangione-Smith, 2005] and *Field Programmable Gate Array* (FPGA) [Song et al., 2005, Song and Lockwood, 2005, Bu and Chandy, 2004] are able to cope with higher event throughputs, but they are much more expensive and lack the flexibility of software-based implementations. Moreover, being centralized and not scalable, they do not represent a long-term solution to the problem of analyzing high volume event streams.

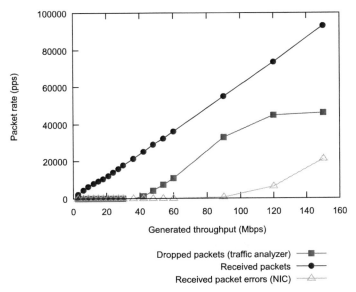

Figure 1. Capacity of a NIDS for increasing input traffic.

2.2. Complexity of the environment

In order to guarantee high levels of accuracy, any IDS needs to monitor all the events that are relevant to the analysis algorithms. Hence, a centralized IDS needs to gather all the relevant events from a single point. While this requirement can be fulfilled in simple network scenarios (for example, through a network switch that support SPAN ports), it is impossible to satisfy it in environments typical of modern information systems, that are characterized

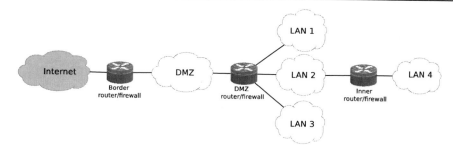

Figure 2. Capacity of the traffic analyzer for increasing input traffic.

by multiple network levels for operational and security purposes. Indeed, local networks are fragmented in multiple isolated sub-networks, each characterized by different security policies enforced by routers, packet filters, application gateways and VPN concentrators.

Even in a simplified network topology as the one shown in Figure 2 we can identify a DMZ and four LANs, where: the DMZ hosts the machines that are directly reachable from hosts connected to the Internet, such as Web servers, SMTP servers, public FTP servers; the first three LANs host local machines that do not need to be reachable from the Internet, such as the production machines used by the employees; the fourth LAN, that represents the inner portion of the network, is used to segregate sensitive targets that need special protection, such as a database server that has to be isolated from the other hosts. Separation among the different sub-networks is implemented through the deployment of routers with firewalling capabilities.

In a similar network it is possible to identify different spots in which a NIDS could be deployed. For example, it is possible to monitor all the network traffic reaching and leaving the protected network by installing one NIDS between the border router and the DMZ. While this solution can provide an accurate analysis of all the network packets flowing through the network perimeter, it does not allow the network administrator to monitor the traffic exchanged within the LANs, and between the LANs and the DMZ. Moreover, this deployment strategy does not take into account possible attack traffic that is blocked by the border firewall, and that could be useful to detect the preliminary phases of an incoming attack. The latter issue can be addressed by deploying the NIDS between the border router and the Internet, with the possible drawbacks of a higher volume of traffic to be analyzed, an increased number of false positives and no improvements in the coverage of the inner LANs. The only way to provide a complete coverage of the whole network environment is to deploy several NIDS sensors, for example, one in each LAN. A proliferation of independent IDS sensors would cause a proportional increase in alert management efforts.

The same considerations are also applicable to the context of SIEM, since intrusion detection systems represent one of the most valuable sources of security events that can be gathered, analyzed and correlated by a SIEM. Moreover, a SIEM needs to gather heterogeneous security events (such as logs from servers, network appliances, authentication and authorization systems, ...). The segregation of these information sources in different sub-networks makes it difficult or impossible for a centralized SIEM to gather all the required information and security events.

2.3. Crumbling network perimeter

Novel forms of interconnection, such as *tunneling* and *mobility*, are playing an important role in modern networks. For example, tunneling technologies, such as VPNs, are widely used to extend the logical perimeter of a local network across wide areas and untrusted links. Mobility-enabled networks allow mobile nodes to dynamically roam across different networks and to change their point of connection. These technologies make it difficult to establish the physical and logical perimeters that an IDS has to monitor. Moreover, node mobility can prevent a NIDS to understand network boundaries, because the traffic does not follow any predictable path. Similarly, node mobility and dynamic network membership complicate the configuration and the analysis algorithms of traditional SIEMs.

2.4. Compliance to defense-in-depth principles

A modern security infrastructure that aims to comply to defense-in-depth principles has to consider threats and defenses at different levels, including network security, operating system security, application security, data security, identity management, user authentication and authorization. We should consider that each of these attributes is monitored through a multitude of algorithms and techniques (just recently some integrated proposals is appearing on the market). As a consequence, an effective security infrastructure has to rely on heterogeneous intrusion detectors disseminated throughout the protected environment. Even in the simplest case of a NIDS and a HIDS, some cooperation technique is necessary to integrate heterogeneous tools in a unified and coherent alerting interface.

3. Cooperative Security Architectures

The first solution to the problems highlighted in the previous section was based on the dissemination of several independent IDSs in the monitored environment. This approach is preferable to a single IDS architecture because it increases the coverage of a complex network scenario composed by several sub-networks. However, the deployment of multiple independent and not cooperative IDSs does not represent an effective solution. A set of independent IDSs, where each one monitors just a part of a complex environment, prevents the adoption of modern intrusion detection algorithms operating on a complete knowledge of the state of the monitored environment (namely, *stateful* analysis) in order to detect even the simplest and most common IDS evasion techniques [Ptacek and Newsham, 1998] and distributed attacks. Independent IDSs cannot implement stateful algorithms, hence some cooperation techniques are needed to allow distributed IDSs to communicate by exchanging their state information. Moreover, we should not forget that the deployment of several independent IDSs, each generating alerts that have to be manually validated by a human operator, multiplies the burden of analyzing and managing security events and the time wasted in dealing with false positives. For these reasons, we do not investigate further the architectures consisting of multiple independent components that do not include systems and algorithms for security event management.

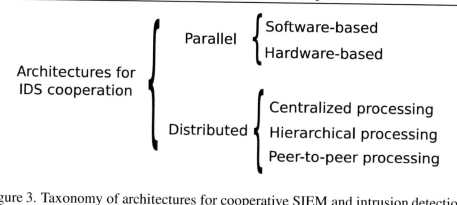

Figure 3. Taxonomy of architectures for cooperative SIEM and intrusion detection.

We classify cooperative security architectures according to two main characteristics:

◇ the architecture that enables cooperation among multiple components, and
◇ the cooperation strategies.

It is important to consider that any system for the analysis of security events is composed by three main functional units, each executing a specific task. The first component, namely the *sensor*, gathers all the events that have to be analyzed. The second component, namely the *event analyzer*, executes the algorithms for the analysis of the events gathered by the sensor. The last element, namely the *alert manager*, elaborates the alerts generated by the event analyzer. Alert processing operations can vary widely, ranging from a simple alert materialization to complex aggregation and correlation of multiple alerts.

We classify cooperative architectures for intrusion detection and security events management on the basis of how they implement and/or replicate the three main functionalities. The first important distinction shown in Figure 3 is between *parallel* and *distributed* architectures.

In parallel architectures, the sensor and the alert processor components are not replicated, while there are multiple event analyzers, processing in parallel different subsets of the same event stream coming from one event source. Parallel architectures can be further classified upon the solutions used to implement the centralized sensor component, or *event dispatcher*. The architectures relying on custom hardware, such as ASIC, FPGA and NP, are included in the *hardware-based* category, whilst the parallel architectures based on standard COTS hardware are defined *software-based*.

On the other hand, distributed architectures for intrusion detection and security event management are characterized by a replication of the sensor and the event analyzer components. Hence, a distributed architecture is able to gather events from multiple sources, and to analyze all the monitored event streams through distributed and independent security event analyzers. It is possible to distinguish different distributed architectures on the basis of the structure of the alert manager: a *centralized management* scheme means that the alert manager function is concentrated in one component; in the *hierarchical management* scheme, the alert manager is distributed among several machines that are arranged as a hierarchy; in the *peer-to-peer management* class, the alert processing function is distributed among a set of peer nodes.

Parallel and distributed architectures are analyzed in Section 4 and Section 5, respectively. A further taxonomy that classifies cooperative architectures for intrusion detection and security events management on the basis of their cooperation methods is presented in Section 6.

4. Parallel Architectures for Intrusion Detection and Security Events Management

A *parallel* architecture for intrusion detection and security event management leverages the computational capacity of multiple sensors and event analyzers to process events gathered from one source. The motivation is that a traditional centralized IDS can monitor the entire event stream until its architecture has a sufficient capacity to analyze all data. When the capacity is insufficient, a parallel architecture is used to split the event flow in multiple smaller streams analyzed concurrently by its multiple parallel components. The parallel architectures proposed in literature refer to the analysis of network traffic, hence we can limit our analysis to sets of homogeneous Network IDSs (NIDSs) where the relevant events are represented by network packets.

As a reference, consider the analysis of network traffic flowing through a high capacity link. Depending on the link utilization and on the computational complexity of the intrusion detection algorithms, the amount of network packets can easily overwhelm commonly deployed NIDSs. (See Section 2.1 for the performance characterization of a NIDS built on COTS hardware components.) In this scenario, a parallel NIDS architecture can be used to partition the network traffic into several subsets, small enough to be managed by one parallel NIDS without packet loss.

Several parallel IDS architectures have been proposed in literature, such as [Kruegel et al., 2002, Schaelicke et al., 2005, Xinidis et al., 2006, Colajanni and Marchetti, 2006, Charitakis et al., 2003, Alam et al., 2004, Xinidis K and Markatos, 2005, Le et al., 2008, Vallentin et al., 2007, Foschini et al., 2008]. While each of these works presents new and original contributions, their architectures are characterized by some similarities that allow us to highlight common design patterns. The typical structure of a generic parallel architecture for intrusion detection is shown in Figure 4. All the events generated by the *event source* are received by the *event dispatcher*, that acts as centralized sensor and routes each event to the parallel event analyzers. The generated alerts are received by the *alert aggregator*, that simplifies alert and event management processes by aggregating and correlating related alerts and by providing one well defined interface for alert materialization and analysis. The components of the architecture can be monitored and configured through a unified *management interface*. From a high level of abstraction, the whole parallel architecture (bounded by the gray box in Figure 4) is functionally equivalent to a centralized IDS having one event input interface, one alert output interface and a management console for configuration and monitoring purposes.

Besides the ability to analyze a higher event throughput, a parallel architecture has other benefits over a centralized implementation. The inherent modularity of a parallel architecture makes it flexible, and allows to easily increase (or diminish) the highest sustainable

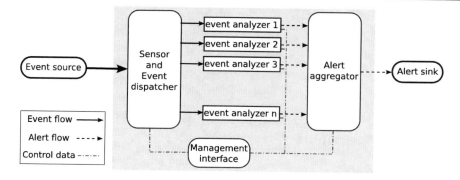

Figure 4. A model of a parallel NIDS architecture.

event throughput by adding (removing) components to (from) the system, and reconfiguring the event dispatcher. This property makes it easy to adapt a parallel architecture to the performance requirement of any specific deployment scenario in an almost transparent way. Moreover, parallel architectures are characterized by high scalability. Depending on the nature of the analysis algorithm applied by the NIDSs, on the granularity of the event dispatching algorithm and on the performance of the event dispatcher, the highest event throughput sustainable by the parallel architecture can scale almost linearly with respect to the number of IDSs [Colajanni and Marchetti, 2006].

These benefits come at the price of a complex architecture, that is significantly more difficult to deploy, configure and maintain with respect to a monolithic IDS. In particular, the main issues are related to:

- the design and implementation of the event dispatcher,

- the consequences of event dispatching on the reliability of the analysis results,

- the design and implementation of the alert aggregator.

Being the only component that receives the complete event flow coming from the source, the event dispatcher represents a bottleneck and a single point of failure for the whole parallel architecture. Several designs have been proposed for the implementation of an event dispatcher that is able to receive, classify and deliver events at very high rates. It is possible to classify the parallel IDS architectures depending on whether the event dispatcher has been implemented through some specialized hardware components (Section 4.1) or in software running on COTS, unmodified hardware (Section 4.2).

We should consider that all modern IDSs rely on *stateful* analysis algorithms, where an IDS incrementally builds an internal state that reflects the current state of the monitored environment. This contextual information is then used to improve the analysis reliability of each event, reducing both false positive and false negative rates. Stateful analysis algorithms became popular because they allow to counter many IDS evasion techniques [Ptacek and Newsham, 1998] that an attacker can leverage to perform illicit activities without being detected by a stateless IDS.

For example, a stateful NIDS is able to reconstruct the flow of data transmitted between any two endpoints by tracking and reassembling all the concurrently open TCP connections.

This task increases the computational complexity and memory requirements of the event analyzer, but it can be easily implemented in a centralized IDS that analyzes all the events produced in the monitored environment. On the other hand, when an event analyzer is part of a parallel architecture, it is able to analyze just the fraction of events that the event dispatcher routes directly to it, because it does not receive the entire contextual information needed by a stateful analysis algorithm.

Different strategies have been proposed to design stateful parallel IDSs. Some of them rely on the ability of the event dispatcher to enforce event routing policies that preserve event flows, thus guaranteeing that each IDS receives all the events that are relevant to its detection algorithm. A thorough description of event distribution algorithms and policies is in Section 6.2. Another approach allows parallel (and also distributed) IDSs to share information among their components, thus obtaining the missing contextual information from the cooperative sensors rather than from the incoming events. These approaches are discussed in Section 6.3.

A parallel IDS architecture should also provide an effective alert aggregation mechanism that is able to cluster alerts generated by different IDSs and related to the same intrusion. Manual validation of alerts generated automatically by an IDS is a complex and time-consuming task, and without an effective alert aggregator it would be necessary to multiply this effort by the number of event analyzers on which the parallel architecture relies. While cooperation through alert aggregation is a challenging and still open problem (discussed in Section 6.1), the context of parallel architectures requires just an aggregation of homogeneous alerts, generated by several instances of the same IDS. This assumption eliminates all the issues related to the interpretation and fusion of heterogeneous information, and greatly simplifies the alert correlation process.

4.1. Hardware-based parallel architectures

A hardware event dispatcher represents the simplest solution for the deployment of a parallel NIDS architecture. Several vendors sell network appliances that are able to split a high throughput traffic flow in smaller subsets, that can be forwarded to an array of parallel NIDSs for analysis. These appliances are usually based on the know-how used to produce hardware load balancers for clusters of Web servers. Hence they have the ability to distribute network traffic while preserving transport-level flows (TCP connections and UDP sessions).

Examples of commercial hardware appliances that can be used as event dispatchers are the Radware SecurFlow™ [Radware, 2012] as well as all the appliances belonging to the TopLayer Intelligence Distribution System Balancer (IDSB) product family [Corero, 2012a] and Cisco *Catalyst* switches supporting *EtherChannel Load Balancing* (ECLB) [Cisco Systems, 2012]. All these products are able to handle multi-Gigabit traffic flows by coupling high speed traffic distribution backplanes together with *Application Specific Integrated Circuits* (ASICs) for network packet classification and dispatching. Moreover, besides traffic dispatching, these hardware appliances offer other useful features, such as traffic filtering and shaping, SLA monitoring and integrated graphical management interfaces.

Hardware producers can afford to implement well-established traffic dispatching algorithms in ASICs, while hardware-based research prototypes are realized through programmable hardware components, such as *Field programmable Gate Arrays* (FPGAs) and *Network Processors* (NPs). Commercial event dispatchers represent a viable solution, specifically designed to facilitate deployment and configuration, but they lack the flexibility and IDS specific optimizations that are typical of academic prototypes.

An example of research prototype implemented through FPGA is presented in [Schaelicke et al., 2005]. This event dispatcher achieves a network packet distribution that is balanced and flow-preserving by applying hash functions to IP addresses and port numbers contained in the packet headers. The result of the hash function is used as the index in a table in which each cell is associated to a destination NIDS. Since all the network packets belonging to the same traffic flow have the same IP addresses and port numbers, they are always forwarded to the same destination NIDS. Uniform load distribution can be achieved by dynamically adapting the associations between cells in the hash table and NIDS sensors. However, whenever a cell is reassigned to a different sensor by the dynamic load distribution algoritm, the flows are not preserved.

An event dispatcher realized through programmable Network Processors has been proposed in [Xinidis K and Markatos, 2005] and [Xinidis et al., 2006], where the implementation relies on an Intel® IXP1200 Network Processor [Intel®, 2012]. Even this event dispatching policy is hash-based: a hash function is computed on relevant fields of the network packet header and its result is used to determine the destination NIDS.

Besides the basic event dispatching algorithm, the event dispatcher proposed in [Xinidis K and Markatos, 2005] and [Xinidis et al., 2006] introduces two novel improvements that lead to a noticeable reduction of the computational load of the parallel NIDSs: *early filtering* and *locality buffering*. The main idea behind early filtering is to execute simple filtering operations (based only on the packet header and involving only packets without payload) directly within the event dispatcher, thus reducing the number of packets analyzed by the NIDSs. Locality buffering can be used to reorder network packets so to increase the efficiency of the NIDS analysis. This goal is achieved by sending similar packets (e.g., packets belonging to the same protocol) back-to-back to the same NIDS, thus increasing temporal and spatial locality and allowing a more efficient use of CPU caches.

It is also worth noticing that the architectures proposed in [Xinidis K and Markatos, 2005] and [Xinidis et al., 2006] differ from the model of parallel NIDS architecture presented in Figure 4. While their event dispatcher can be used for a parallel NIDS, they are designed to support a parallel *Network Intrusion Prevention System* (NIPS). As a result, the event flow is not unidirectional (as in Figure 4) but bidirectional. This means that, after the analysis, all licit network packets are sent back by the array of parallel event analyzers to the event dispatcher, and then the event dispatcher forwards them to their destination.

4.2. Software-based parallel architectures

The implementation of an event dispatcher based on standard, unmodified hardware components is appealing for two main reasons: software-based solutions are cheaper than hardware-based appliances; moreover, they are more flexible, because any change in the dispatching algorithm or configuration does not require the replacement or the reprogramming of some hardware component.

On the other hand, using COTS hardware components poses limitations to the complexity of the event dispatching algorithm. As it is represented by a single component, the highest event throughput manageable by the whole architecture is bounded by the event dispatcher speed. In order to keep the event dispatching cost as low as possible, all the proposed event dispatching algorithms are based on simple computations on small and fixed-size fields of the packet headers. Hybrid solutions where the event dispatcher is based on specific hardware and all the rest of the parallel architecture is based on commodity hardware is a viable solution to augment the architecture capacity.

From an architectural perspective, the simplest event dispatcher is represented by a single host. This solution is proposed in [Alam et al., 2004, Charitakis et al., 2003, Le et al., 2008].

In particular, in [Alam et al., 2004] the event dispatcher (called *traffic splitter*), splits the flow of network packets according to a set of static rules that classify each packet on the basis of a five-element tuple: source IP address, destination IP address, source port number, destination port number and transport-level protocol. The traffic dispatching rules are derived by automatic analysis of a set of policies defined by the system administrator. Each policy is composed by two parts. The first part defines a class of network packets by specifying constraints on some of the elements in the tuple. All the network packets that satisfy all these constraints belong to the class defined by the policy. The second part specifies which NIDS must analyze the network packets belonging to the class defined by the policy. This rule-based approach is used to enforce a *flow preserving* traffic splitting, that allows a single NIDS to receive a complete traffic flow, and prevents network packets belonging to the same flow to be scattered among different sensors.

As already seen in Section 4.1, flow-preserving properties can also be achieved through a hash-based scheme that does not require a system administrator to explicitly define a set of traffic splitting policies. The event dispatcher proposed in [Charitakis et al., 2003], called *nIDS splitter*, distributes the incoming network packets to a set of parallel NIDSs based on the result of a hash function computed on selected fields of the packet header. Moreover, it implements the two IDS-specific optimization used by [Xinidis K and Markatos, 2005] and [Xinidis et al., 2006]: early filtering and locality buffering. While these improvements can reduce the CPU load of the parallel analyzer up to about 20%, they also increase the computational load of the nIDS splitter, that represents the bottleneck of the proposed architecture. Hence it is unclear whether these techniques are really useful for parallel architectures composed by a high number of NIDSs.

Another monolithic traffic splitter has been proposed in [Le et al., 2008]. Its main novelty is represented by the network packet dispatching and flow correlation algorithm, based on on-line clustering of similar traffic flows, while its architecture is similar to these proposed in [Alam et al., 2004] and [Charitakis et al., 2003].

In the event dispatchers analyzed so far, one machine is used to perform the following three tasks: event gathering, event classification and event forwarding. However, it is possible to assign these tasks to different machines. For example, in the architecture proposed in [Vallentin et al., 2007] the event dispatcher (represented in Figure 5) consists of two physical components. The first element gathers all the packets from the network and classifies them using a hash-based technique. Instead of forwarding the classified packets

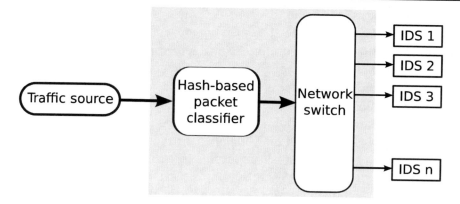

Figure 5. Two-layered event dispatcher proposed in [Vallentin et al., 2007].

to the network interface to which the destination NIDS is connected, it rewrites just the destination MAC address of the Ethernet frame with the MAC address of the corresponding NIDS sensor. After that, all network packets are sent to a standard network switch, that leverages the rewritten destination MAC address to forward each network packet to its destination NIDS.

The network switch allows a system to reduce both the number of NICs needed by the event dispatcher and its CPU usage, since all the rewritten packages are blindly forwarded to the single output NIC without the need for MAC-based packet routing. Another optimization is the implementation of the hash-based packet classification and MAC rewriting algorithms entirely in kernel-space based on the Click modular router [Kohler et al., 2000]. Authors of [Vallentin et al., 2007] also propose an alternative implementation based on FPGA.

Another two-layered event dispatcher is presented in [Foschini et al., 2008]. The first layer receives all the network packets and associates to each packet a number, that is the value of a monotonically increasing packet counter. After having been numbered, all the network packets are sent to the second layer, that implements a simple round-robin packet distribution scheme: incoming packets are evenly distributed among all the NIDSs without any inspection. This design choice keeps the computational cost of packet forwarding as low as possible. However it is not flow preserving, since there is no guarantee that network packets belonging to the same flow will be received and analyzed by the same NIDS (indeed, the probability of a complete flow to be analyzed by the same NIDS is low, and decreases with both the number of packets and the number of NIDSs used by the architecture). Hence, the applicability of this dispatching strategy is limited to architectures employing stateless intrusion detection algorithms.

An event dispatching scheme that is able to leverage the low cost of round-robin dispatching together with flow preserving properties has been presented in [Kruegel et al., 2002]. This event dispatcher is composed by four layers, as shown in Figure 6. The first layer is represented by a *scatterer*, the second layer is composed by an array of m *slicers*, the third layer is represented by a *switch*, and the fourth and final layer is an array of n *reassemblers*, where n is also the number of parallel NIDSs that the whole parallel architecture supports.

The scatterer gathers network packets at line speed, and distributes them to a set of m

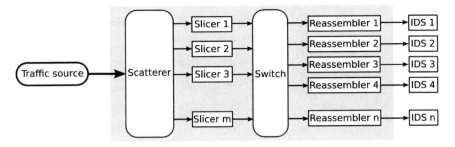

Figure 6. Four-layered event dispatcher proposed in [Kruegel et al., 2002].

slicers to which it is directly connected. In principle, the scatterer can use any algorithm to distribute packets among the slicers, since flow-preserving properties are not required at this stage. Given that the scatterer is a centralized component that represents a possible bottleneck for the whole parallel architecture, it is important to keep the computational complexity of scattering operations as low as possible, hence the scatterer distributes network packets to the slicers according to a stateless, round-robin algorithm. As a consequence, each slicer receives $1/m$-th of the total amount of network packets processed by the scatterer. Before forwarding a network packet to one of the slicers, the scatterer overwrites its source MAC address with the value of a monotonically increasing counter, used as sequence number. Since the scatterer performance is critical, this activity is implemented in kernel space.

Slicers are used to classify the incoming subset of network packets according to a flow-preserving algorithm. The authors of [Kruegel et al., 2002] propose a rule-based slicing algorithm similar to that implemented in [Alam et al., 2004]. Since it is possible to decrease the load on the slicers by increasing their number, an event dispatcher with enough slicers can leverage complex slicing algorithms that involve analysis of both the packet headers and its payload. However, for testing purposes authors restrict the evaluation of their event dispatcher to slicing rules based only on network packets' IP addresses. Once a slicer has determined to which event analyzer a network packet has to be dispatched, it overwrites its destination MAC address with a logical identifier. As an example, if a network packet satisfies the slicing rules for the event analyzer number 2, the destination MAC address will be substituted with the value 00:00:00:00:00:02. It is possible for one network packet to comply with several slicing rules, each associated to a different destination NIDS. In this case, a copy of the packet is created for each sensor that require its analysis.

After being classified by the slicers, network packets are forwarded to the switch for the actual packet routing. By using a switch to mediate packet forwarding between the array of slicers and the array of reassemblers it is possible to decouple these two layers. A direct communication would require the deployment of a fully connected mesh network, and the installation of at least n output NICs in each slicer and m input interface in each reassembler. On the other hand, the use of a network switch makes it possible to use only one output interface for each slicer and only one input interface for each reassembler, independently of the values of m and n. The only constraint implicit in using a switch for packet routing is the need to configure the input NIC of each reassembler with the MAC address that corresponds to its logical identifier, as used by the slicer. As an example, the input interface of the reassembler in front of the IDS number 2 has to be 00:00:00:00:00:02.

After having been routed by the switch, each network packet is forwarded to a reassembler. Each reassembler acts as a buffer in which network packets are temporarily stored and reordered with respect to the sequence number that the scatterer wrote in the source MAC address field of each network packet. Reassembling operations are necessary because network packets are processed in parallel by different slicers, and because the complexity of slicing operations can differ from packet to packet, depending on the set of slicing rules and the nature and size of each packet. After being processed by the reassembler, an ordered flow of packets is forwarded to the directly connected IDS for the actual packet analysis.

An   evolution   of   this   event   dispatcher   has   been   proposed in [Colajanni and Marchetti, 2006] and [Andreolini et al., 2007].   From the architectural point of view, the main difference is the absence of the reassembler layer, and the network switch is directly connected to the array of parallel IDSs. This optimization can be implemented because the NIDSs used in the parallel architecture already perform network packet reordering, as is the case of modern NIDSs. Another important consequence is that the scatterer is no longer required to overwrite the source MAC address of each packet with its sequence number, thus leading to a further reduction in the complexity of the operations performed by the scatterer and to an increased scalability for the whole parallel architecture. Other important differences are related to the introduction of novel load balancing algorithms and IDS state management techniques, and are described in Sections 6.2 and 6.3, respectively.

5. Distributed Architectures for Intrusion Detection and Security Event Management

A *distributed* IDS architecture is characterized by several intrusion detection components that cooperate for the analysis of event streams produced by different sources. It is worth to observe that in our definition a distributed IDS architecture does not consist just of a set of distributed sensors and event analyzers, but also of multiple alert and security event managers (SIEM) that can aggregate and correlate low-level security events coming from the event analyzers. Unlike a parallel IDS architecture that is functionally equivalent (for intrusion detection) to one centralized IDS, a truly distributed architecture enlarges the IDS functionalities because it can generate high-level *activity reports* resulting from aggregation, correlation and synthesis of low-level security events. A distributed IDS is suitable to complex and heterogeneous system/network scenarios where sources are physically distributed even on a geographical scale. A high-level description of complex attack patterns allows human operators to correlate malicious activities involving multiple systems instead of dealing with one low-level alert at a time. Moreover, the possibility of integrating the output of multiple, possibly heterogeneous, sensors and event analyzers allows distributed IDS architectures to implement the powerful abstraction of a *hybrid* IDS that leverage, aggregate and correlate low-level alerts coming from NIDSs, HIDSs, application-specific IDSs and log analyzers for a multitude of applications and services.

We classify the distributed architectures for intrusion detection and security event management in three categories depending on the cooperation model adopted for security event

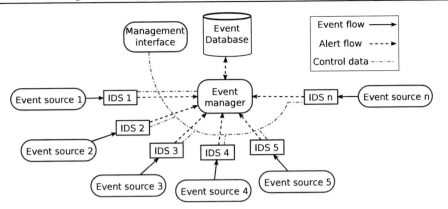

Figure 7. Distributed IDS based on a centralized scheme for the aggregation and analysis of security events.

processing: *centralized processing* (Section 5.1), *hierarchical processing* (Section 5.2), and *peer-to-peer processing* (Section 5.3).

5.1. Centralized processing

The simplest and most widely adopted approach (e.g., [Snapp et al., 1991, Snapp et al., 1988, Kemmerer, 1998, Bass, 1999, Bass, 2000, Wu et al., 2003, Wang et al., 2004, Zhang et al., 2005]) for aggregating and correlating security events coming from multiple event analyzers is based on a centralized SIEM scheme, as in Figure 7.

This architecture consists of several sensors and event analyzers (each couple is represented as a numbered IDS), each analyzing events produced by different (possibly heterogeneous) sources. All these low-level security events are relayed to a centralized *event manager*, that aggregates, fuses and correlates them. Low-level and high-level aggregated security events are then stored in an *event database*. Stored events can be accessed by the event manager, depending on the requirements of the specific aggregation and correlation algorithms. A *management interface* allows remote monitoring and administration of all the distributed IDSs and of the event managers.

A similar architecture has been initially envisioned in the paper [Snapp et al., 1991], published in 1991. In this seminal work, all the high level functions of the centralized component in Figure 7 (event manager, event database and management interface) are implemented in one logical node, called *central manager*. The central manager receives alerts generated by two classes of distributed sensors, called *host manager* (HIDS) and *LAN managers* (NIDS). In modern terms, it is possible to conclude that this paper described a centralized SIEM architecture for the management of heterogeneous security events. A prototype implementation of the architecture proposed in [Snapp et al., 1991] has been described in [Snapp et al., 1988].

NSTAT is another early prototype of a centralized SIEM for a distributed IDS [Kemmerer, 1998]. This architecture, based on the STAT framework for intrusion detection [Ilgun et al., 1995], consists of a STAT process that acts as a centralized alert aggregator by fusing the alerts coming from multiple, distributed USTAT sensors in one audit trail.

Other proposals of similar architectures focus on novel strategies for aggregation and correlation of security events. Notable examples are [Bass, 1999], [Wang et al., 2004], and [Bass, 2000], in which data fusion strategies are applied to the IDS context. Interesting data clustering schemes for alert classification have been discussed in [Zhang et al., 2005].

The distributed architecture proposed in [Wu et al., 2003] focuses mainly on secure communications between the distributed sensors (called *elementary detectors*) and the centralized event management element (namely, the *manager*). The solution is at multiple levels: a private key is assigned to each elementary detector to sign messages; all communications are mediated by a *message queue* element that wraps each message in a logical envelope. The main elements of the envelope are a per-sender and monotonically increasing message counter, a SHA1 digest computed over the elementary detector's private key, the message counter, and the message itself. This scheme prevents poisoning attacks to the architecture through the insertion of fake messages or multiple replications of the same alert sniffed from the network.

Besides research efforts and academic prototypes, distributed IDS architectures characterized by a centralized event manager nowadays represent a commercial solution in enterprise network scenarios. Almost all the major vendors in the field sell hardware appliances that implement the functions of event manager, event database and management interface, and that can be used to monitor and to gather alerts from multiple distributed IDSs. A partial list is represented by the Sourcefire defence center[TM] [Sourcefire®, 2012], TopLayer's SecureCommand[TM] [Corero, 2012b], Cisco's and Hewlett-Packard's *HP OpenView Node Sentry* [Cisco and Hewlett-Packard, 2012], Datamation® Dragon IDS/IPS [Enterasys®, 2012] and Qbik's NetPatrol [QBIK, 2012]. Similar architectures are also built upon open source software (e.g., Prelude SIEM [Prelude IDS technologies, 2012]).

5.2. Hierarchical processing

Distributed architectures for intrusion detection and security event management find their natural deployment in large and complex networks, characterized by a high number of subnets and hosts, where monitoring and low-level analysis is carried out by several distributed sensors. However, with the increase in size and complexity of the monitored environment, the computational capacity of one centralized event manager becomes a limit to the architecture scalability.

Hierarchical processing schemes [Staniford-Chen et al., 1996, Debar and Wespi, 2001, Zhang et al., 2001b,   Zhang et al., 2001a,   Chu et al., 2005,   Xue et al., 2003, Balasubramaniyan et al., 1998, Colajanni et al., 2008a, Ragsdale et al., 2000] aim to increase the scalability of a distributed SIEM based on one centralized unit. The main idea is to reduce the workload of the centralized event manager by building a hierarchy of intermediate managers, each processing a subset of alerts and relaying their partial results to the event managers at the higher tier. An example of hierarchical scheme for intrusion detection is shown in Figure 8.

As any other distributed architecture, a hierarchical scheme consists of several dis-

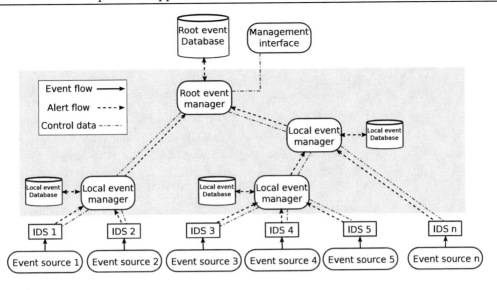

Figure 8. Distributed IDS based on a hierarchical architecture for security event management.

tributed and possibly heterogeneous sensors, each analyzing events coming from a different source. Unlike a centralized scheme (Figure 7) where the low-level alerts are forwarded to one aggregator, the hierarchical scheme leverages a multitude of *local event managers*, organized at different layers. Each local event manager belonging to the lowest layer receives alerts from a subset of the distributed sensors. These events are aggregated and correlated locally, and the partial results generated by the local analysis are relayed to a local manager belonging to a higher layer. As a result of the local aggregation and correlation, the number of events relayed by a local manager is much smaller than the total number of received alerts. Using proper aggregation and correlation algorithms, the information that is relevant to an event analysis algorithm is maintained and forwarded to the higher levels of the architecture. The *root event manager* is the highest security event manager that receives and correlates partial results that are representative of all the activities performed in the monitored environment.

It is worth noticing that it is not necessary for the event management hierarchy to be shaped as an *n*-ary tree, or to be perfectly balanced. The in-degree of each element in the hierarchy, modeled as a directed graph, can be adapted to the characteristics of each scenario. Similarly, the height of the sub-trees connecting the sensors to the root event manager can also vary.

GrIDS is the first example of hierarchical processing scheme for SIEM [Staniford-Chen et al., 1996] that is specifically tailored to worm detection. In GrIDS, each local event manager is composed by two software modules: an *engine* and a *software manager*. Engines belonging to the lowest level are responsible for collecting alerts generated by NIDS and HIDS (called *network sniffers* and *point IDS* in this 1996 paper). These alerts are used to build a graph that represents the traffic flows among the monitored hosts. Each engine then forwards its graph to the higher-level engine, that fuses all the received graphs and relays its aggregated results to an engine positioned in a higher level of the hierarchy. This fusion and relaying procedure is repeated until the root engine is reached. Each engine is coupled with a software manager that has to build and manage the architecture hierarchy.

Other hierarchical architectures following the model in Figure 8 are proposed in [Debar and Wespi, 2001], [Zhang et al., 2001b], [Zhang et al., 2001a]. The authors in [Debar and Wespi, 2001] present a new alert representation, that allows a easier classification of heterogeneous alerts. Their formal description has been used as a basis for the development of the widely used Intrusion Detection Message Exchange Format (ID-MEF) [IETF Intrusion Detection Working Group, 2006], that now is a standard for IDS interoperability proposed by the IETF Intrusion Detection Working Group. The works proposed in [Zhang et al., 2001b] and [Zhang et al., 2001a] explore new alert aggregation schemes based on neural networks and statistical classification, on top of a standard hierarchical architecture.

The hierarchical architecture presented in [Colajanni et al., 2008a] is specifically designed for efficient gathering and analysis of self-spreading malware (e.g., Internet worms) rather than on their detection. The sensors are operational IDSs (also called honeypots) and the local alert aggregators (called *managers*) cooperate by relaying only unknown malware binaries to higher-level managers. This distributed filtering process guarantees that the root alert manager (*called coordinator*) receives and analyzes only new malware specimens, thus avoiding duplicate analysis of the same malware.

LDIDS [Chu et al., 2005] is an interesting twist on the basic hierarchical scheme proposed in Figure 8. Although the scheme is purely hierarchical, each intermediate component embeds both an event manager and a sensor. Hence all the building blocks of the architecture are functionally equivalent.

While a hierarchical architecture can scale much better than a centralized architecture, both approaches suffer of a single point of failure: the event manager in a centralized scheme, the root event manager in a hierarchical scheme. Moreover, a failure of any local event manager within the hierarchy causes the complete isolation of all the sensors that are connected to the root event manager through the failed local event manager.

This issue is acknowledged and mitigated in [Balasubramaniyan et al., 1998] and [Ragsdale et al., 2000] by introducing some redundancy in the hierarchical scheme. In [Balasubramaniyan et al., 1998], each local event manager can relay its partial aggregation results to more than one higher-level monitors, thus creating multiple redundant paths toward the root monitor. This design choice makes the architecture able to tolerate the failure of some intermediate managers, at the expense of an increased complexity in the architecture design and management. In [Ragsdale et al., 2000], each local event manager is associated with a *surrogate agent*, whose aim is to take over the director's duties in case of a failure.

Another problem affecting hierarchical architectures is represented by the lack of load balancing among the intermediate nodes. Indeed, a hierarchical scheme can be overloaded by workloads that are relatively small compared to the aggregated computational capacity of the entire architecture. If only one of the event sources of Figure 8 starts producing a high throughput event stream, then the load of the local event managers that are in the path between the event source and the root event manager increase. Eventually, one overloaded intermediate event manager may begin to drop security events or partial aggregation results, while the load of other event managers in different paths may be negligible.

5.3. Peer-to-peer processing

Distributed architectures for intrusion detection and security event manage-
ment based on a peer-to-peer scheme have been proposed   [White et al., 1996,
Ingram et al., 2000, Janakiraman et al., 2003, Locasto et al., 2005, Marchetti et al., 2009,
Malan and Smith, 2005,   Vlachos et al., 2004,   Li et al., 2006,   Duma et al., 2006,
Yegneswaran et al., 2004] to address the single point of failure issue that is intrinsic
in centralized and hierarchical designs.

The common goal is to avoid a centralized event manager module and to distribute its
functions among the peers that belongs to the distributed SIEM architecture. High scalability and, in some cases, better load balancing are other benefits of peer-to-peer schemes.
However, we should keep in mind that the lack of a centralized event manager poses also
new challenges. Since there is not an entity with a complete view on the environment, it
is necessary to devise new intrusion detection and security event management algorithms
based on partial knowledge, and to define event routing techniques that enable each distributed event manager to receive all the required information.

The first example of a completely distributed and flat architecture for intrusion detection has been described in [White et al., 1996], published in 1996. In this solution a set of
cooperating security managers (CSM) is installed on several hosts belonging to the same
LAN. Each CSM acts as a HIDS and as a NIDS that analyzes just the network packets
received by the host in which the CMS is installed. CMSs cooperate by exchanging "relevant events" through TCP connections. This require each CMS to know the IP addresses
and ports of all the other CMSs, thus limiting the dynamic scalability of the proposed system. While both the detection algorithms and the communication scheme are now obso-
lete, this remains a seminal paper for purely distributed intrusion detection. Another example of purely distributed IDS that does not rely on peer-to-peer overlays is represented
by [Ingram et al., 2000] in which distributed IDS agents communicate by broadcasting UDP
packets. This communication scheme limits the applicability of the proposed architecture
to a single LAN.

Scalability issues have been addressed by many other distributed architectures leveraging peer-to-peer overlays for communication.   A first step in this direction has
been taken by *Indra* [Janakiraman et al., 2003] that is based on a Pastry overlay network [Rowstron and Druschel, 2001], and it leverages Scribe [Castro et al., 2002] for efficient group communication among peers. Besides scalability, other fundamental benefits
inherited from peer-to-peer overlays are its ability to gracefully handle churn, node failure
and link disruption. These properties make it possible to build and maintain a SIEM distributed over a large scale with minimal human intervention. While defining a scalable and
extensible architecture, the paper in [Janakiraman et al., 2003] does not detail the intrusion
detection algorithms to be implemented on top of Indra.

Several peer-to-peer IDSs and SIEMs focus on the detection of Internet
worms [Vlachos et al., 2004, Locasto et al., 2005, Malan and Smith, 2005].   Since worm
epidemics represent an Internet-scale phenomenon, distributed SIEM that leverage a high
number of heterogeneous sensors that are geographically distributed and connected to sev-

eral different autonomous systems are perfectly suited for the detection of self-replicating malware and worms spreading over the Internet. By correlating partial evidence of worm infections collected by only a few of the cooperative sensors, a largely distributed architecture can generate early warnings as soon as the worm starts to spread, and with a low false positive rate. Early warnings are then distributed to all the peers that cooperate in the distributed SIEM architecture. Information about the spreading of new worms can be received by peers even before the worms reach the network in which the peer is deployed, thus allowing the network administrator to deploy proactive countermeasures. Early warnings represent the main advantage of large-scale peer-to-peer distributed SIEM architectures, as well as a strong incentive for new peers to join. Examples of host-based approaches for distributed worm detection are *NetBiotic* [Vlachos et al., 2004] and *Wormboy* [Malan and Smith, 2005]. NetBiotic is a peer-to-peer overlay based on the Jxta framework [jxt, 2012] where peers cooperate by exchanging security alerts generated by a log file analyzer. Wormboy aims to detect worm infections by recognizing suspicious temporal consistencies among process invocation traces shared by the cooperative peers. A different approach is followed by *Worminator* [Locasto et al., 2005] and by the peer-to-peer architecture proposed in [Duma et al., 2006], in which each peer cooperates by sharing security events generated by a NIDS.

A peer-to-peer and hybrid SIEM architecture, that is able to leverage both NIDSs and low-interaction honeypots as distributed sensors, is presented in [Marchetti et al., 2009]. This architecture is not only able to detect Internet worms, but also to capture a copy of their binary code. Binary payloads are then distributed among the cooperative sensors using the peer-to-peer overlay network based on Pastry. A hash function is computed on each binary payload, and its result is used to determine which cooperative node will be responsible for the malware analysis. This distribution strategy guarantees a fair load balancing and a high analysis efficiency, since it prevents different cooperative nodes to perform duplicate analysis of identical malware specimens. The same paper also provides an interesting evaluation of the architecture resilience to the failure of cooperative sensors, and a comparison of load balancing between architectures based on peer-to-peer overlays and hierarchical architectures.

A drawback of peer-to-peer SIEM architectures is represented by the cooperation among nodes belonging to different and untrusted organizations. Cooperation by the exchange of security events may reveal sensitive information to cooperative nodes, such as the structure of the internal network, or the fact that some machines have been compromised. Moreover, it is possible for an attacker to deploy a rogue cooperative node, and then to issue false security events in order to reduce the quality of the aggregated alerts and activity reports generated by the whole architecture. Some of these problems have already been considered and solved, although only partially. For example, all the cooperative nodes participating to Indra [Janakiraman et al., 2003] have to be trusted and identified by means of private keys, distributed through a centralized key server. Since this centralized solution limits the architecture scalability, authors also theorize the possibility of using distributed trust schemes, such as the *Web of Trust* borrowed from PGP [Zimmermann, 1995].

The problem of information confidentiality is considered in Worminator [Locasto et al., 2005], that proposes a novel IP address anonymization scheme. In this peer-to-peer scheme, Bloom filters are used to allow correlation based on IP addresses without revealing the actual IP addresses to other collaborative nodes. A set of IP addresses is added to a Bloom filter, that is shared among the collaborative node. Each node can add new addresses to the Bloom filter and check whether some known IP addresses have already been inserted in the Bloom filter by another node. It is not possible for any collaborative node to recover unknown IP addresses from the Bloom filter alone.

Another trust-aware event management scheme has been proposed in [Duma et al., 2006]. In this architecture based on JXTA [jxt, 2012] each peer maintains a list of already known peers, each associated with a trust value. Trust values are constantly updated to reflect the perceived utility of previously generated security events. As an example, the trust of a peer is increased if an event coming from the same peer is followed by a real attack. Trust values are used to weight the security events, thus giving more importance to events coming from peers that are known to be trustworthy.

All the peer-to-peer architectures discussed so far are characterized by a completely flat architecture, in which all peers are equals. A different design is followed by the *Cyber Desease DHT* [Li et al., 2006] peer-to-peer architecture where there are two kinds of cooperative nodes: IDSs and *sensor fusion centers* (SFC). The IDSs produce alerts, that are sent to one of the SFCs for fusion. A limited number of IDSs characterized by high connectivity and computational power are selected to serve as SFCs, thus behaving as supernodes for the CDDHT overlay.

DOMINO is another interesting peer-to-peer scheme much more complex than the other architectures described in this section [Yegneswaran et al., 2004]. The cooperative nodes used by DOMINO belong to three classes: the *axis overlay*, the *satellite communities* and the *terrestrial contributors*. The axis overlay is the class of nodes organized as a peer-to-peer network implemented through Chord [Stoica et al., 2003]. This overlay can be extended by nodes belonging to satellite communities, that is, groups of nodes that run a local instance of the DOMINO software. Satellite communities are organized as a hierarchical architecture, where the nodes belonging to the same satellite community route their alerts towards one node, working as a root local aggregator for its community. This nodes transmits the collected data to the nodes on the axis overlay. Finally, the terrestrial contributors are distributed nodes that supply the axis overlay with security events (generated by IDSs) without direct interaction among themselves, in a way similar to distributed IDSs belonging to a centralized processing scheme. Hence, we can consider DOMINO as a hybrid distributed architecture that integrates design patterns typical of centralized, hierarchical and peer-to-peer schemes.

6. Cooperation Methods for Parallel and Distributed Architectures

Parallel and distributed architectures for aggregation and correlation of security events represent the basic infrastructure that allow communications and cooperation among multiple components. Several different cooperation methods can be implemented on top of these architectures. Figure 9 proposes a classification of solutions for SIEM based on the methods of cooperation. We identify three main cooperation strategies: *security event aggregation and correlation*, *load distribution* and *state information exchange*.

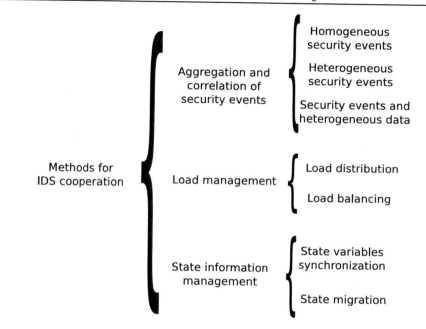

Figure 9. Taxonomy of methods and algorithms for cooperative SIEM and Intrusion Detection.

We can distinguish event aggregation and correlation strategies according to the nature of the events that are aggregated. The simplest and most used aggregation algorithms rely on the *correlation of homogeneous information*, such as alerts generated by different instances of the same IDS software. An evolution of this approach is represented by algorithms that are able to handle *heterogeneous IDS alerts*, generated by different intrusion detection software that is adopted by state of the art hybrid and distributed IDSs. Finally, we consider methods that aggregate IDS alerts and *heterogeneous data* coming from different domains, such as logs, vulnerability repositories and software configuration information.

When an architecture has to deal with multiple components, it is important to consider how the load is distributed among them. The simplest choice is to adopt some form of *static load distribution*, while the most complex and modern solutions are represented by *dynamic load balancing* strategies.

The possible ways to exchange state information among the components of cooperative IDSs rely on completely different schemes: *state variable synchronization* requires cooperative IDSs to exchange continuous updates on the value of atomic state variables; *state migration* is realized through on-demand exchange of IDS state snapshots. We should consider that these forms of cooperation are quite innovative. Their benefits have been demonstrated in literature and in research prototypes, but they have not yet been implemented in commercial IDSs.

6.1. Security event management

Security event management plays an important role for both parallel and distributed IDS architectures. Depending on their configuration and on the monitored environment, each IDS can produce huge amounts of alerts, each requiring manual validation by a human operator. Without suitable event fusion techniques [Maggi et al., 2009], this burden is multiplied by the number of IDSs that compose a parallel or a distributed IDS architecture to the extent that the use of multiple IDSs would be impracticable.

Event management can achieve other useful results, such as alert clustering [Julisch, 2003, Cuppens, 2001, Dain and Cunningham, 2001], reduction of false positives [Pietraszek, 2004, Zhai et al., 2004], alert ranking and prioritization [Morin et al., 2002, Colajanni et al., 2008b] and reconstruction of complex multistep attacks [Zhou et al., 2007, Manganiello et al., 2011, Marchetti et al., 2011b, Marchetti et al., 2011a]. The description of a comprehensive approach to the correlation of alerts generated by IDSs can be found in [Valeur et al., 2004], while a survey about the most relevant results on IDS alert correlation is in [Sadoddin and Ghorbani, 2006].

The goal of alert management algorithms is similar, hence we prefer to classify them on the basis of their inputs:

- management of homogeneous security events (Section 6.1.1);

- management of heterogeneous security events (Section 6.1.2);

- management of heterogeneous security events and integration with information coming from other sources, such as repositories of software vulnerabilities, host configuration and sensors placement (Section 6.1.3).

6.1.1. Management of homogeneous security events

Homogeneous security events are produced by different instances of the same type of intrusion detection software. SIEM algorithms that fall in this category can only be used in cooperative IDS architectures that are based on homogeneous event analyzers. For this reason, the event aggregation and correlation algorithm does not need to normalize alerts before processing them. Moreover, it can leverage application specific information, such as signature identifiers that are used by an IDS and that are not comparable between different IDSs.

Several commercial and open source alert softwares also fall in this category, such as the *Basic Analysis and Security Engine* (BASE) [Jonson, 2012] tailored for the analysis of alerts produces by the Snort NIDS, and the Check Point software [Check Point software technologies, 2012] that manages alerts produced in the context of the *IPS software Blade*.

Some examples of alert management schemes are described in [Julisch, 2003, Julisch, 2001], where the techniques are borrowed from the data mining domain and adapted to cluster similar NIDS alerts. Other instances of more complex aggregation and correlation algorithms for the management of homogeneous security alerts leverage several machine-learning techniques aiming to recognize and reconstruct complex multistep attack strategies [Manganiello et al., 2011, Marchetti et al., 2011b]. Since simple attacks and intrusions are often foiled by modern design principle and defense strategies, multistep attacks are on the rise, and it is possible to anticipate that the need robust algorithms for their automatic identification will grow in the near future.

6.1.2. Management of heterogeneous security events

One of the main benefits of distributed IDS and SIEM architectures is their ability to leverage heterogeneous event sources, thus complying to the best practices of the so called in-depth defense. The first intuitive problem is that heterogeneous event analyzers produce heterogeneous security events, that are not directly comparable among themselves. Hence the first goal is to adopt some common format to aggregate and correlate heterogeneous events. An important effort in this direction is represented by the *Intrusion Detection Message Exchange Format* (IDMEF) [Debar et al., 2007] that proposes a standard syntax for the representation of security alerts. This standard is already supported by several IDSs. For example, Prelude SIEM [Prelude SIEM,], that is is a widespread Open Source software, adopts IDMEF for the management of alerts generated by heterogeneous event analyzers.

While standard formats can simplify event management by defining common syntax rules, they do not bridge the semantic gap existing among events generated by different IDSs. Other solutions for the correlation of heterogeneous events are based on a reduced set of characteristics that preserve the same meaning, and that are directly comparable. As an example, several papers exploits temporal locality principles by clustering events that are "near" in time [Viinikka et al., 2009, Maggi et al., 2009].

A third class of approaches is based on the definition of attack scenarios (e.g., [Templeton and Levitt, 2000, Cuppens and Miège, 2002, Ning et al., 2004]). For example, the phases of attacks based on multiple actions are defined manually through a custom attack definition language. Heterogeneous alerts referring to some steps of a complex attack are then fused in one high-level alert.

6.1.3. Management of security events and other data sources

The most recent and interesting results in literature aim to integrate information coming from heterogeneous data sources with the purpose of validating and ranking IDS alerts and heterogeneous security events. The goal is to reduce false positives and to simplify security event management by human operators or even to guide reaction of some IPS in the right direction.

The first paper in this field describes the M2D2 formal data model for IDS alert correlation [Morin et al., 2002]: it proposes an alert management scheme in which IDS alerts are correlated with information about the monitored information systems and information about software vulnerabilities. Each data source is formally defined, and the aggregation process is specified rigorously. However, we are not aware of any product or prototype that takes advantage of the M2D2 formalism.

The use of multiple information related to the monitored environment has also been proposed in [Valeur et al., 2004]. The comprehensive alert management scheme uses an *asset database*, containing structured information on the characteristics of the monitored environment, to verify whether it is vulnerable to the attacks described by IDS alerts and other security events. If some protected assets is vulnerable to the detected attack, then the related alerts are ranked with high priority. This helps the human operator to focus on alerts related to real threats for their organization.

Further steps in this direction are taken in [Colajanni et al., 2008b, Colajanni et al., 2010]. Rather than relying on a single asset database, and on one source for vulnerability information, this paper proposes the use of custom wrappers that are able to acquire useful data from multiple and heterogeneous data sources. As an example, several open and unstructured vulnerability databases can be consulted, thus obtaining complete information on a large number of vulnerabilities. The effectiveness of the proposed scheme is demonstrated through a prototype based on Prelude SIEM [Prelude SIEM,].

Another original approach for the validation of security events is proposed in [Bolzoni et al., 2007]. The main idea is to correlate IDS alerts with the responses generated by the systems that are targeted by the attack. If the attacked systems continues to behave normally after the attack, then chances are that the attack has not been effective. On the other hand, if anomalies are found in the system, then the system is assumed to be compromised, so the priority of the alert is augmented.

6.2. Load management

The distribution of the computational load among several IDSs represents the raison d'être of the parallel IDS architectures. As described in Section 4, load distribution in this case is carried out by the centralized event dispatcher, that splits the incoming event stream into multiple subsets, each small enough to be managed by each event analyzer. Load management is also important for distributed, hierarchical and peer-to-peer schemes, where several event processors contribute to the analysis.

We distinguish between *load distribution* and *load balancing* schemes. The former algorithms aim to distribute the load statically among the multiple components of a parallel or distributed architecture. The latter algorithms introduce some dynamic principles in the distribution of the load.

6.2.1. Load distribution

Static load distribution is widely employed by most parallel IDS architectures [Kruegel et al., 2002, Charitakis et al., 2003, Xinidis K and Markatos, 2005, Xinidis et al., 2006, Vallentin et al., 2007]. In these cases, the strategy implemented by the event dispatcher to distribute the load among the sensors and event analyzers does not change. For example, the architecture in [Kruegel et al., 2002] implements a rule-based event dispatching, where it is responsibility of the system administrator to devise the best set of event distribution rules that is flow-preserving and that does not overload any parallel event analyzer. The event distribution schemes proposed in [Charitakis et al., 2003, Xinidis K and Markatos, 2005, Xinidis et al., 2006, Vallentin et al., 2007] are based on some hash function, hence the destination sensor is determined by the content of each event.

Rule-based approaches give more control to the system administrator, and makes it possible to deploy IDSs that are optimized to perform a specific analysis task. As an example, if the event dispatching rules are designed to route to a specific NIDS only network packets that do not use TCP as a transport layer protocol, then this NIDS can be configured without all the attack signatures that are related to application-level protocols. The elimination of useless signatures makes the pattern matching process more efficient. On the other hand, static rule-based event dispatching schemes are prone to uneven load distribution among event analyzers. This is especially true in the context of network traffic analysis, whose workload is characterized by high variability over time, traffic bursts and sudden spikes [Crovella, 2001, Fishman and Adan, 2006].

Hash-based event dispatching strategies do not require an explicit definition of event dispatching rules, and can achieve a fine-grain event distribution. However, the administrator has less control on the characteristics of the events that are routed towards each IDS. Moreover, static hash-based event dispatching schemes do not solve load unbalancing problems among the parallel sensors. If too many events hash to the same value or to different values mapped to the same IDS, its computational capacity can easily be overloaded.

In distributed IDS architectures, the event distribution is statically determined by their placement that implicitly defines the event source monitored by each IDS. As an example, an HIDS deployed within a host is able to analyze just the events produced by the host itself, while a NIDS deployed in a branch of a switched network is able to gather just the events related to that segment.

The distribution of the load related to event management in hierarchical (Section 5.2) and peer-to-peer (Section 5.3) SIEM architectures open another class of problems. In hierarchical architectures, the computational load related to local event management is determined by the event management algorithms. Each local event manager forwards its partial results to event managers at the higher level (see Figure 8), hence the flow distribution is statically determined by the hierarchy structure. On the other hand, in peer-to-peer architectures both the computational load and the alert flow can be controlled by the event management algorithm implemented on top of the peer-to-peer overlay.

6.2.2. Load balancing

The main goal of dynamic algorithms is to solve the load unbalance problems (and overload risks) that are intrinsic in any static load distribution scheme.

For example, the event dispatcher proposed in the parallel IDS architectures in [Alam et al., 2004, Colajanni and Marchetti, 2006, Andreolini et al., 2007, Le et al., 2008, Schaelicke et al., 2005] can detect whether any parallel IDS is overloaded. In such a case, one or more traffic flows assigned to the overloaded component are dynamically reassigned to another IDS. In case of rule-based event dispatchers [Alam et al., 2004, Colajanni and Marchetti, 2006, Andreolini et al., 2007], the destination associated with one or more rule is modified consequently. Similarly, hash-based event distribution schemes [Le et al., 2008, Schaelicke et al., 2005] are adapted by modifying the associations between hash values and destinations.

Load balancing schemes require a dynamic evaluation of the load state of the parallel IDSs. The typical approach is to use a collector that periodically gathers load samples from each IDS. In [Andreolini et al., 2007], the load of the parallel IDS is measured by applying linear aggregation functions on a sequence of load samples. Load detection algorithms based on aggregation of load samples are shown to be reliable and to reduce both the number of balancing operations and the packet loss rate.

Another issue related to dynamic load balancing is the need to dynamically reassign some traffic flows that are undergoing stateful analysis. As an example, consider a network traffic flow, such as a TCP connection, that is associated to the i-th analyzer. Since the event distribution scheme applied by the event dispatcher is flow preserving, then the i-th analyzer has received all the network packets belonging to this connection, and is able to perform a stateful analysis of this traffic flow. However, due to a load balancing operation, the traffic flow associated to the currently open connection is reassigned from the i-th to the j-th analyzer. As a consequence, the j-th analyzer starts to receive network packets belonging to a TCP connection that is already open, without having all the information that is necessary to perform a stateful analysis. Hence, we have two alternatives: the simplest, although less reliable, choice is to combine dynamic load balancing with stateless analyses on reassigned event flows; otherwise, if we want to preserve stateful analyses, then we have to integrate some mechanisms for state information migration in the load balancing process. This latter approach is proposed in some recent papers [Sommer and Paxson, 2005, Colajanni and Marchetti, 2006, Colajanni et al., 2007]. In such cases, the previously considered j-th analyzer does not receive just the network packets belonging to an open connection, but also all state information generated by the i-th NIDS referring to that connection that is necessary to perform a stateful analysis. Algorithm and techniques that enable cooperation through the exchange of state information among analyzers of parallel and distributed IDS architectures are described in the following section.

6.3.   State information management

All modern IDSs perform a *stateful* traffic analysis, where each event is not analyzed as an independent entity, but it is considered as related to a set of state information that are generated by related events. Stateful intrusion detection implies that a traffic analyzer has to build and maintain state information for each event flow. This function has greatly improved the analysis reliability, at the expense of an increase in computational complexity and memory requirements.

As a network-oriented motivation for stateful analysis, we can consider the effect of packet fragmentation, possibly the simplest NIDS evasion technique. An attacker can easily divide a network packet containing an attack in two different IP fragments (for example by setting a low MTU). Then the NIDS receives two network packets, none of which contains the attack signature. If the NIDS is *stateless*, the analysis of each packet is based only on information included in the packet itself, and since none of the two fragmented packets contains enough information to recognize an intrusion, the attack is not detected. On the other hand, if the NIDS is stateful, the analysis of the first attack fragment results from the storage of its partial payload. When the second fragment is received, its payload is merged with the payload of the other fragment. Payload reconstruction allows the NIDS to detect the attack.

The generation and storage of an internal state is commonly carried out by traditional IDSs, where all the events are received by a single event analyzer. However, when the events are processed by multiple event analyzers, as in parallel and distributed IDS architectures, the global state is fragmented because each event analyzer has only a limited view of the global state. In parallel IDS architectures this problem is mitigated by flow preserving event dispatching algorithms (described in Section 4), but flows are not preserved in all parallel IDS architecture that adopt dynamic load balancing.

Distributed IDS architectures are able to perform stateful analysis on all the events that are gathered from the same source, when these events are processed by the same event analyzer. The complete state of the whole monitored environment can be inferred by aggregating the security events generated by the distributed event analyzers. However, in some cases even the stateful analysis of the events gathered from one source is impossible, possibly resulting in stealth intrusion that cannot be detected by state-of-the art IDSs. For example, let us consider a distributed architecture consisting of two NIDSs each analyzing the network traffic flowing on a different LAN segment that allows some forms of node mobility across LANs (e.g., Mobile IPv4 [Charles E. Perkins, 2002] and IPv6 [Perkins and Johnson, 1996], 802.11r standard [IEEE Computer Society, 2008]). These technologies allow a mobile node to change its point of attachment to the network without disrupting open connections. This feature can be abused by malicious mobile nodes to perform stealth mobility-based attacks, by sending a fragment of the attack in a LAN and the remaining attack fragment from a second LAN. Since no of the two NIDSs has analyzed the whole traffic, it is impossible to perform a stateful traffic analysis that is needed to recognize the fragmented attack signature [Colajanni et al., 2011b].

The two main approaches to allow a dynamic exchange of internal state information among parallel and distributed IDS architectures are based on the synchronization of state variables and state migration.

A mechanism for state variable synchronization has been proposed in [Sommer and Paxson, 2005]. It is implemented for the BroNIDS [Paxson, 1999], and has been used in the parallel architecture described in [Vallentin et al., 2007]. The event analyzer of Bro is divided in two layers: an event engine and a policy script. The event engine analyzes all the received network packets, and generates high-level events that represent the network activities occurring in the monitored network links. These high level events are then analyzed by the policy script layer, in which attack patterns and network policies are described through a custom policy definition language. Policies can leverage atomic variables and more complex data structures. All the cooperative instances of Bro label a subset of these variable and data structures as synchronized. If an event triggers the update of a synchronized variable in one of the cooperative Bro instances, then this instance is responsible for generating an update message and for sending the update message to any other cooperative Bro NIDS through a *push*-based communication scheme. Ideally, all the variables that are synchronized among different instances of Bro share the same value, hence a modification in the internal state of any instance is propagated towards all the others. Some synchronization problem may occur because the time to generate and forward an update message is not null, hence the propagation of state updates suffers of some delays.

State migration has first been proposed in the parallel architecture presented in [Colajanni and Marchetti, 2006], while a more detailed description of its internals, together with a performance evaluation of an implementation based on the Snort NIDS [Snort, 2012], is proposed in [Colajanni et al., 2007]. Snort is a signature-based NIDS that performs stateful traffic analysis by reassembling the content of network packets belonging to the same traffic flows, such as TCP connections or communication over UDP. For each transport level flow, a set of state information is built and maintained by the *stream_5* pre-processor. This state information is constantly updated after the receipt of any packet belonging to the same flow, hence signature-based pattern matching algorithms are not suitable to a state management scheme based on state variable synchronization. If two cooperative instances of Snort were to cooperate in this way, each NIDS would be forced to create an update message after the analysis of each TCP or UDP packet. To avoid this huge overhead, state migration is modeled as an on-demand transfer of all the state information that is related to a specific flow, rather than on a continuous update of state variables. All the cooperative Snort instances are provided with an XMLRPC module [Winer, 2007] that handles remote invocations of two remote procedures: *state import* and *state export*. The state export RPC takes as its parameter the identifier of one or more transport-level flows, and returns a serialized representation of the related state information, as maintained by the stream_5 preprocessor. The state import RPC takes as its parameter the serialized representation of the state of one or more transport-level flows, that is merged with the set of state information currently owned by the cooperative Snort instance.

State migration can be performed only when needed, thus avoiding useless overhead when the sharing of state information is not needed. As an example, the event dispatcher of a parallel and load balanced IDS architecture can use the state export and state import remote procedure calls to migrate only the state information that is related to a dynamically reassigned TCP connection. Similarly, a NIDS belonging to a distributed architecture can ask for the state information related to the TCP connections opened by a mobile node right after the mobility event is detected [Colajanni et al., 2011a].

7. Open Issues and Research Perspectives

Some areas in the field of cooperative intrusion detection and cooperative SIEM can be considered as mature. Nowadays, several architectures, algorithms and products that enable cooperation among parallel and distributed IDSs architectures exist. However, the continuously changing scenario of modern information systems and the growth in the number, complexity and heterogeneity of the environments that have to be monitored, present new challenges for cooperative security architectures and SIEM solutions.

One major goal is to enhance the interoperability of heterogeneous analysis engines, with the goal of combining stateful analysis of security events together with load balancing and node mobility management. An open issue for IDS cooperation is represented by the lack of a common format for the dissemination of internal state information generated by stateful IDSs. Existing solutions allow state information exchange among instances of the same software for intrusion detection, but they prevent heterogeneous stateful IDSs to cooperate by sharing their internal state information.

Moreover, cooperation among parallel and distributed IDS architectures is performed through event distribution and alert aggregation and correlation, while the event analysis engines are still independent of each other. Truly distributed and real-time event analysis is still an open research area.

Other research opportunities concern IDS alert aggregation and correlation. Although many results exist, human intervention is still needed for alert validation, especially in distributed systems that rely on several heterogeneous intrusion detection approaches. Fusion of security events generated by network IDS, host IDS and operational IDS together with other heterogeneous information sources is also a recent field, that is still open to original ideas and approaches.

References

[jxt, 2012] (Visited March 2012). Jxta[TM]commmunity project homepage. `http://java.net/projects/jxta/`.

[Alam et al., 2004] Alam, M., Javed, Q., Akbar, M., M.R.U.Rehman, and Anwer, M. (2004). Adaptive load balancing architecture for snort. In *Proc. of the Internationale Conference on Networking and Communication (INCC 2004)*, Lahore, Pakistan.

[Andreolini et al., 2007] Andreolini, M., Casolari, S., Colajanni, M., and Marchetti, M. (2007). Dynamic load balancing for network intrusion detection systems based on distributed architectures. In *Network Computing and Applications, 2007. NCA 2007. Sixth IEEE International Symposium on*.

[Balasubramaniyan et al., 1998] Balasubramaniyan, J. S., Garcia-Fernandez, J. O., Isacoff, D., Spafford, E. H., and Zamboni, D. (1998). An architecture for intrusion detection using autonomous agents. In *Proc. of the 14th Annual Computer Security Applications Conference (ACSAC 1998)*.

[Bass, 1999] Bass, T. (1999). Multisensor data fusion for next generation distributed intrusion detection systems. In *Proc. of the 1999 DoD-IRIS National Symposium on Sensor and Data Fusion (NSSDF)*.

[Bass, 2000] Bass, T. (2000). Intrusion detection systems and multisensor data fusion. *Communications of the ACM*, 43(4):99–105.

[Bolzoni et al., 2007] Bolzoni, D., Crispo, B., and Etalle, S. (2007). Atlantides: an architecture for alert verification in network intrusion detection systems. In *Proc. of the 21st conference on Large Installation System Administration Conference (LISA'07)*.

[Bu and Chandy, 2004] Bu, L. and Chandy, J. A. (2004). FPGA based network intrusion detection using content addressable memories. In *Proc. of the 12th Annual IEEE Symposium on Field-Programmable Custom Computing Machines (FCCM)*, Napa, CA, USA.

[Castro et al., 2002] Castro, M., Druschel, P., Kermarrec, A.-M., and Rowstron, A. (2002). Scribe: a large-scale and decentralized application-level multicast infrastructure. *IEEE Journal on Selected Areas in Communications*, 20(8):1489–1499.

[Charitakis et al., 2003] Charitakis, I., Anagnostakis, S., and Markatos, E. P. (2003). An active traffic splitter architecture for intrusion detection. In *Proc. of the 11th IEEE/ACM International Symposium on Modeling, Analysis and Simulation of Computer Telecommunications Systems (MASCOTS 2003)*, Orlando, FL, USA.

[Charles E. Perkins, 2002] Charles E. Perkins (2002). Mobile IP. *IEEE Communications Magazine*, 40(5):66–82.

[Check Point software technologies, 2012] Check Point software technologies (Visited March 2012). IPS SmartEvent Software Blade homepage. http://www.checkpoint.com/products/softwareblades/ips-smartevent.html.

[Cho and Mangione-Smith, 2005] Cho, Y. and Mangione-Smith, W. (2005). A pattern matching co-processor for network security. In *Proc. of the 42nd ACM Design Automation Conference*, Anaheim, CA, USA.

[Chu et al., 2005] Chu, Y., Li, J., and Yang, Y. (2005). The architecture of the large-scale distributed intrusion detection system. In *Proc. of the Sixth International Conference on Parallel and Distributed Computing Applications and Technologies (PDCAT '05)*.

[Cisco and Hewlett-Packard, 2012] Cisco and Hewlett-Packard (Visited March 2012). HP OpenView Node Sentry. http://www.cisco.com/warp/public/756/partnership/hp/sentry.pdf.

[Cisco Systems, 2012] Cisco Systems (Visited March 2012). Configuring IPS High Bandwidth Using EtherChannel Load Balancing. http://www.cisco.com/univercd/cc/td/doc/product/iaabu/csids/csids12/eclbips5.pdf.

[Clark et al., 2004] Clark, C. R., Lee, W., Schimmel, D. E., Contis, D., Kon, M., and Thomas, A. (2004). A hardware platform for network intrusion detection and prevention. In *Proc. of the Workshop on Network Processors and Applications at HPCA (NP-3)*, Madrid, Spain.

[Colajanni et al., 2011a] Colajanni, M., Dal Zotto, L., Marchetti, M., and Messori, M. (2011a). Defeating nids evasion in mobile ipv6 networks. In *Proc. of the 12th IEEE International Symposium on a World of Wireless, Mobile and Multimedia Networks,(WoWMoM 2011)*, Lucca, Italy.

[Colajanni et al., 2011b] Colajanni, M., Dal Zotto, L., Marchetti, M., and Messori, M. (2011b). The problem of nids evasion in mobile networks. In *Proc. of the 4th IFIP International Conference on New Technologies, Mobility and Security (NTMS 2011)*, Paris, France.

[Colajanni et al., 2007] Colajanni, M., Gozzi, D., and Marchetti, M. (2007). Enhancing interoperability and stateful analysis of cooperative network intrusion detection systems. In *Proc. of the 3rd ACM/IEEE Symposium on Architecture for networking and communications systems, (ANCS '07)*.

[Colajanni et al., 2008a] Colajanni, M., Gozzi, D., and Marchetti, M. (2008a). Collaborative architecture for malware detection and analysis. In *Proc. of the IFIP 23rd International Information Security Conference (SEC '08)*.

[Colajanni et al., 2008b] Colajanni, M., Gozzi, D., and Marchetti, M. (2008b). Selective alerts for the run-time protection of distributed systems. In *Proc. of the Ninth International Conference on Data Mining, Protection, Detection and other Security Technologies (DATAMINING 2008)*.

[Colajanni and Marchetti, 2006] Colajanni, M. and Marchetti, M. (2006). A parallel architecture for stateful intrusion detection in high traffic networks. In *Proc. of the IEEE/IST Workshop on "Monitoring, attack detection and mitigation" (MonAM 2006)*, Tuebingen, Germany.

[Colajanni et al., 2010] Colajanni, M., Marchetti, M., and Messori, M. (2010). Selective and early threat detection in large networked systems. In *Proc. of the 10th IEEE International Conference on Computer and Information Technology (CIT 2010)*, Bradford, UK.

[Corero, 2012a] Corero (Visited March 2012a). Intelligence Distribution System Balancer - IDSB. http://www.corero.com/en/products_and_services/idsb.

[Corero, 2012b] Corero (Visited March 2012b). SecureCommand™IPS Centralized Management Solution. http://www.corero.com/en/products_and_services/ips.

[Crovella, 2001] Crovella, M. (2001). *Performance Evaluation with Heavy-Tailed Distributions*. Springer.

[Cuppens, 2001] Cuppens, F. (2001). Managing alerts in a multi-intrusion detection environment. In *Proc. of the 17th Annual Computer Security Applications Conference (ACSAC '01)*.

[Cuppens and Miège, 2002] Cuppens, F. and Miège, A. (2002). Alert correlation in a cooperative intrusion detection framework. In *SP '02: Proceedings of the 2002 IEEE Symposium on Security and Privacy*, page 202, Washington, DC, USA. IEEE Computer Society.

[Dain and Cunningham, 2001] Dain, O. and Cunningham, R. K. (2001). Fusing a heterogeneous alert stream into scenarios. In *In Proc. of the 2001 ACM workshop on Data Mining for Security Applications*, pages 1–13.

[Debar et al., 2007] Debar, H., Curry, D., and B., F. (2007). The Intrusion Detection Message Exchange Format. RFC 4765.

[Debar and Wespi, 2001] Debar, H. and Wespi, A. (2001). Aggregation and correlation of intrusion-detection alerts. In *Proc. of the 4th International Symposium on Recent Advances in Intrusion Detection RAID 2001*.

[Duma et al., 2006] Duma, C., Karresand, M., Shahmehri, N., and Caronni, G. (2006). A trust-aware, p2p-based overlay for intrusion detection. *Proc. of the 17th International Conference on Database and Expert Systems Applications (DEXA'06)*.

[Enterasys®, 2012] Enterasys® (Visited March 2012).   Enterasys Delivers Distributed Intrusion Prevention System. `http://www.enterasys.com/company/press-release-item.aspx?id=748`.

[Fishman and Adan, 2006] Fishman, G. and Adan, I. (2006). How heavy-tailed distributions affect simulation-generated time averages. *ACM Trans. on Modeling and Computer Simulation*, 16(2):152–173.

[Foschini et al., 2008] Foschini, L., Thapliyal, A. V., Cavallaro, L., Kruegel, C., and Vigna, G. (2008). A parallel architecture for stateful, high-speed intrusion detection. In *ICISS '08: Proceedings of the 4th International Conference on Information Systems Security*.

[IEEE Computer Society, 2008] IEEE Computer Society (2008). IEEE standard for information technology-telecommunications and information exchange between systems-local and metropolitan area networks-specific requirements part 11: wireless lan medium access control (mac) and physical layer (phy) specifications amendment 2: fast basic service set (bss). *IEEE Std 802.11r-2008 (Amendment to IEEE Std 802.11-2007 as amended by IEEE Std 802.11k-2008)*, pages c1–108.

[IETF Intrusion Detection Working Group, 2006] IETF Intrusion Detection Working Group (2006). The intrusion detection message exchange format. `http://www.ietf.org/internet-drafts/draft-ietf-idwg-idmef-xml-16.txt`.

[Ilgun et al., 1995] Ilgun, K., Kemmerer, R. A., and Porras, P. A. (1995). State transition analysis: A rule-based intrusion detection approach. *IEEE Transactions on Software Engineering*, 21(3):181–199.

[Ingram et al., 2000] Ingram, D. J., Kremer, H. S., and Rowe, N. C. (2000). Distributed intrusion detection for computer systems using communicating agents. In *Proc. of 2000 Command and Control Research and Technology Symposium*.

[Intel®, 2012] Intel® (Visited March 2012). Intel® IXP1200 Network Processor. `http://www.intel.com/intelpress/sum_ixp1200.htm?wapkw=ixp1200`.

[Janakiraman et al., 2003] Janakiraman, R., Waldvogel, M., and Zhang, Q. (2003). Indra: A peer-to-peer approach to network intrusion detection and prevention. In *Proc. of the 12th IEEE International Workshops on Enabling Technologies (WETICE'03)*.

[Jonson, 2012] Jonson, K. (Visited March 2012).   BASE homepage.   `http://sourceforge.net/projects/secureideas/`.

[Julisch, 2001] Julisch, K. (2001). Mining alarm clusters to improve alarm handling efficiency. In *Proc. of the 17th Annual Computer Security Applications Conference (ACSAC '01)*.

[Julisch, 2003] Julisch, K. (2003). Clustering intrusion detection alarms to support root cause analysis. *ACM Transactions on Information Systems Security*, 6(4):443–471.

[Kemmerer, 1998] Kemmerer, R. A. (1998). Nstat: A model-based real-time network intrusion detection system. Technical report, University of California at Santa Barbara, Santa Barbara, CA, USA.

[Kohler et al., 2000] Kohler, E., Morris, R., Chen, B., Jannotti, J., and Kaashoek, M. F. (2000). The click modular router. *ACM Trans. Comput. Syst.*, 18(3):263–297.

[Kruegel et al., 2002] Kruegel, C., Valeur, F., Vigna, G., and Kemmerer, R. (2002). Stateful intrusion detection for high-speed networks. In *Proc. of the IEEE Symposium on Research on Security and Privacy*, Oakland, CA, USA.

[Le et al., 2008] Le, A., Boutaba, R., and Al-Shaer, E. (2008). Correlation-based load balancing for network intrusion detection and prevention systems. In *SecureComm '08: Proceedings of the 4th international conference on Security and privacy in communication netowrks*.

[Li et al., 2006] Li, Z., Chen, Y., and Beach, A. (2006). Towards scalable and robust distributed intrusion alert fusion with good load balancing. In *Proc. of the 2006 SIGCOMM workshop on Large-scale attack defense (LSAD '06)*.

[Lippmann et al., 2000] Lippmann, R., Haines, J. W., Fried, D. J., Korba, J., and Das, K. (2000). Analysis and results of the 1999 darpa off-line intrusion detection evaluation. In *Proc. of the Third International Workshop on Recent Advances in Intrusion Detection*, Toulouse, France.

[Liu et al., 2004] Liu, R.-T., Huang, N.-F., Chen, C.-H., and Kao, C.-N. (2004). A fast string-matching algorithm for network processor-based intrusion detection system. *ACM Trans. Embed. Comput. Syst.*, 3(3).

[Locasto et al., 2005] Locasto, M., Parekh, J., Keromytis, A., and Stolfo, S. (2005). Towards collaborative security and p2p intrusion detection. In *Proceedings from the Sixth Annual IEEE SMC Information Assurance Workshop (IAW '05)*.

[Maggi et al., 2009] Maggi, F., Matteucci, M., and Zanero, S. (2009). Reducing False Positives In Anomaly Detectors Through Fuzzy Alert Aggregation. *Information Fusion*.

[Malan and Smith, 2005] Malan, D. J. and Smith, M. D. (2005). Host-based detection of worms through peer-to-peer cooperation. In *Proc. of the 3rd workshop on rapid malcode (WORM'05)*.

[Manganiello et al., 2011] Manganiello, F., Marchetti, M., and Colajanni, M. (2011). Multistep attack detection and alert correlation in intrusion detection systems. In *Proc. of the 5th International Conference on Information Security and Assurance (ISA 2011)*, Brno, Czec Republic.

[Marchetti et al., 2011a] Marchetti, M., Colajanni, M., and Manganiello, F. (2011a). Framework and models for multistep attack detection. *International Journal on Security and its Applications (IJSIA)*, 5(4):73–92.

[Marchetti et al., 2011b] Marchetti, M., Colajanni, M., and Manganiello, F. (2011b). Identification of correlated network intrusion alerts. In *Proc. of the 3rd IEEE International Workshop on Cyberspace Safety and Security (CSS 2011)*, Milan, IT.

[Marchetti et al., 2009] Marchetti, M., Messori, M., and Colajanni, M. (2009). Peer-to-peer architecture for collaborative intrusion and malware detection on a large scale. In *Proc. of the 12th Information Security Conference (ISC 2009)*.

[Morin et al., 2002] Morin, B., M, L., Debar, H., and Ducass, M. (2002). M2d2: A formal data model for ids alert correlation. In *In Proc. of the 5th International Symposium on Recent Advances in Intrusion Detection (RAID 2002*, pages 115–137.

[Ning et al., 2004] Ning, P., Cui, Y., Reeves, D. S., and Xu, D. (2004). Techniques and tools for analyzing intrusion alerts. *ACM Transactions on Information and System Security*, 7(2):274–318.

[Paxson, 1999] Paxson, V. (1999). Bro: a system for detecting network intruders in real-time. *Computer Networks: The International Journal of Computer and Telecommunication Networking*, 31(23-24):2435–2463.

[Perkins and Johnson, 1996] Perkins, C. E. and Johnson, D. B. (1996). Mobility support in ipv6. In *Proc. of the 2nd annual international conference on Mobile computing and networking (MobiCom '96)*.

[Pietraszek, 2004] Pietraszek, T. (2004). Using Adaptive Alert Classification to Reduce False Positives in Intrusion Detection. In Verlang, S., editor, *Proc. of the Seventh International Symposium on Recent Advances in Intrusion Detection (RAID 2004)*, volume 3224 of *Lecture Notes in Computer Science (LNCS)*.

[Prelude IDS technologies, 2012] Prelude IDS technologies (Visited March 2012). Prelude ids homepage. http://www.prelude-ids.org/.

[Prelude SIEM,] Prelude SIEM. Prelude SIEM Home Page.

[Ptacek and Newsham, 1998] Ptacek, T. H. and Newsham, T. N. (1998). Insertion, evasion, and denial of service: Eluding network intrusion detection. Technical report, Secure Networks, Inc., Suite 330, 1201 5th Street S.W, Calgary, Alberta, Canada, T2R-0Y6.

[QBIK, 2012] QBIK (Visited March 2012). NetPatrol. http://www.wingate.com/products/netpatrol/features.php?fid=68.

[Radware, 2012] Radware (Visited March 2012). Radware: Application delivery secureflow fireproof. http://www.radware.com/Products/ApplicationDelivery/SecureFlow/FireProof.aspx.

[Ragsdale et al., 2000] Ragsdale, D., Carver, C., Humphries, J., and Pooch, U. (2000). Adaptation techniques for intrusion detection and intrusion response systems. In *Proc. of the IEEE International Conference on Systems, Man, and Cybernetics (SMC 2000)*.

[Rowstron and Druschel, 2001] Rowstron, A. I. T. and Druschel, P. (2001). Pastry: Scalable, decentralized object location, and routing for large-scale peer-to-peer systems. In *Proc. of the IFIP/ACM International Conference on Distributed Systems Platforms (Middleware '01)*.

[Sadoddin and Ghorbani, 2006] Sadoddin, R. and Ghorbani, A. (2006). Alert correlation survey: framework and techniques. In *Proc. of the 2006 International Conference on Privacy, Security and Trust (PST '06)*, New York, NY, USA. ACM.

[Schaelicke et al., 2005] Schaelicke, L., Wheeler, K., and Freeland, C. (2005). Spanids: a scalable network intrusion detection loadbalancer. In *Proc. of the 2nd conference on Computing frontiers*, Ischia, Italy.

[Snapp et al., 1991] Snapp, S., Brentano, J., Dias, G., Goan, T., Grance, T., Heberlein, L., Ho, C.-L., Levitt, K., Mukherjee, B., Mansur, D., Pon, K., and Smaha, S. (1991). A system for distributed intrusion detection. In *Compcon Spring '91. Digest of Papers from the IEEE Computer Society Thirty-sixth International Conference*.

[Snapp et al., 1988] Snapp, S. R., Brentano, J., Dias, G. V., Goan, T. L., Heberlein, L. T., Ho, C.-L., Levitt, K. N., Mukherjee, B., Smaha, S. E., Grance, T., Teal, D. M., and Mansur, D. (1988). *Internet besieged: countering cyberspace scofflaws*, chapter DIDS (distributed intrusion detection system)—motivation, architecture, and an early prototype, pages 211–227. ACM Press/Addison-Wesley Publishing Co., New York, NY, USA.

[Snort, 2012] Snort (Visited March 2012). Snort home page. http://www.snort.org.

[Sommer and Paxson, 2005] Sommer, R. and Paxson, V. (2005). Exploiting independent state for network intrusion detection. In *Proc. of the 21st Annual Computer Security Applications Conference*, Tucson, AZ, USA.

[Song and Lockwood, 2005] Song, H. and Lockwood, J. W. (2005). Efficient packet classification for network intrusion detection using fpga. In *Proc. of the 2005 ACM/SIGDA 13th International Symposium on Field-Programmable Gate Arrays (FPGA 05)*, Monterey, CA, USA.

[Song et al., 2005] Song, H., Sproull, T., Attig, M., and Lockwood, J. (2005). Snort offloader: A reconfigurable hardware NIDS filter. In *Proc. of the 15th International Conference on Field Programmable Logic and Applications (FPL)*, Tampere, Finland.

[Sourcefire®, 2012] Sourcefire® (Visited March 2012). Sourcefire Defense Center™. http://www.sourcefire.com/security-technologies/network-security/centralized-management.

[Staniford-Chen et al., 1996] Staniford-Chen, S., Cheung, S., Crawford, R., Dilger, M., Frank, J., Hoagland, J., Levitt, K., Wee, C., Yip, R., and Zerkle, D. (1996). Grids - a graph-based intrusion detection system for large networks. In *Proc. of the 19th National Information Systems Security Conference*.

[Stoica et al., 2003] Stoica, I., Morris, R., Liben-Nowell, D., Karger, D. R., Kaashoek, M. F., Dabek, F., and Balakrishnan, H. (2003). Chord: a scalable peer-to-peer lookup protocol for internet applications. *IEEE/ACM Transactions on Networking*, 11(1):17–32.

[Templeton and Levitt, 2000] Templeton, S. J. and Levitt, K. (2000). A requires/provides model for computer attacks. In *Proc. of the 2000 workshop on New security paradigms (NSPW '00:)*, pages 31–38, New York, NY, USA. ACM.

[Valeur et al., 2004] Valeur, F., Vigna, G., Kruegel, C., and Kemmerer, R. A. (2004). A comprehensive approach to intrusion detection alert correlation. *IEEE Transactions on Dependable and Secure Computing*, 1(3):146–169.

[Vallentin et al., 2007] Vallentin, M., Sommer, R., Lee, J., Leres, C., Paxson, V., and Tiereney, B. (2007). The NIDS cluster: Scalable, Stateful Network Intrusion Detection on Commodity Hardware. In *Proc. of the International Symposium on Recent Advances in Intrusion Detection (RAID)*.

[Viinikka et al., 2009] Viinikka, J., Debar, H., Mé, L., Lehikoinen, A., and Tarvainen, M. (2009). Processing intrusion detection alert aggregates with time series modeling. *Information Fusion*, 10(4):312–324.

[Vlachos et al., 2004] Vlachos, V., Androutsellis-Theotokis, S., and Spinellis, D. (2004). Security applications of peer-to-peer networks. *Computer Networks: The International Journal of Computer and Telecommunications Networking*, 45(2):195–205.

[Wang et al., 2004] Wang, Y., Yang, H., Wang, X., and Zhang, R. (2004). Distributed intrusion detection system based on data fusion method. In *Proc. of the Fifth World Congress on Intelligent Control and Automation (WCICA 2004)*.

[White et al., 1996] White, G., Fisch, E., and Pooch, U. (1996). Cooperating security managers: a peer-based intrusion detection system. *Network, IEEE*, 10(1):20–23.

[Winer, 2007] Winer, D. (2007). XMLRPC.

[Wu et al., 2003] Wu, Y.-S., Foo, B., Mei, Y., and Bagchi, S. (2003). Collaborative intrusion detection system (cids): A framework for accurate and efficient ids. In *Proc. of the 19th Annual Computer Security Applications Conference*.

[Xinidis et al., 2006] Xinidis, K., Charitakis, I., Antonatos, S., Anagnostakis, K. G., and Markatos, E. P. (2006). An active splitter architecture for intrusion detection and prevention. *IEEE Transactions on Dependable and Secure Computing*, 03(1):31–44.

[Xinidis K and Markatos, 2005] Xinidis K, K. G. A. and Markatos, E. P. (2005). Design and implementation of a high-performance network intrusion prevention system. In

Proc. of the 20th International Information Security Conference (SEC 2005), Chiba, Japan.

[Xue et al., 2003] Xue, Q., Sun, J., and Wei, Z. (2003). Tjids: an intrusion detection architecture for distributed network. In *Proc. ot the 2003 IEEE Canadian Conference on Electrical and Computer Engineering CCECE 2003*.

[Yegneswaran et al., 2004] Yegneswaran, V., Barford, P., and Jha, S. (2004). Global intrusion detection in the domino overlay system. In *In Proc. of the 11th Annual Network and Distributed System Security Symposium (NDSS'04)*.

[Zhai et al., 2004] Zhai, Y., Ning, P., Iyer, P., and Reeves, D. S. (2004). Reasoning about complementary intrusion evidence. In *Proc. of the 20th Annual Computer Security Applications Conference (ACSAC '04)*.

[Zhang et al., 2005] Zhang, Y.-F., Xiong, Z.-Y., and Wang, X.-Q. (2005). Distributed intrusion detection based on clustering. In *Proc. of 2005 International Conference on Machine Learning and Cybernetics*.

[Zhang et al., 2001a] Zhang, Z., Li, J., Manikopulos, C. N., Jorgenson, J., and Ucles, J. (2001a). HIDE: a hierarchical network intrusion detection system using statistical pre-processing and neural network classification. In *Proc. of the 2001 IEEE Workshop on Information Assurance and Security*.

[Zhang et al., 2001b] Zhang, Z., Li, J., Manikopulos, C. N., Jorgenson, J., and Ucles, J. (2001b). A hierarchical anomaly network intrusion detection system using neural network classification. In *Proc. of 2001 WSES Conferemce on Neural Networks and Applications (NNA '01)*.

[Zhou et al., 2007] Zhou, J., Heckman, M., Reynolds, B., Carlson, A., and Bishop, M. (2007). Modeling network intrusion detection alerts for correlation. *ACM Transactions on Information System Security*, 10(1):4.

[Zimmermann, 1995] Zimmermann, P. (1995). Pretty good privacy: public key encryption for the masses. *Building in big brother: the cryptographic policy debate*, pages 93–107.

In: Advances in Security Information Management
Editors: G. Suarez-Tangil and E. Palomar

ISBN: 978-1-62417-204-5
© 2013 Nova Science Publishers, Inc.

Chapter 5

ON THE PERFORMANCE EVALUATION OF INTRUSION DETECTION SYSTEMS

Rashid Munir,* Adeeb Alhomoud, Irfan Awan and Jules Pagna Disso
School of Computing, Informatics and Media
University of Bradford, UK

Abstract

Intrusion detection is essential to keep the enterprise secure and it should be appropriately designed to meet all the security requirements. There are several commercial and open source tools intrusion detection system (IDS) used to prevent a wide variety of attacks, but the performance of these toolkits is still in doubt. In general, expert operators exploit different toolkits and techniques to optimize the detection and prevention tasks. Currently, Security Information and Event Management (SIEM) systems play an important role in dealing with the security threats generated within the network. In this chapter, our main focus is to describe different approaches for evaluating the performance of any kind of IDS. In this regard, two different experiments have been performed on a specifically designed test bench to replicate extensive enterprise network traffic. In our first experiment, we analyze the performance of Snort —which is perhaps the most commonly used tool in current SIEM systems— at a discrete level by enabling and disabling rules, and the detection engine. Results enable us to draw conclusions about the performance limitations of Snort. Our second experiment is devoted to comparing a novel tool called Suricata with Snort, under three different platforms (Linux, FreeBSD and ESXi server).

Keywords: Security Information and Event Management (SIEM), Performance, Intrusion Detection Systems (IDS), Snort, Suricata

*E-mail address: R.Munir@bradford.ac.uk

1. Introduction

Due to the tremendous increase in the use of computers as a part of our daily routine, and also due to the nature of this use, security managers and professionals should be ready to respond and react to any type of security challenge occurring in various domains, e.g. businesses, industries and organizations, as well as in social and domestic circles. Moreover, e–businesses are experiencing additional concerns regarding security as these types of businesses are now considered an indispensable part of buying, selling and interacting with other organizations.

Traditionally, two major components have been used to counter security threats, namely firewalls and network intrusion detection systemd (NIDSs). So far, firewalls have been considered a major deterrent to network threats. However, it has been proved that firewalls cannot provide full protection against data leakage or hidden and multi–thread attacks. In order to provide protection against these malicious attacks, more sophisticated tools for intrusion detection and prevention are needed specifically for analyzing the traffic in depth and classifying it properly. Perhaps the most sophisticated tool, which is also used in forensic computing, is the concept of honeypot [Honeynet, 2010]. This technique helps to give an early warning about possible attempts at unauthorized use and even different types of malware have been launched against information systems. However, honeypots have also been covertly used by hackers to evade detection tools. For example, attackers can use simple and automatic techniques to spread worms on a target system. Melissa [Burstein, 2003] and Blaster [Bailey et al., 2005] are the earliest examples of viruses distributed in such a way.

Nowadays, among the most widely–used techniques for providing a holistic intrusion detection framework are Security Information and Event Management (SIEM) systems. SIEM systems integrate all IDS reports and threats generated by the network. Conceptually, SIEM is a combined solution of two different products, namely SIM (Security Information Management) and SEM (Security Event Management) [Swift, 2006]. SIM is applied to monitoring software applications running on computers. It is mainly devoted to displaying graphs and, charts and to generate reports, which are collected in real–time mostly in the way of generated events. SIM also refers to the correlation of events, console view and notification. Conversely, SEM is based on reporting log data and long–term storage.

Furthermore, SIEM systems are used to provide an intelligent framework to discover potential hidden relationships between events. Events include IDS alerts, system logs, system alerts, and other data generated by security tools. For instance, SIEM systems can result in an intriguing prediction tool for unknown attacks as they provide a global picture of the detected attack (e.g. serious multi–step attacks whose reported alerts need to be correlated) [Swift, 2006]. However, there is still a need to optimize the cooperation between different IDS sensors aimed at maximizing the detection coverage.

Despite all these tactics, intrusion detection is still a big challenge for information security, especially as current platforms such as web services, remote access and distributed databases have raised new issues in terms of network security. To protect these technologies against security attacks, more sophisticated tools are needed to provide an accurate and reliable protection against malware [Kumar et al., 2005]. Moreover, some efforts have been made to evaluate the performance of existing IDSs. Most of these evaluations are based on well–known data sets or on moderate traffic, whilst others use real traffic but do not provide any comparison with other IDS [Alserhani et al., 2009a, ?, ?]. Thus, our aim in this chapter is to focus on the experimentation and evaluation of two IDSs in a real environment under high–speed network traffic and to provide detailed comparisons with other IDSs in terms of packet drops, alerts, etc. The significance of the results and calculated data has been analyzed to present considerable insights into further enhancements of IDSs.

Organization: The rest of this chapter is organized as follows: Section 2 briefly describes the main characteristics of current SIEMs. In Section 3 we further elaborate on the different approaches which can be used to measure the performance evaluation of any IDS. In particular, we focus on two different types of experiments to evaluate Snort and Suricata. In Section 4 we state some conclusions.

2.   Information Sources for the SIEM

We will start by describing the main sources which report security information to SIEM systems.

2.1.   Firewalls

In current networking environments, firewall and anti–virus software are the normal personal and small business protection mechanisms that are applied to keep a host present in a secure network. A firewall is a widely–used security tool that may also be found integrated in a large number of operating systems. It is used to control the unauthorized traffic running in a system, and also to react against malicious traffic. The security requirements of organizations and the nature of online activities are key factors that are used to determine the efficiency of a firewall installed in a network. The firewall concept was first introduced in 1980, when most of the world's population was unfamiliar with the concept of the Internet. The reason behind this was the Morris attack, which occurred in 1988. This attack damaged the Berkeley University, UC San Diego, Lawrence Livermore, and NASA Ames Research Centre networks. Scientists such as Dodong Sean James and Elohra from Digital Equipment Corporation (DEC) wrote the first white paper on firewalls and introduced a new packet–filtering system in a firewall. The enhancement enabled packet data to be allowed or discarded based on rules that were defined by the administrator of that network. Two different kinds of firewall exist: stateless and stateful. The former hold all the information related to packet–filtering but provides less security than a stateful firewall. The latter resembles a router due to its packet–filtering capability. A stateful firewall describes information regarding connections, defining whether they are connected or disconnected,and hence whether data are allowed or not.

2.2.   Intrusion Detection System

SIEM comprises a wide range of technologies and IDS reports are essential inputs for SIEM systems [Innella, 2001]. Basically, IDSs are hardware, software or a combination of both, which generate alerts when any of the incomming or outgoing packets match an established

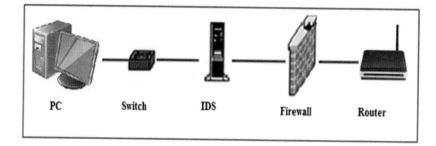

Figure 1. A generic intrusion detection system.

pattern [Antonatos et al., 2004]. The idea of the IDS was first introduced by James Anderson in 1980, when he distinguished between the characteristics of anomalous and normal behaviour in the anomaly detection approach [?].

IDSs generally comprise several components operating in conjunction with one another in order to offer protection against malicious activities. The main IDS components are sensors, console and engine [Alhomoud et al., 2011]. Sensors sense the traffic on a network and send it to the detection engine for further analysis which is mostly based on matching the packet content against a series of pre–established rules. An alert is generated after a match occurs. The console monitors the events running in the system and controls the activity of alerts and sensors. In general, IDSs falls into two categories: network–based systems and host–based systems [Magalhaes, 2004]. Figure 1 depicts the generic location of the IDS in a network.

- **Network–based Intrusion Detection System (NIDS)** NIDS monitors all the network traffic in order to detect malicious packets that contain intrusions such as a Denial of Service (DoS) attack or port scans in a network. After detecting a malicious packet, NIDS informs the network administrator or blocks that malicious packet to avoid the intrusion. Snort and Suricata are two examples of NIDS. Firewalls do not provide full security against data leakage or hidden and multi–threaded attack. However, NIDS provides a valuable service in this regard. A false positive is one of the major limitations of NIDS [Julisch, 2003].

- **Host-based Intrusion Detection System (HIDS)** HIDS only analyzes the traffic running on host machines. An example of HIDS is OSSEC [Hay et al., 2008]. OSSEC is a software tool that can be ran on various operating systems such as Open BSD, MacOS, Windows and Solaris. HIDS works as an agent, which monitors all the information about system calls, the file system and the Windows registry, thereby producing log files and performing editing activities inside the host machine.

- **Anomaly–based Intrusion Detection System (AIDS)** Anomaly–based IDS receives traffic from the host machine, observes that traffic and compares the pattern of the traffic with the baseline. The baseline defines a normal networking activity in terms of bandwidth, protocol type, ports, etc [Bradley, 2011]. AIDS is also able to detect novel zero–day attacks.

- **Signature-based Intrusion Detection System (SIDS)** Signature–based methods are knowledge–based techniques in which the attack pattern matches well–defined rules previously established to detect security violation [Bradley, 2011]. Perhaps, the most important feature of SIDSs is the capacity to handle a huge amount of network traffic, because when traffic comes into a target machine the IDS starts examining and comparing each packet with the database of rules and, during this process, the IDS drops some packets because of heavy traffic on the network [Salour and Su, 2007].

2.3.   Intrusion Prevention System (IPS)

Intrusion prevention systems not only detect malicious activities but also pro–actively react to prevent detected intrusions or alleviate their consequences. For instance, IPS can actively terminate TCP connections or drop malicious packets. We can find several IPS systems according to where the monitoring is taking place. Firstly, Network–based Intrusion Prevention System (NIPS), monitors the whole network for malicious activity. Secondly, Network Behaviour Analysis (NBA) examines only unusual flows of traffic. Thirdly, Wireless Intrusion Prevention System (WIPS) examines traffic running on a wireless network. And, as a final example, Host–based Intrusion Prevention System (HIPS) monitors the malicious activity running on a single host by the installation of a single piece of software.

3.   IDS Performance Evaluation

The evaluation of IDS performance is paramount in order tounderstand the capabilities of SIEM systems. Therefore, we perform two different types of experiment to evaluate Snort and Suricata's performance in terms of packet–handling capability. Specifically, each of the two has diverse ways of measuring IDS performance. The first experiment is based on using Snort to enable and disable rules and preprocessors. The second experiment compares the findings from the first experiment with Suricata. Our hope is that these experiments will help network and security analysts to select the most suitable IDS for their SIEM.

For a better understanding of the experiments, we first describe both Snort and Suricata IDS.

3.1.   Preliminaries

3.1.1.   Snort

Snort is an open–source rule–based IDS developed by Marty Roesch in 1998. Snort detects malicious network traffic by analyzing incoming and outgoing packets and matches them with an enormous number of rules. In fact, version 3.0 of Snort contains almost 8000 of them [Roesch et al., 1999]. Snort is considered as one of the most active sensor and a core sensor for current SIEM. It is capable of performing packet–logging and real–time traffic analisis on the network [Alserhani et al., 2009b]. Snort inspects packet header, performs protocol analyses and detects a range of network threats by using content/signature matching algorithms. Additionally, Snort can analyze protocol infrastructure, inspect traffic, detect probes and log the network activity. [Kohlenberg et al.,]

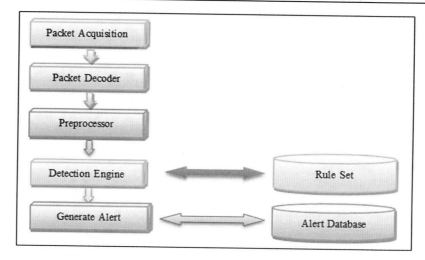

Figure 2. Snort Architecture.

Snort architecture comprises four components: (i) packet–sniffing, (ii) preprocessor, (iii) detection engine, and (iv) output device, as depicted in Figure 2. On the one hand, packet–sniffing collects data from the network and dumps this information. In cases of packet–sniffing, Snort collects data from the network and displays them as they are on the screen as a TCP dump mode using *libpcap* and *winpcap* libraries. On the other hand, packet acquisition monitors packet arriving time, and calculates total length of the packet.

Furthermore, packet–processing is done by the preprocessor. A preprocessor is a program that is used to normalize the raw packets and check those against anomaly–based behaviour (plug–in), for example HTTP plug–in. The plug–in provides the facility to manage the application at traffic flow time. The plug–in also avoids unwanted traffic–processing which can cause an overload on the network. Snort can have several processors; *packet defragmentation*, *stateful inspection session* and *application layer preprocessor* are the three most important ones.

Thus, Snort examines and processes each packet individually, decoding packet structures and examining protocols and related behaviour for anomaly–based detection (no–rule–based detection). After processing the packets, the detection engine checks misuse according to some configured rules. When malicious content is identified in a package, Snort queues subsequent traffic for further inspection. If network traffic volume is higher than processing limitations, Snort drops packets without analyzing them.

3.1.2. Suricata

Suricata is an open–source rule–based IDS/IPS. It monitors sniffed network traffic with the help of rule sets and generates alerts when any suspicious event takes place [Alhomoud et al., 2011]. Suricata is an Open Information Security Foundation (OISF), which is part of, and funded by, the USA's Department of Homeland Security's Directorate for Science and Technology's Host Program (Homeland Open Security Technology) and the Navy's Space and Naval Warfare Systems Command (SPAWAR) [Spawar, 2010].

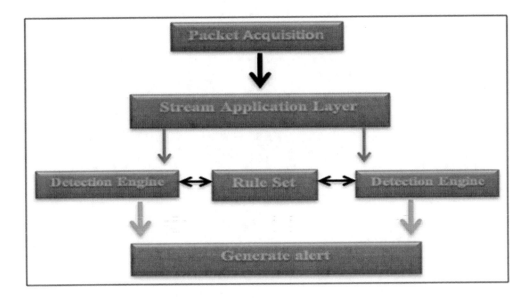

Figure 3. Suricata Architecture.

Like most IDSs it is designed to fit within existing network security components. The first release of Suricata runs on a Linux 2.6 platform and supports both inline and passive traffic monitoring configurations capable of handling multiple gigabit traffic levels. Suricata works as a multi–threaded engine.

The source code for the Suricata configuration file is written as a YAML file. In comparison with Snort, Suricata can process from one packet to hundreds of thousands of packets at a time. There is indeed a trade–off between performance and the use of memory (RAM).

Similarly to Snort, Suricata decodes packets and forwards them to the preprocessor before analyzing them. The defragmentation session contains three options: prealloc, timeout and max–frag. Furthermore, the detection engine is the core of any IDS, where network traffic is analysed. In contrast to Snort, rules are divided into four different categories according to the priority assigned to their processing: default, high, medium and low. A group of high volume gives a high performance and uses more memory, whereas a smaller volume of groups uses less memory and gives a lower performance. The detection engine has the capability to accomplish the balance between performance and memory.

Figure 3 depicts the packet–acquisitioning mode. Suricata detects a packet from the network and forwards it to the packet decoder. After decoding the packet, the stream application layer performs three actions on the packet: (i) it checks whether the network connection is correct or not, (ii) determines whether TCP network traffic is coming in a packet or not; and (iii) it reconstructs the original stream by stream assembly. Furthermore, packets are inspected by the detection engine as depending on the number of packets, more than one detection engine is used in the inspection procedure.

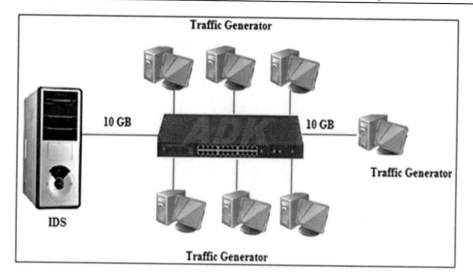

Figure 4. Test Bench.

3.2. Experiment 1: Performance evaluation of the Snort IDS in terms of enabling/disabling rules and preprocessors

Perhaps the main goal of the existing SIEM tools is to reach the ability to deal with a huge volume of traffic for packet–processing without any packet loss. In other words, packet loss is one of the most significant problems faced today by networking teams, and it is still very much an open issue. This section is devoted to evaluating the performance of one of the most used SIEM tools, namely Snort, under heavy traffic conditions, paying special attention to its packet–handling capability by enabling and disabling rules. We also concentrate on Snort preprocessors, and evaluate the causes of any packet drop occurred during packet–processing. All these tests are performed on frequent protocols, namely TCP and UDP, and our conclusions will be drawn by using specific values. Moreover, our analysis uses LAN traffic V2 Enhanced tool which is designed to generate the traffic.

Our network consists of more than six high–performance PCs which are connected via a ProCurve Series 2900 switch using a 1.0 Gigabit Ethernet cable, and two 10 Gigabit cables as shown in Figure 4. A ProCurve Series 2900 switch [Alserhani et al., 2009a] is used to configure all traffic transmitted over the network and sent to the spanning port. Each machine runs both Snort and Suricata tools to monitor the software's traffic. Two 10 Gigabit cards have been used, one for connecting IDSs for monitoring traffic via the monitoring port, and the other one to connect to a high–performance PC to generate more traffic as needed. A number of packets are generated from source to destination. For TCP connection, the maximum data size is 65,536 and for UDP the maximum data size is 65,507.

As mentioned above, signature–based IDSs compare packets' patterns with those in a database of rules, in order to find any similarity. The first experiment was performed on Snort in which 8,000 rules were loaded. Thus, in our first experiment we evaluate the impact of disabling and enabling rules on the packet–dropping. Note that we do not give

Table 1. Performance of Snort at 10 Mbps

All rules	All preprocessors	Packets Analysed %	Packets Dropped %	Application Usage %
Disable	Disable	100	0	2
Disable	Enable	100	0	9
Enable	Enable	98.527	1.473	24
Enable	Disable	99.074	0.926	16

Table 2. Performance of Snort at 100 Mbps

All rules	All preprocessors	Packets Analysed %	Packets Dropped %	Application Usage %
Disable	Disable	99.880	0.120	8
Disable	Enable	98.689	1.311	20
Enable	Enable	90.628	9.372	30
Enable	Disable	92.858	7.142	26

any importance to the number of packets generated, but to the number of packets received at the application level (Snort/Suricata), so we can see how many packets have been analyzed and how many are dropped. All the information (packets dropped, packets received and packets analyzed) is reported as a summary afterwards. Moreover, central processing unit (CPU) overhead has been calculated from the system task manager.

3.2.1. Scenarios

Packet drop is a major issue in SIEM systems as loss of sensors data can lead to decorrelation of ongoing attacks. The following scenarios are tested during the performance evaluation in Snort. Each scenario is evaluated by both enabling and disabling rules and preprocessors.

A. Performance of Snort at 10 Mbps

Experiments undertaken with a workload speed of 10 Mbps are summarized in Table 1. Experiments show that the application receives approximately 6 million packets. Comparing performance measured with and without preprocessors, we can see an increase of the CPU usage up to 9%. Specifically, in both cases the overall usage of the CPU is low and no packet is dropped. On the other hand, when rules are enabled, the CPU usage increases up to 16% and a relatively small percentage of packet drops is observed (0.926%). Furthermore, when both rules and processors are enabled, the application usage rises to 24% and packet loss to 1.4%.

B. Performance of Snort at 100 Mbps

Experiments undertaken with a workload speed of 100 Mbps are summarized in Table 2. Comparing performance measured with and without rules and preprocessors, we

Table 3. Performance of Snort at 400 Mbps

All rules	All preprocessors	Packets Analysed %	Packets Dropped %	Application Usage %
Disable	Disable	99.948	0.40	15
Disable	Enable	97.132	2.868	31.9
Enable	Enable	78.981	21.019	47.5
Enable	Disable	87.473	15.527	38

Table 4. Performance of Snort at 800 Mbps

All rules	All preprocessors	Packets Analysed %	Packets Dropped %	Application Usage %
Disable	Disable	99.834	1.20	25
Disable	Enable	96.613	3.387	48
Enable	Enable	74.775	25.224	72
Enable	Disable	87.745	18.2	59

can see an increase of the CPU usage up to 30% and a significant packet loss of almost 10%.

C. Performance of Snort at 400 Mbps

Experiments undertaken with a workload speed of 400 Mbps (Table 3) show a non–neglected increase of the CPU consumption even when rules and preprocessors are disabled (15%). Additionally, as expected, the percentage of packet loss is increased up to 21%.

D. Performance of Snort at 800 Mbps

Experiments undertaken with a workload speed of 800 Mbps also show an increase of the CPU consumption when rules and preprocessors are disabled (25%). Additionally, the usage of the CPU is rises to 72% and the percentage of packets dropped is 25%. In fact, the lower the CPU usage, the fewer packets dropped as shown in Table 4.

E. All rules are disabled, only preprocessors are enabled

The aforementioned scenarios indeed represent an interesting way of understanding the relationship between rules and processors in terms of CPU usage and packet loss. Regarding all scenarios considered, i.e., 10, 100, 400 and 800 Mbps we can conclude that there is no substantial packet loss in Snort when all rules are disabled, as depicted in 5. More than 90% of packets were analyzed by the preprocessors, and the IDS was able to cope with the increasing bandwidth. However, disabling rules disallow the detection engine.

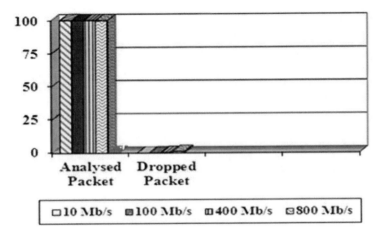

Figure 5. All rules are disabled only preprocessors are enabled.

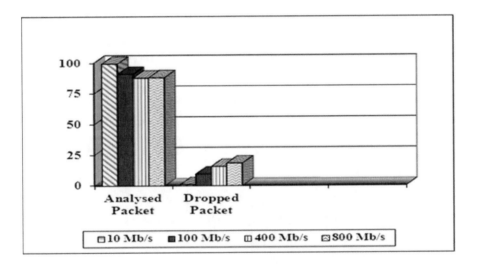

Figure 6. All rules are enabled and only preprocessors are disabled.

F. All rules are enabled and only preprocessors are disabled

Regarding all scenarios in which preprocessors are disabled, i.e. 10, 100, 400 and 800 Mbps, we can conclude that bandwidth of 10 Mbps drops a non–significant number of packets as shown in Figure 5, whereas when the bandwidth is increased, the packets start dropping on a linear basis. Additionally, we can also observe that rules consume more resources than preprocessors.

G. All rules and preprocessors are enabled

In the scenario where all rules are enabled and processors disabled, we observed that more packets are dropped, as shown in Figure 7. However, if both of them are enabled

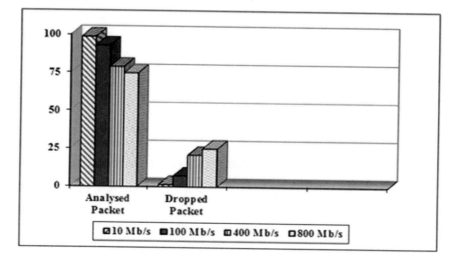

Figure 7. All rules and preprocessors are enabled.

at the same time, then the dropping occurs more rapidly. Thus, we can conclude that CPU usage and packet loss are directly proportional to the bandwidth.

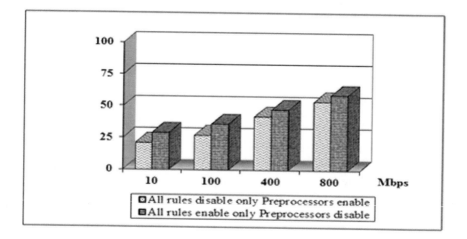

Figure 8. Performance of Snort at different bandwidths.

H. Performance of Snort at different bandwidths

Figure 8 gives a clear insight into the packet drop capability of Snort in terms of workload. Similarly, we can infer that packet drop rate also increases with the bandwidth. However, the packet drop is more acute in the detection engine than in the processors. It has also been observed that Snort performs better with low bandwidth.

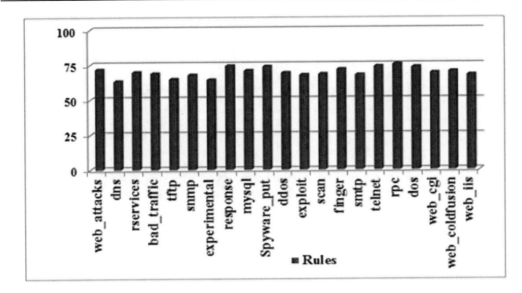

Figure 9. One rule is enabled and all preprocessors are disabled.

Furthermore, rules use more CPU workload than preprocessors. Interested readers can consult [Munir et al., 2011] for a detailed guideline to evaluate IDS performance.

I. One rule is enabled and all preprocessors are disabled

Additionally, we have evaluated different experiments where Snort is configured with a single rule at a time, and results are depicted in Figure 9. We observed that, in general, almost all rules have a similar CPU usage. However, some differences are shown, and in an advantage scenario this information could be used to disable subsets of rules when the type of attack is not likely to occur.

J. One preprocessor is enabled and all rules are disabled

Similarly, we have evaluated several experiments where only one processor is enabled at a time; and results are described in Figure 10. This can also help the analyst to assess the performance of the most commonly–used preprocessors.

3.2.2. Analysis

Resulting experiments show that Snort performance depends basically on: (i) the amount of memory; (ii) the network processor; and (iii) the frequency of the CPU. Different scenarios proved that bandwidth and CPU workload are deeply related. In fact, the increase of Snort workload in particular, and SIEM sensors in general, pose a challenge to attack detection.

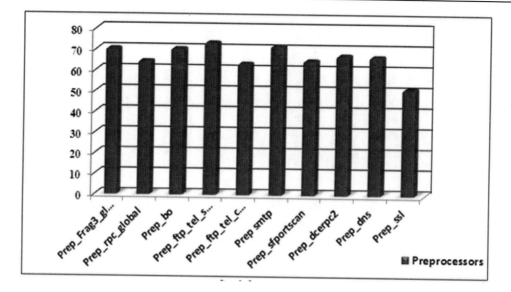

Figure 10. One preprocessor is enabled and all rules are disabled.

3.3. Experiment 2: Performance evaluation comparison of SIEM tools (Snort vs. Suricata)

The configuration of network detectors is paramount for SIEM systems. This section presents a number of performance test benches evaluating Suricata IDS. In addition, these experiments are performed on three different platforms, ESXi server, Linux 2.6 and FreeBSD. Finally, in the results and analysis, a comparison of the performances of the two IDS systems is provided together with some recommendations as to the ideal environment for both IDSs. The selected IDSs used in this section for the experiments are the latest versions of Snort (v2.9.0.4) and Suricata (v1.0.2).

3.3.1. Scenarios

Test scenarios are designed to evaluate the performance of the newly developed IDS Suricata and compare it with Snort on different operating systems. Both IDSs are subjected to the same tests under exactly the same conditions. In order to obtain more accurate results, all scenarios are tested on different packet sizes (1470, 1024, 512) for the different protocols, TCP and UDP. Additionally, the tests are performed for speed ranging from 250 Mbps, 500 Mbps, 750 Mbps, 1.0 Gbps, 1.5 Gbps, and 2.0 Gbps. In all these scenarios, Suricata and Snort are configured to load and run a similar number of rules. The assessment of the performance of the best IDS in terms of packet–handling can be tackled by using different packet sizes. In fact, different packet sizes can help to determine which IDS is the more reliable in terms of packet drop and CPU performance.

A. Performance of IDSs on ESXi sever

In this scenario, two virtual enterprise data centre are built on an ESXi server

[Lowe, 2009] with both Snort and Suricata. The ESXi server is equipped with 4 GB of memory; 2 GB are allocated to the virtual Linux hosted in the ESXi server. All the IDS machines have the same amount of memory. Both Snort and Suricata are subjected to heavy traffic on both protocols, TCP and UDP, with different packet sizes at different speeds, in order to collect more accurate results. A network card is used in the ESXi server to establish a connection from the management PC to enable the management of the virtual host. The monitoring of the network card used for the management of the ESXi server has been disabled from the ProCurve switch.

B. Performance of IDSs on Linux 2.6

In this scenario, Snort and Suricata are installed on a Linux 2.6 server, running Ubuntu 10.10. The machine has been configured to monitor traffic using the 10 Gbps card.

C. Performance of IDSs on FreeBSD

In this scenario, Snort and Suricata are installed on a FreeBSD server running the latest version 8.1. The FreeBSD has been configured to operate with a 10–Gbps network card as well. Both IDS systems are operated separately on the same platforms.

3.3.2.   Result and Analysis

Resulting performance analyses are described in this section for each of the aforementioned scenarios. For a better understanding of the results, this section has been divided into two subsections: TCP and UDP traffic.

TCP   We first discuss the performance of Snort and Suricata while analyzing TCP traffic. Figure 11 illustrates the performance of both IDS tools using a packet size of 512 kilobytes. On the one hand, we have observed that Suricata drops some packets in the early stages (250 Mbps). We also observed that the virtual Linux behaves inefficiently, dropping 35.4% of the packets. Furthermore, Suricata drops a small number of packets (0.6%) on FreeBSD, and none on Linux2.6. These behaviours are similar in the 500 Mbps scenario and worsen at 1.0 Gbps (26.5% of dropped packets on Linux 2.6, 36.7% on FreeBSD and 47.2% on virtual Linux).

On the other hand, Snort showed a better performance as there are no packet drops recorded at 250 Mbps and 500 Mbps on any of the platforms evaluated. However, Snort starts dropping a small number of packets (1.1% in the worst case, i.e. virtual Linux) at 750 Mbps. It is at over 1.0 Gbps that Snort starts dropping a significant number of packets (from 2.8% to 30% on virtual Linux), and the number remains steady on the rest.

When increasing the packet size to 1024 kilobytes, Suricata starts recording a high packet loss, as depicted in Figure 12, especially on virtual Linux. It is worth mentioning that Suricata's performance is in general slightly better with smaller packets, but it still performs worse than Snort at 1024 kilobytes.

For larger packet sizes, we observed a similar pattern performance. Some differences are shown at speeds of 1.5 Gbps or higher, as depicted in Figure 13. Specifically, we

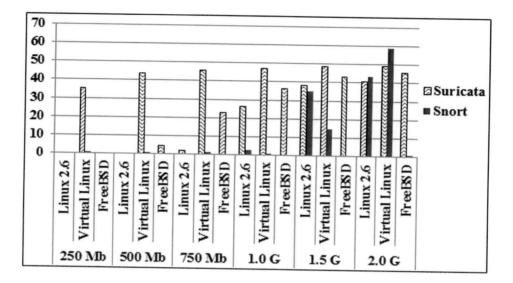

Figure 11. Comparison chart of Snort and Suricata (512) TCP.

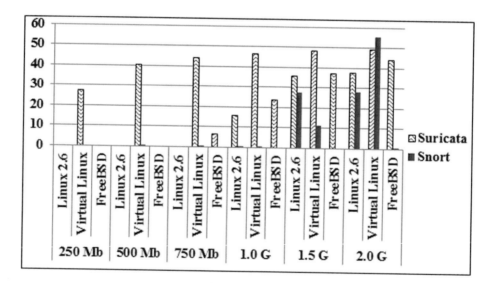

Figure 12. Comparison chart of Snort and Suricata (1024) TCP.

observed that the number of drops decreased, especially with Snort.

UDP   Similarly to the TCP scenario, we performed several experiments comparing different packet sizes at different bandwidths. Figure 14 illustrates the results. In general Suricata
drops about 40% of the packets when using a packet size of 512. At slow speeds, Snort per-

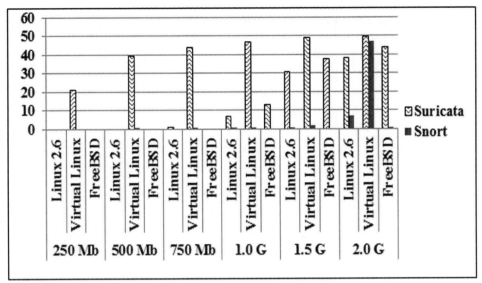

Figure 13. Comparison chart of Snort and Suricata (1470) TCP.

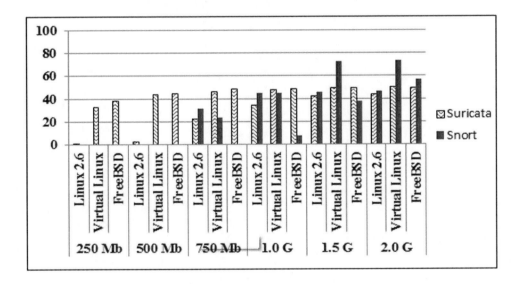

Figure 14. Comparison chart of Snort and Suricata (512) UDP.

forms better than Suricata. Nonetheless, some distributions such as Linux 2.6 always show a better performance by Suricata than by Snort. When the generated traffic reaches the speed of 500 Mbps, Suricata still has a high performance, but remains steady. However, Snort's packet loss grows as the speed increases. Nonetheless, Snort's performance is better when considering only FreeBSD. When the generated traffic reaches 1.5 Gbps or higher,

Table 5. IDS CPU usage and packet drops (UDP traffic–packet size–1.0 Gbps)

Platform	Snort	Snort	Suricata	Suricata
	CPU usage (%)	Packet drop (%)	CPU usage (%)	Packet drop (%)
Linux	27	31.43	68	8.9
FreeBSD	21	3.24	24.5	43.6

Snort starts dropping a high number of packets, exceeding the 73% of packet loss.

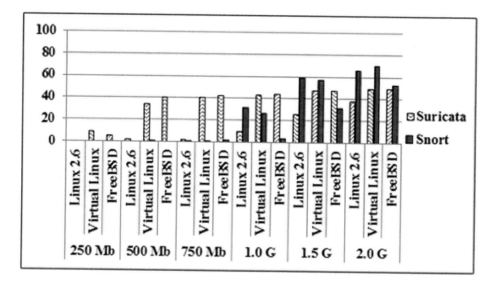

Figure 15. Comparison chart of Snort and Suricata (1024) UDP.

When increasing the packet size to 1024 kilobytes, experiments show that Snort still performs worse than Suricata at high bandwidth, but better at slow ones, as depicted in Figure 15. On the other hand, Suricata reaches a high number of packet drops on FreeBSD (up to 40.2%) and on virtual Linux (33.9%). However, it does not show any packet losses on Linux 2.6. Suricata's performance at the speeds of 250, 500 and 750 Mbps is acceptable as it does not exceed 0.33%. The overall performance of Snort at 750 Mbps is significantly better on the virtual Linux and FreeBSD, as Snort only records 1.2% packet drops. At higher speeds (1.0 Gbps), the best performance is shown by Snort on FreeBSD with only 3.24% of packet drop, while the best performance for Suricata is on Linux 2.6 at 8.9%. At the speeds of 1.5 Gbps and 2.0 Gbps, both IDSs drop a high number of packets.

When considering bigger UDP packet size, Snort proves to have a very good performance, not exceeding a packet loss ratio of 1.15%, as depicted in Figure 16. We can conclude that Snort is capable of handling packets of size 1470 better than Suricata.

We have recorded the CPU usage of both Snort and Suricata on all three platforms during our tests. Table 5 shows an excerpt of CPU usage and packet loss. As can be observed, Snort on FreeBSD uses only 21% of CPU and drops 3.24% of packets, while Suricata has

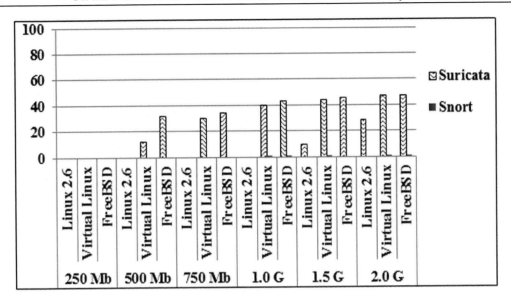

Figure 16. Comparison chart of Snort and Suricata (1470) UDP.

Table 6. Percentage of attacks detected

Speed	Snort(%)	Suricata (%)
1.0 Gbps	100	98
1.5 Gbps	100	91.8
2.0 Gbps	99.7	66.8

a similar CPU usage and drops 43.6%. On the other hand, Suricata's performance shows a different result on Linux. It drops fewer packets than Snort, but it has a higher CPU usage.

Attacks detection rate (Alerts)   To evaluate performance of both IDSs in heavy and mixed traffic, a Denial of Service (DoS) attack is generated while launching a number of attacks. Results are shown in Table 6 and they demonstrate that Snort shows better results.

Further analysis, summarized in Tables 7 and 8, shows that Suricata performs better on Linux 2.6, while Snort performs best on FreeBSD, especially when handling high speeds.

3.3.3.   Summary of Analysis

Experiment 2 focuses on determining the efficiency and performance of a novel IDS: Suricata. Experiments are also compared with Snort, a well–known IDSs. Both IDSs are evaluated on different platforms, protocols, network packet sizes and different network–transfer speeds. Experiments show that a significant number of packet drops while using virtualization. In fact, the physical memory (RAM) allocated on the host machine is actually allocated on the virtual RAM and is often swapped to hard disk [Abdallah and Hassan, 2010]. The overhead of the machine is increased and the number of arriving packets is higher than

Table 7. IDSs ideal operating systems (TCP traffic–Packet size 1024)

Speed (M/G bps)	Suricata ideal Platform	Snort ideal Platform
500	Linux2.6	Linux2.6 or FreeBSD
750	Linux2.6	Linux2.6 or FreeBSD
1.5	Linux2.6	FreeBSD
2.0	Linux2.6	FreeBSD

Table 8. IDSs ideal operating systems (UDP traffic–Packet size 1024)

Speed (M/G bps)	Suricata ideal Platform	Snort ideal Platform
500	Linux2.6	Linux2.6 or FreeBSD
750	Linux2.6	Linux2.6
1.5	Linux2.6	FreeBSD
2.0	Linux2.6	FreeBSD

the machine's capability. Thus, the number of packet drops increases as a consequence. It is also observed that, in some cases, Snort drops more packets in Linux 2.6 than in a virtual Linux, whereas Suricata does not report such misbehaviour. We can therefore conclude that Suricata performed better on Linux 2.6 comparing to FreeBSD and virtual Linux, but it does not perform better than Snort.

Conclusion

This chapter presents an insight into how IDS performs in different environments through a number of experiments. Specifically, we employ two different ways of evaluating the performance and efficiency of two SIEM sensors: Snort and Suricata IDS. The experiments evaluate the performance of both IDSs by enabling and disabling rules and preprocessors.

Results shown in the first experiment indicate that there is a strong correlation between bandwidth and application usage. When comparing overhead used by the detection engine and the preprocessor used by the IDSs, we observed that the overhead increases as we add rules to the detector engine. We also observed that the packet drop increases when there is a boost in application usage. Additionally, we observed that the performance of Snort depends intrinsically on memory hardware, CPU usage and the Network Interface Card (NIC) saturation. Finally, our experiments show that Snort generally performs better than Suricata at low bandwidth.

Results from the second experiment confirm that there is a significant number of packet drops when using virtualization. In fact, physical memory (RAM) is allocated on the host machine by means of virtual RAM memory, which is often swapped to hard disk. Additionally, we can conclude that Suricata performs better on Linux 2.6 if we compare it with FreeBSD and virtual Linux. However, Suricata does not perform better than Snort.

We hope that our experiments will provide researchers with detailed guidelines to evaluate the performance of SIEM tools.

References

[Abdallah and Hassan, 2010] Abdallah A. and Hassan, T. (2010). Formalizing delegation and integrating it into role-based access control models. *Journal of Information Assurance and Security*, 5:021–030.

[Alhomoud et al., 2011] Alhomoud, A., Munir, R., Disso, J., Awan, I., and Al-Dhelaan, A. (2011). Performance evaluation study of intrusion detection systems. *Procedia Computer Science*, 5:173–180.

[Alserhani et al., 2009a] Alserhani, F., Akhlaq, M., Awan, I., Mellor, J., Cullen, A., and Mirchandani, P. (2009a). Evaluating intrusion detection systems in high speed networks. In *Information Assurance and Security, 2009. IAS'09. Fifth International Conference on*, volume 2, pages 454–459. IEEE.

[Alserhani et al., 2009b] Alserhani, F., Akhlaq, M., et al. (2009b). Snort performance evaluation. In *Proceedings of Twenty Fifth UK Performance Engineering Workshop (UKPEW 2009), Leeds, UK*.

[Antonatos et al., 2004] Antonatos, S., Anagnostakis, K., Markatos, E., and Polychronakis, M. (2004). Performance analysis of content matching intrusion detection systems. In *Applications and the Internet, 2004. Proceedings. 2004 International Symposium on*, pages 208–215. IEEE.

[Bailey et al., 2005] Bailey, M., Cooke, E., Jahanian, F., Watson, D., and Nazario, J. (2005). The blaster worm: Then and now. *Security & Privacy, IEEE*, 3(4):26–31.

[Bradley, 2011] Bradley, T. (2011). Introduction to intrusion detection systems. http://netsecurity.about.com/cs/hackertools/a/aa030504.htm.

[Burstein, 2003] Burstein (2003). Survey of cybercrime in the united states, a. *Berkeley Tech. LJ*, 18:313.

[Hay et al., 2008] Hay, A., Cid, D., and Bray, R. (2008). *OSSEC host-based intrusion detection guide*. Syngress.

[Honeynet, 2010] Honeynet (2010). Honeynet project challenges.

[Innella, 2001] Innella, P. (December 6, 2001). An introduction to ids.

[Julisch, 2003] Julisch, K. (2003). Using root cause analysis to handle intrusion detection alarms.

[Kohlenberg et al.,] Kohlenberg, T. et al. Snort ids and ips toolkit, 2007.

[Kumar et al., 2005] Kumar, V., Srivastava, J., and Lazarević, A. (2005). *Managing cyber threats: issues, approaches, and challenges*, volume 5. Springer Verlag.

[Lowe, 2009] Lowe, S. (2009). *Mastering VMware vSphere 4*. Sybex.

[Magalhaes, 2004] Magalhaes, R. (2004). Host-based ids vs network-based ids.

[Munir et al., 2011] Munir, R., Alhomoud, A., et al. (2011). Performance analysis of ids (snort). In *Proceedings of Twenty Seventh UK Performance Engineering Workshop (UKPEW 2011), Bradford, UK*.

[Roesch et al., 1999] Roesch, M. et al. (1999). Snort-lightweight intrusion detection for networks. In *Proceedings of the 13th USENIX conference on System administration*, pages 229–238. Seattle, Washington.

[Salour and Su, 2007] Salour, M. and Su, X. (2007). Dynamic two-layer signature-based ids with unequal databases. In *Information Technology, 2007. ITNG'07. Fourth International Conference on*, pages 77–82. IEEE.

[Spawar, 2010]   Suricata.   `https://redmine.openinfosecfoundation.org/projects/suricata/wiki/Suricata_User_Guide/`.

[Swift, 2006] A practical application of sim/sem/siem automating threat identification'.

In: Advances in Security Information Management
Editors: G. Suarez-Tangil and E. Palomar

ISBN: 978-1-62417-204-5
© 2013 Nova Science Publishers, Inc.

Chapter 6

COMPLEX EVENT PROCESSING BASED SIEM

Vincenzo Gulisano, Ricardo Jiménez Peris, Marta Patiño Martinez,
*Claudio Soriente and Valerio Vianello**
Universidad Politécnica de Madrid, Spain

Abstract

Correlation engines are a key component of modern SIEMs. They employ user-defined rules to process input alerts and identify the minimal set of meaningful data that should be provided to the final user. As IT systems grow in size and complexity, the amount of alerts generated by probes is constantly increasing and centralized SIEMs (i.e., SIEMs with a single-node correlation engine) start to show their processing limits.

In this chapter we present a novel parallel correlation engine to be embedded in next generation SIEMs. The engine is based on Complex Event Processing and on a novel parallelization technique that allows to deploy the engine on an arbitrary number of nodes in a shared-nothing cluster. At the same time, the parallel execution preserves semantic transparency, i.e., its output is identical to the one of an ideal centralized execution. Our engine scales with the number of processed alerts per second and allows to reach beyond the processing limits of a centralized correlation engine.

Keywords: Security Information and Event Management (SIEM), Parallel Correlation Engine, Salability, Complex Event Processing

1. Introduction

Security Information Management Systems (SIEMs) represent an effective tool to monitor complex systems and help security IT staff to identify and react to security threats. SIEMs provide reliable information abstraction and correlation so that the amount of information delivered to the final user is free of background noise and identifying real threats as well as their sources becomes easier. The heart of a SIEM is its correlation engine that employs user-defined rules to process input alerts and identify the minimal set of meaningful data that should be provided to the final user.

---

*E-mail address: {vgulisano,rjimenez,mpatino,csoriente,vvianello}@fi.upm.es

As IT systems keep growing and become more complex, current SIEMs [AlienValult, 2010, PreludeIDS Technologies, 2010] start to show their limits. Current SIEMs that rely on a centralized correlation engine can not cope with massive amount of information produced by large and complex infrastructures and are forced either to shed the load or to queue up alerts and delay their processing. This is not an option in many scenarios where no information can be discarded and real-time processing of alerts and timely discovery of threats is a must.

Motivation. Complex Event Processing (CEP) [Abadi et al., 2003, Abadi et al., 2005, Chen et al., 2000, Chandrasekaran et al., 2003, Shah et al., 2003] represents a promising tool to improve current SIEMs. They can process large amounts of information in real time and provide information abstraction and correlation, similarly to SIEM correlation engines. Within the context of CEPs, an alert is called an *event*, a directive is a *query* and the rules of a directive are referred to as *operators*.

Some CEPs offer distributed processing [Shah et al., 2003, Abadi et al., 2005] and, at a first glance, might seem as a perfect match to overcome the single-site execution limitations of current SIEMs. However, the scalability achieved by previous CEP proposals is still limited due to single node bottlenecks (e.g. [Abadi et al., 2005]) or high distribution overhead (e.g. [Shah et al., 2003]). In particular, current distributed CEPs try to overcome the processing limit of a centralized execution either with inter-query parallelism or intra-query parallelism via inter-operator parallelism [Cherniack et al., 2003].

The former allows to run different queries on different nodes. Intra-query parallelism through inter-operator parallelism, deploys different operators on different nodes so that the per-event load at each node decreases. However, both options still require the whole data flow to pass through a single node, that is, no real parallelism is achieved.

Providing real parallelism (i.e., intra-operator parallelism) in CEPs is a challenging task. A naïve way to achieve it, also known as *intra-partition* parallelism, dictates to replicate an operator on several nodes and have each node processing a fraction of the input. Partitioning the input data over several processing unit is an ad-hoc (hence, error-prone) process. This strategy allows to overcome the processing capacity of a centralized system because no node processes the whole input data; however, intra-partition parallelism is a poor match for SIEMs, where correlation of all the available information is key to threat discovery. Indeed, with intra-partition parallelism, events that once correlated might reveal a threat, could be processed by different nodes and the threat might remain hidden.

Contributions. This chapter proposes a novel approach to alert correlation in SIEM systems. We propose to use CEP systems as the underlying correlation engine of a SIEM, in order to improve their scalability and applicability in scenarios where massive amount of alerts must be processed with strict timing requirements.

We introduce a novel parallelization technique for CEP systems that achieves intra-operator parallelism [Gulisano et al., 2010]. The proposed technique allows to deploy any query operator on an arbitrary number of nodes in a shared-nothing environment.

The logical input stream of alerts is partitioned in many physical streams that flow in parallel through the system so that no node is required to process the whole input. The parallel system enables throughput rates far beyond the ones allowed by a single processing node while guaranteeing the correctness of a centralized execution. The result is a highly-scalable CEP that can process massive amount of input data on-the-fly and that is a perfect candidate to enhance state of the art SIEM correlation engines.

Organization.   Section 2 provides an overview of Complex Event Processing introducing basic terminology and operators. Section 3 introduces our novel parallelization technique that allows the correlation engine to scale with the input load while guaranteeing that no threats are missed. Section 4 provides a concrete example of how to convert a SIEM directive in a CEP query while Section 5 provides some concluding remarks.

2.   Complex Event Processing

Complex Event Processing (CEP) finds patterns of interest over streams of data. A data stream S is an infinite sequence of events $e_0, e_1, e_2, \ldots$. All events of a stream share a "schema" that defines the number and type of their attributes; attribute A_i of event e is referred to as $e.A_i$. We assume events are timestamped at data sources that are equipped with well-synchronized clocks managed through, e.g., NTP [Mills, 2003]. In case data sources clock synchronization is not feasible, we assume events are timestamped at the entry point of the CEP system. In either case, we refer to the timestamp of event e as $e.ts$, that is, timestamp is an additional attribute of all schemas.

Table 1 provides a sample schema of a security event; it lists relevant attributes that will be used in the examples throughout the chapter. Pair $Plugin\_id$ and $Plugin\_sid$, identify the sensor that generated the event (e.g, SNORT) and the event type (e.g., FINGER probe 0 attempt), respectively. Src_IP, Src_Port and Dst_IP, Dst_Port specify the two endpoints that were interested by the event. ts is the timestamp generated when the event was recorded.

Table 1. Sample security event schema

$Plugin\_id$	Id of the device that generated the event
$Plugin\_sid$	Id of the type of event
Src_IP	Source IP address
Src_Port	Source port number
Dst_IP	Destination IP address
Dst_Port	Destination port number
ts	Timestamp

CEP allow users to specify pattern of interests over incoming data through *continuous queries*. The latter is "continuosly" executed over the streaming data, so that each time a pattern of interest is identified, the result is presented to the user.

A continuous query is defined over one or more input streams and can have multiple output streams. Queries are modeled as an acyclic direct graph made of "boxes and arrows". Each box (operator) represents a computational unit that performs an operation over events input through its incoming arrow(s) and outputs resulting events over its outgoing arrow(s).

Each arrow (stream) represents a data flow. An arrow between two boxes means that the second box consumes events produced by the first one.

Typical query operators of CEP systems are similar to relational algebra operators. They are classified depending on whether they keep state information across input events. Stateless operators (e.g., Map, Union and Filter) do not keep any state across events and perform one-by-one computation; that is, each incoming event is processed and an output event is produced, if any.

Stateful operators (e.g., Aggregate and Join) perform operations on multiple input events; that is, each incoming event updates the state information of the operator and contributes to the output event, if any. Because of the infinite nature of data streams, stateful operators keep state information only for the most recent incoming events. This technique is referred to as *windowing*. Windows can be defined over a period of time (e.g., events received in the last hour) or over the number of received events (e.g., last 100 events).

In the following we introduce the basic processing tasks of a SIEM correlation engine and map them to a CEP operator, providing examples of both its syntax and semantic. Readers interested in CEP are referred to [Garofalakis et al., 2012].

2.1. Transforming Events

Raw information conveyed by incoming events might need further processing before being used for correlation. For example, in order to reduce the per-event processing overhead and allow higher throughput, events attributes that are not required for correlation, should be removed as soon as the event reaches the engine. Other transformations include, time-zone translation of the event timestamp, conversion among metrics (e.g., Celsius degrees to Fahrenheit degrees), etc.

Event transformation in CEP systems is performed by the Map operator. The latter is a generalized projection operator defined as

$$M\{A'_1 \leftarrow f_1(e_{in}), \ldots, A'_n \leftarrow f_n(e_{in})\}(I, O)$$

with I and O that denote the input and output stream, respectively. e_{in} is a generic input event, $\{A'_1, \ldots, A'_n\}$ is the schema of the output stream and $\{f'_1, \ldots, f'_n\}$ is a set of user-defined functions. Each input event is transformed according to the set $\{f'_1, \ldots, f'_n\}$ and the resulting event is propagated over the output stream. The output stream schema might differ from the input one, but the output event preserves the timestamp of the input one. Figure 1 shows a sample Map operator that extracts source IP address and port from each incoming event. The latter event complies with the schema of Table 1 while output events have attributes Src_IP, Src_Port, ts. The syntax of the operator in Fig. 1 is

$$M\{A'_1 = e_{in}.Src\_IP, A'_2 = e_{in}.Src\_Port, A'_3 = e_{in}.ts\}(I, O)$$

2.2. Filtering Events

One of the main tasks of the correlation engine is to remove background noise from the incoming streams of alerts. A basic technique to reduce the load of alerts of interest is to look into each event and choose whether it is relevant or not, based on its content. For

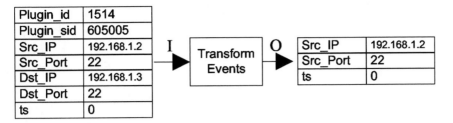

Figure 1. Extracting attributes from incoming events.

example, if the engine is monitoring a particular subnetwork, events related to nodes outside of the monitored set, can be safely discarded.

The CEP operator that is used either to discard events or to route events to different output streams, depending on the event content is the Filter operator. It is similar to a case statement and it is used to route input events over multiple output streams. The Filter operator is defined as

$$F\{P_1, \ldots, P_m\}(I, O_1, \ldots, O_m[, O_{m+1}])$$

where I is the input stream, $O_1 \ldots, O_m, O_{m+1}$ is an ordered set of output streams and $P_1, \ldots, P_m$ is an ordered set of predicates.

The number of predicates equals the number of output streams and each input event is forwarded over the output stream associated to the first predicate that the event satisfies. That is, e_{in} is forwarded over O_j where $j = \min_{1 \le i \le m}\{i \mid P_i(e_{in}) = TRUE\}$.

Events that satisfy none of the predicates are output on stream O_{m+1}, or discarded if output $m + 1$ has not been defined.

Predicates are defined over the attributes of the input event and include comparisons between two attributes (e.g., $e_{in}.Src\_Port = e_{in}.Dst\_Port$)or comparisons between an attribute and a constant(e.g., $e_i n.Dst\_Port = 22$).

Figure 2 shows a sample Filter operator that routes events based on their $Plugin\_ID$ attribute. SNORT events ($Plugin\_ID = 1001$) are routed over output O_1, while CISCO Pix events ($Plugin\_ID = 1514$) are forwarded over output stream O_2; as no additional output stream has been specified, events with $Plugin\_ID \notin \{1001, 1514\}$ are discarded. The syntax of the operator in Fig. 2 is

$$F\{e_{in}.Plugin\_id = 1001, e_{in}.Plugin\_id = 1514\}(I, O_1, O_2)$$

2.3. Merging Events

SIEM correlation engines collect event from a multitude of sources, so that events need to be merged in a unique stream before further processing. In CEP systems, the Union operator merges two or more input streams with the same schema into a single output stream. Input events are propagated over the output stream in FIFO order. The Union operator is defined as

$$U\{\}(I_1, \ldots, I_n, O)$$

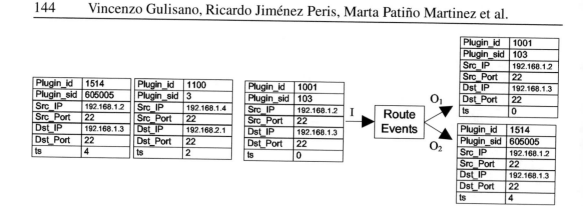

Figure 2. Route SNORT and CISCO Pix events, discard others.

where $I_1, \ldots, I_n$ is a set of input streams and O is the only output stream; all streams share the same schema. Figure 3 shows a sample Union operator that merges streams from two SNORT sensors into a single output stream, propagated for further processing. The operator syntax is

$$U\{\}(I_1, I_2, O)$$

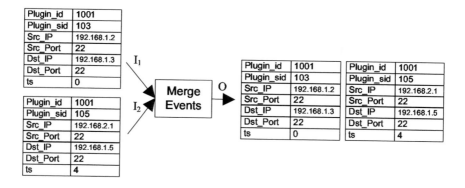

Figure 3. Merge SNORT events from two different sensors.

2.4. Aggregating Events

In some scenarios, only little information can be inferred from single events, while a greater knowledge can be obtained aggregating multiple events together. For example, each new connection to a given node might be of little interest, while the number of connections over the last, e.g., minute, hour, day, might provide a greater amount of information.

The Aggregate operator is used in CEP systems to provide information related to group of incoming events. The operator computes an aggregate function (e.g., average, count, etc.) over a window of its input stream. It is defined as

$$Ag\{Wtype, Size, Advance, A'_1 \leftarrow f_1(W), \ldots, A'_n \leftarrow f_n(W),$$
$$[Group - by = (A_{i_1}, \ldots, A_{i_m})]\}(I, O)$$

Events over input stream I are stored in the current window W until it becomes full. $Wtype$ specifies the window type that can be either time-based ($Wtype = time$) or event-based ($Wtype = numEvents$). If the window is time-based, it is considered full if the time distance between the incoming event and the earliest event in the window exceeds the window $Size$. In case of event-based windows, a window is full if it contains $Size$ events.

Once a window is full, an output event is produced. Output events are propagated over stream O and have timestamp equal to the timestamp of the earliest event in the current window. The output event schema is $\{A'_1, \ldots, A'_n\}$ and $\{f_1, \ldots, f_n\}$ is a set of user-defined functions (e.g., sum, count, average, etc.) computed over all events in the window.

After an output event has been propagated, the window is updated (or "slid" forward) and stale events are discarded according to parameter $Advance$. If $Wtype = time$ and e_{in} is the current input event, a event e in the current window is discarded if $e_{in}.ts - e.ts > Size$. If $Wtype = numEvents$, the earliest $Advance$ events are discarded from the current window.

Finally, the parameter Group-by is optional and is used to define equivalence classes over the input stream. In particular, assume Group-by= A_i, where A_i is an attribute of the input schema. Then, the Aggregate operator handles separate windows for each possible value of A_i.

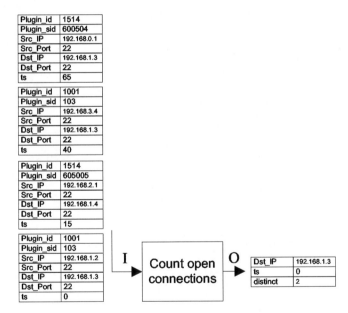

Figure 4. Count open connections for each server on a per-minute basis.

To further clarify the semantic of operators based on windows, we refer to the Aggregate operator of Figure 4. The operator counts the number of open connections for each server (i.e., Group-by= Dst_IP) during the last minute (i.e, $Size = 60$), with an advance of twenty seconds (i.e., $Advance = 20$). It is defined as

$$Ag\{time, 60, 20, A'_1 = count(), Group - by = e_{in}.Dst\_IP\}(I, O)$$

Figure 4 shows the sequence of input events. Three events refer to a connection to IP address 192.168.1.3 (Dst_IP) and their timestamps are 0, 40 and 65, respectively. One event refers to a connection to IP address 192.168.1.4 and is generated at time 15.

Figure 5 shows the window evolution as the above events are received by the operator. In the following, we provide detailed steps of the operator behavior as events are received.

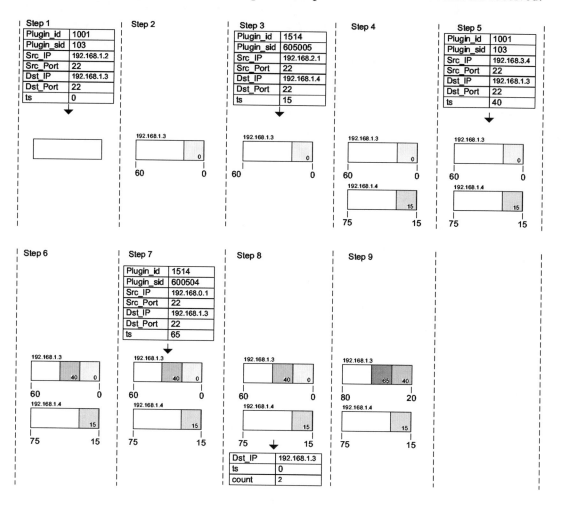

Figure 5. Aggregate Sample Time-Based Window Evolution.

- **Step 1**. Event relative to IP address 192.168.1.3 (Dst_IP) with timestamp 0 is received.

- **Step 2**. As this is the first event relative to IP 192.168.1.3, a new window is created and the event is stored (recall that Group-by= Dst_IP).

- **Step 3**. Event relative to IP address 192.168.1.4 with timestamp 15 is received.

- **Step 4**. As for the previous event, there is no window for events relative to IP 192.168.1.4, so a new window is created and the event is stored.

- **Step 5**. Event relative to IP address 192.168.1.3 with timestamp 40 is received.

- **Step 6**. A window for IP address 192.168.1.3 is already defined. No event currently stored in the window is discarded as the timestamp difference between the input event (40) and the earliest event in the window (0) is smaller than the window size (i.e., 60 seconds). The incoming event is stored in the window.

- **Step 7**. Event relative to IP address 192.168.1.3 with timestamp 65 is received.

- **Step 8**. The window relative to IP address 192.168.1.3 must produce an output as the timestamp difference between the incoming event (65) and the earliest event in the window (0) is greater than the window size. The output event is produced considering the events currently stored in the window (the ones with timestamp 0 and 40).

- **Step 9**. After the output is produced, the window is slid forward of *Advance* time units until the timestamp of the incoming event falls within the current window. Finally, the incoming event is stored. In the example, the event with timestamp 0 is discarded; in general, any event with timestamp between 0 and 20 would be removed.

2.5.   Correlating Events

The ultimate goal of the SIEM engine is to correlate events coming from different input streams and extract information of interest. For example, a successful brute-force attack can be detected correlating a number of denied login attempts followed by one successful login event.

The Join operator can be used in CEP systems to correlate events from different sources. It is a binary operator defined as

$$J\{P, Wtype, Size\}(S_l, S_r, O)$$

S_l, S_r are two input streams referred to as *left* and *right*, respectively, while O denotes the output stream. P is a predicate over pairs of events (one from each input stream), that is, the Join predicate include comparisons between attributes of the same event or between attributes of different events. Parameters $Wtype$ and $Size$ are windows parameters similar to the ones in the Aggregate operator.

The Join operator keeps two separate windows, W_l, W_r, for each input stream. Events arriving on the left (resp. right) stream are stored in the left (resp. right) window and used to update (i.e., slide forward) the right (resp. left) window. If $Wtype = time$, upon arrival of event $e_{in} \in S_l$, window W_r is updated removing all events e such that $e_{in}.ts - e.ts \geq Size$. If $Wtype = NumEvents$, upon arrival of event $e_{in} \in S_l$, window W_r, if full, is updated removing the earliest event.

After window update, for each $e \in W_r$, the concatenation of events e_{in} and e is produced as a single output event if $P(e_{in}, e) = TRUE$.

Window update, predicate evaluation and output propagation for input events over the right stream are performed in a similar fashion.

Figure 6 shows a join operator that receives events from SNORT and CISCO Pix sensors. Events coming from the two streams are matched any time they refer to the same source IP address (Src_IP) and their distance in time is less than 10 seconds. The syntax

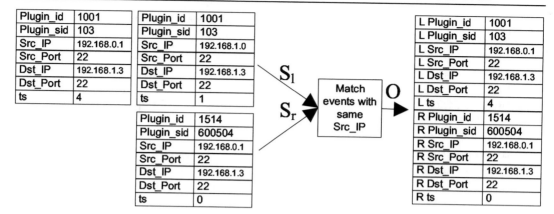

Figure 6. Match SNORT and CISCO Pix events with the same Src_IP.

of the Join operator is

$$J\{P = (left.e_{in}.Src\_IP = right.e_{in}.Src\_IP), time, 10\}(S_l, S_r, O)$$

3. Parallel Complex Event Processing

The ultimate goal of a SIEM is to detect **all** threats. As SIEMs are used to monitor sensitive infrastructure, all attempted or successful attacks must be discovered and any piece of information must be carefully analyzed.

Our goal in architecting a parallel correlation engine is to make sure that the parallel system identifies all threats, just as a centralized one. At the same time, we must minimize distribution overhead, in order to make parallelization cost-effective. If a parallel system provides the same results of its centralized counterpart, the former is said to be *semantically transparent*. In the following, we provide details on how to parallelize each of the operators presented in Section 2.

Semantic transparency for stateless operators is straightforward. Assume a stateless operator, e.g., a Filter, is parallelized and distributed over multiple nodes; that is, the same operator is deployed on multiple nodes and each instance processes a fraction of the input events. As stateless operators process events one-by-one, no matter which event will be processed by which instance of the parallel operator, the final outcome will match the one of a centralized execution.

However, semantic transparency becomes challenging with stateful operators. As a stateful operator keeps state across input events, we must guarantee that all events that are aggregated/correlated in a centralized execution, are processed by the same instance of the parallel operator. As an example, let us consider an Aggregate operator deployed over multiple nodes that is used to compute the number of open connections for each server during the last hour. We must ensure that all the events related to open connections for a particular server are processed by the same Aggregate instance in order to provide the correct results, that is, the semantic provided by the distributed operator is equal to the semantic of the centralized one.

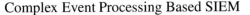

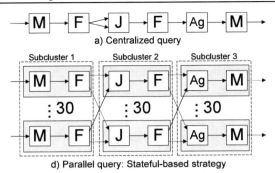

a) Centralized query

Subcluster 1   Subcluster 2   Subcluster 3

: 30   : 30   : 30

d) Parallel query: Stateful-based strategy

Figure 7. Query Parallelization Strategy.

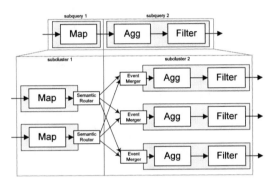

Figure 8. Subquery parallelization.

This section provides details of the proposed parallelization technique and the rationale behind our design.

3.1. Query Parallelization Strategy

Our query parallelization strategy aims at reducing the communication overhead among nodes. The rationale is that, in order to guarantee semantic transparency, communication is required only before stateful operators. Therefore, we define the parallelization unit (called *subquery*) according to stateful operators of a query. Each query is split into as many subqueries as stateful operators, plus an additional one, if the query starts with stateless operators. A subquery consists of a stateful operator followed by all the stateless operators connected to its output, until the next stateful operator or the end of query. If the query starts with stateless operators, the first subquery consists of all stateless operators before the first stateful one.

As the query of Fig. 7.a has two stateful operators plus a stateless prefix, Fig. 7.b shows three subqueries. The first one contains the prefix of stateless operators, and the next two, one stateful operator with the following stateless operators. Assuming a cluster (i.e., a set) of 90 nodes, each subquery is deployed on a subcluster of 30 nodes. Data flows from one subcluster to the next one, until the output of the system. All instances of a subcluster run the same subquery, called *local subquery*, for a fraction of the input data stream, and produce a fraction of the output data stream.

3.2. Semantic Transparency

Once the query has been partitioned, semantic transparency requires that input events are carefully distributed to each subquery containing a stateful operator. That is, the output of a subquery feeding its downstream (i.e., following) counterpart must be carefully arranged so that, if the downstream subquery has a stateful operator, events that must be aggregated/correlated together are received by the same instance of the stateful operator.

In this section we show how to parallelize a query and achieve semantic transparency by means of the sample query in Fig. 8. The latter provides the IP address of the servers that managed a number of connections above a given threshold over the last hour, every ten minutes. It receives a stream of events with the schema of Table 1. The Map operator is used to extract relevant fields from incoming events. The Aggregate has windows defined over time with $Size = 3600$ seconds and $Advance = 600$; it groups connections by server (i.e., Group-by= Dst_IP) and counts the number of relevant events per server. Finally, events output by the Aggregate that carry a number of connections greater than a given threshold are forwarded to output by the Filter operator.

As the query has one stateful operator and a stateless prefix, it is split into two subqueries. Subquery1 consists of the Map operator while Subquery2 has the Aggregate and the Filter operators. They are allocated to subcluster 1 and 2, respectively.

To guarantee effective event distribution from one subcluster to the downstream one, output events of each subcluster are assigned to *buckets*. Event-buckets assignment is based on the fields of the event. Given B distinct buckets[1] and event $e = \{A_1, A_2, ..., A_n\}$, its corresponding bucket b is computed by hashing one or more of the event fields[2], e.g., A_i, A_j, modulus B, e.g., $b = Hash(A_i, A_j) \mod B$. All events belonging to a given bucket will be forwarded to and processed by the same node of the downstream subcluster.

In order to distribute the buckets across N downstream nodes, each subcluster employs a *bucket-node map* (BNM). The BNM associates each bucket with a node of the downstream subcluster, so that $BNM[b]$ provides the downstream instance that must receive events belonging to bucket b. In Figure 8, the number of nodes in subcluster 2 is $N = 3$ while B can be set arbitrarily, as long as $B \geq N$.

Event-buckets assignment and BNMs are endorsed by special operators, called *Semantic Router (SR)*. They are placed on the outgoing edge of a subcluster and are used to distribute the output events of the local subquery to the nodes of the downstream subcluster.

As discussed above, semantic transparency requires events that must be aggregated/correlated together to be processed by the same node. However, it is also required that event processing happens in the same order as in a centralized execution. For this reason, we place another special operator, called *Event Merger (EM)*, on the incoming edge of each subcluster. EMs take multiple timestamp-ordered input streams from upstream (i.e., preceding) SRs and feed the local subquery with a single timestamp-ordered merged stream.

The bottom part of Figure 8 shows how the original query is split in subqueries, augmented with SRs and EMs and deployed in a cluster of nodes.

In the following we detail the parallelization logic encapsulated in SRs and EMs for each of the stateful operator we consider.

---

[1] B is a user-defined parameter.

[2] As explained later, the fields used to compute the hash depend on the semantic of the downstream operator.

3.2.1. Semantic Routers

Semantic Routers are in charge of distributing events from one local subquery to all its downstream peers. To guarantee that events that must be aggregated/joined together are indeed received by the same node, SRs located upstream of a stateful subquery must be enriched with *semantic awareness*, that is, they must be aware of the semantics of the downstream stateful operator.

Join operator   Assume a stateful subquery contains a Join operator. In order to guarantee correct distribution of the events, upstream SRs partition their input stream into B buckets and use the BNM to route events to the N nodes where the Join is deployed. The attribute specified in the equality clause of the Join predicate is used at upstream SRs to determine the bucket of an event. That is, let A_i be the attribute of the equality clause, then for each event e, $BNM[Hash(e.A_i) \mod B]$ determines the recipient node to which e should be sent. If the Join predicate contains multiple equality clauses, the hash is computed over all the attributes of those clauses. Therefore, events with the same values of the attributes defined in the equality clause will be sent to the same instance and matched together.

Aggregate operator   If the stateful operator is an Aggregate, its parallelization requires that all events sharing the same values of the attributes specified in the Group-by parameter should be processed by the same instance. In the example of Fig. 8 the Aggregate groups events by their destination IP address. Hence, data partitioning by upstream SRs is performed in a similar way to the Join operator. That is, the set of attributes specified in the Group-by parameter are hashed and the BNM is used to partition the stream across the N instances of the downstream subcluster.

3.2.2. Event Mergers

Just like SRs, Event Mergers (EMs) are key to guarantee semantic transparency. EMs merge multiple timestamp-ordered input streams coming from upstream SRs and feeds the local subquery with a single timestamp-ordered input stream. As a result, the local subquery will produce a timestamp ordered output stream. To guarantee that the output stream is timestamp-ordered, input streams must be carefully merged. In particular, an EM forwards the event with the earliest timestamp, any time it has received at least one event from each input stream. To avoid blocking of the EM, upstream SRs might send dummy events for each output stream that has been idle for the last d time units. Dummy events are discarded by EMs and only used to unblock the processing of other input streams.

4.   Transforming SIEM Directives into CEP Queries

This section presents a sample directive taken from OSSIM SIEM [AlienValult, 2010] and shows how it can be expressed as a CEP query and parallelized through the technique of Section 3

The directive is designed to detect a brute-force attack against a CISCO Firewall and, eventually, its successful result. A first alarm should be raised if an unusual number of

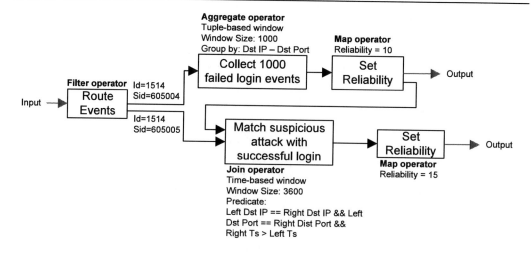

Figure 9. Detect suspicious and successful brute-force attacks.

"denied login" events for a particular connection is generated (e.g., 1000 denied logins). After the first alarm has been triggered, a more severe alarm should be raised if a "permitted login" event is received for the same connection (i.e., the attacker achieved to login to the firewall).

Both denied login and permitted login events are sent from a CISCO Pix sensor ($Plugin\_id$ 1514). Denied login event is identified by $Plugin\_sid$ 605004 while permitted login event by $Plugin\_sid$ 605005. The first alarm sets reliability[3] to 10 while the second alarm sets it to 15.

The query in Figure 9 shows the implementation of the described directive in a CEP system.

The query defines one input and two output streams. Input stream schema is compliant with the one in Table 1 while the output streams share the same schema with attributes Src_ip, Dst_ip and $Reliability$.

Attributes Src_ip and Dst_ip refer to the source and destination IP addresses related to the login attempt.

An initial Filter operator is used to forward only events of interest, i.e., $Plugin\_id = 1514$ and $Plugin\_sid \in \{605004, 605005\}$; all other events are discarded. Events related to a denied login ($Plugin\_id = 1514$ and $Plugin\_sid = 605004$) are processed by an Aggregate operator.

The Aggregate $Wtype$ is set to $numEvents$ and has $Size = 1000$ and $Advance = 1$. Group-by is set to Dst_IP, Dst_Port, that is, the Aggregate keeps separate windows for each port on each destination host. Any time 1000 denied login events are received for the same pair Dst_IP, Dst_Port, an output event is forwarded to the following Map operator. The output event carries information about the attack target (i.e., Dst_IP, Dst_Port) and the timestamp of the earliest denied login event.

The Map operator takes the input event, adds attribute $Reliability = 10$ and forwards the event over the output stream. The events produced by the Map operator are sent to the

---

[3]Reliability is a standard parameter of SIEM systems that defines the trustworthiness of the alarm; that is, only alarms with reliability greater than a given threshold are reported to the user.

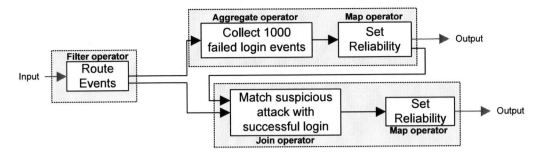

Figure 10. Query Partitioning.

query output and also forwarded to the Join operator for further correlation.

The Join operator is used to correlate suspicious brute-force attempt alarms coming from the Map operator with successful login events forwarded by the Filter.

The Join operator predicate P matches two incoming events if they refer to the same destination (i.e., if they share the same Dst_IP, Dst_Port attributes) and if the successful login event timestamp is greater than the timestamp of the brute-force attempt alarm (i.e., the successful login happens after the brute-force attack). Windows size is equal to 3600 seconds. This implies that two matching events cannot be distant in time more than one hour.

Events produced by the Join operator are forwarded to another Map operator that sets $Reliability = 15$. Produced events are forwarded to the query output.

Figure 10 shows how the query in Fig. 9 is partitioned according to the technique described in Section 3.1

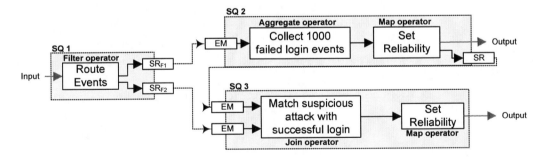

Figure 11. Subqueries with Semantic Routers and Event Mergers.

An initial subquery is allocated for the stateless prefix of the original query (i.e., the Filter operator). Another subquery contains the first stateful operator and its stateless suffix, until the next stateful operator (i.e., the Aggregate operator and Map1 operator). A final subquery is allocated for the Join operator and Map2 operator, that is, the last stateful operator and its stateless suffix.

Once the original query has been partitioned into subqueries, a Semantic Router operator and an Event Merger operator are added for each edge connecting two distinct subqueries. Figure 11 shows the three subqueries (SQ1, SQ2 and SQ3) augmented with Sematic Router and Event Merger operators.

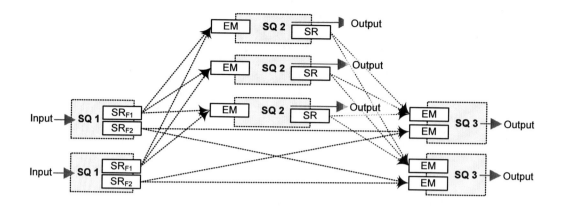

Figure 12. Subquery deployment.

The Filter operator will have one SR for each outgoing edge, SR_{F1} and SR_{F2}. The former will forward events with $Plugin\_id = 1514$ and $Plugin\_sid = 605004$ while SR_{F2} will handle events with $Plugin\_id = 1514$ and $Plugin\_sid = 605005$. The Aggregate operator specifies Group-by= Dst_IP, Dst_Port while the Join operator has the same attribute pair in the equality clause of its predicate. Hence, for each incoming event e_{in}, each SR on the outgoing edge of the first subquery will compute $Hash(e_{in}.Dst\_IP, e_{in}.Dst\_Port) \mod B$ to compute the bucket of the event and then it will look up the BNM to identify the designated recipient among the instances of the downstream subquery.

The subquery containing the Aggregate operator is enriched with an Event Merger on the incoming edge and one Semantic Router to forward output events to the next subquery. Here as well, SR will use attributes of Dst_IP, Dst_Port of each incoming event to compute the bucket of the input event and then the designated receiver among the instances of the downstream subquery.

The subcluster containing the Join operator is enriched with two EM operators, one for each input stream.

Finally, Figure 12 shows subqueries SQ1, SQ2, SQ3, allocated to subclusters of 2, 3 and 2 nodes, respectively.

Conclusion

In this chapter we propose to use Complex Event Processing systems as the correlation engine of next generation SIEMs. We argue that current correlation engines relying on a centralized execution are not suitable for complex scenarios where high-throughput data must be processed with tight timing constraints. We show how Complex Event Processing can be used to express SIEMs directives and provide a novel parallelization technique that allows to parallelize the execution and deploy the engine over an arbitrary number of nodes in a shared-nothing cluster. The parallel system can handle input load far behind the ones afforded by single-node correlation engines. At the same time, our parallelization technique guarantees semantic transparency, i.e., it guarantees that the parallel execution provides the same output of an ideal centralized execution. The result is a highly-scalable correlation engine that can be easily embedded in next generation SIEMs to process massive amount of input data and make sure that no threats are "missed".

References

[Abadi et al., 2005] Abadi, D. J., Ahmad, Y., Balazinska, M., Çetintemel, U., Cherniack, M., Hwang, J.-H., Lindner, W., Maskey, A., Rasin, A., Ryvkina, E., Tatbul, N., Xing, Y., and Zdonik, S. B. (2005). The design of the borealis stream processing engine. In *CIDR 2005*, pages 277–289.

[Abadi et al., 2003] Abadi, D. J., Carney, D., Çetintemel, U., Cherniack, M., Convey, C., Lee, S., Stonebraker, M., Tatbul, N., and Zdonik, S. B. (2003). Aurora: a new model and architecture for data stream management. *VLDB J.*, 12(2):120–139.

[AlienValult, 2010] AlienValult (2010). AlienVault Unified SIEM. http://www.alienvault.com/.

[Chandrasekaran et al., 2003] Chandrasekaran, S., Cooper, O., Deshpande, A., Franklin, M. J., Hellerstein, J. M., Hong, W., Krishnamurthy, S., Madden, S., Raman, V., Reiss, F., and Shah, M. A. (2003). Telegraphcq: Continuous dataflow processing for an uncertain world. In *CIDR*.

[Chen et al., 2000] Chen, J., DeWitt, D. J., Tian, F., and Wang, Y. (2000). Niagaracq: A scalable continuous query system for internet databases. In *ACM SIGMOD International Conference on Management of Data (SIGMOD'00)*, pages 379–390.

[Cherniack et al., 2003] Cherniack, M., Balakrishnan, H., Balazinska, M., Carney, D., Çetintemel, U., Xing, Y., and Zdonik, S. B. (2003). Scalable distributed stream processing. In *CIDR*.

[Garofalakis et al., 2012] Garofalakis, M., Gehrke, J., and Rastogi, R. (2012). *Data Stream Management: Processing High-Speed Data Streams*. Springer.

[Gulisano et al., 2010] Gulisano, V., Jiménez-Peris, R., Patiño-Martínez, M., and Valduriez, P. (2010). Streamcloud: A large scale data streaming system. In *International Conference on Distributed Computing Systems (ICDCS'10)*, pages 126–137.

[Mills, 2003] Mills, D. L. (2003). A brief history of ntp time: memoirs of an internet timekeeper. *Computer Communication Review*, 33(2):9–21.

[PreludeIDS Technologies, 2010] PreludeIDS Technologies (2010). Prelude PRO 1.0. http://www.prelude-technologies.com/.

[Shah et al., 2003] Shah, M. A., Hellerstein, J. M., Chandrasekaran, S., and Franklin, M. J. (2003). Flux: An adaptive partitioning operator for continuous query systems. In *19th International Conference on Data Engineering (ICDE'03)*, pages 25–36.

[Mills, 2003] Mills, D. L. (2003). A brief history of ntp time: memoirs of an internet timekeeper. *Computer Communication Review*, 33(2):9–21.

[PreludeIDS Technologies, 2010] PreludeIDS Technologies (2010). Prelude PRO 1.0. http://www.prelude-technologies.com/.

[Shah et al., 2003] Shah, M. A., Hellerstein, J. M., Chandrasekaran, S., and Franklin, M. J. (2003). Flux: An adaptive partitioning operator for continuous query systems. In *19th International Conference on Data Engineering (ICDE'03)*, pages 25–36.

In: Advances in Security Information Management
Editors: G. Suarez-Tangil and E. Palomar

ISBN: 978-1-62417-204-5
© 2013 Nova Science Publishers, Inc.

Chapter 7

EVADING IDSs AND FIREWALLS AS FUNDAMENTAL SOURCES OF INFORMATION IN SIEMs

Sergio Pastrana,* *José Montero-Castillo,*† *Agustín Orfila*‡
Computer Science Department
University Carlos III of Madrid, Spain

Abstract

A Security Information and Event Management system (SIEM) is typically composed of two parts: a central entity gathering, aggregating, correlating and analysing information and a set of independent monitoring entities in charge of supplying the central entity with suitable information (e.g., intrusion alerts or system logs). Evaluating a SIEM requires evaluating three elements: the central entity, the monitoring systems and the communications between the monitoring systems and the central entity (it must be ensured that the information arriving at the central entity is integral and complete). Nowadays, two of the most important monitoring systems forming a SIEM are Intrusion Detection Systems (IDSs) and firewalls. Such technologies are currently so sophisticated detecting and/or blocking malicious activities that it becomes difficult for an attacker to compromise a system without being detected or blocked. For this reason, a new adversarial model has arisen in the recent years: instead of directly attacking a protected network or system, the attacker tries to bypass the security barriers without raising suspicion. In this chapter, we present and analyse some of the most relevant techniques presented in the literature so as to evade IDSs and firewalls.

Keywords: Security Information and Event Management (SIEM), Evaluation, Evasion, Intrusion Detection, Firewalls

1. Introduction

Nowadays, IT systems are so large and complex that they usually need to be deployed in a decentralized manner. In order to ease such a decentralization process, new paradigms

---

*E-mail address: spastran@inf.uc3m.es
†E-mail address: jmcastil@inf.uc3m.es
‡E-mail address: adiaz@inf.uc3m.es

of computation have appeared in the latest years, for instance, cloud computing. In spite of the important features that decentralized systems have (e.g., availability and scalability), there is still an important challenge to overcome: security. In a decentralized system, the information is usually distributed and replicated among different servers, accessed by a great number of different users and communicated through many different types of links and devices. Consequently, a large variety of problems can arise in a decentralized system: broken links, security vulnerabilities in the operating system installed in a particular server, careless administrators tackling with security options, etc.

In order to secure a decentralized system, it is essential, among other things, to monitor the system and report all the anomalies detected. Such an operation can be performed by a Security Information Event Management system (SIEM), a tool in charge of collecting audit data (data obtained through monitoring), correlating it, analysing it and using the result of the analysis to decide whether abnormal behaviours are present in the system or not. In a SIEM, audit data can come from very different sources: firewalls, Intrusion Detection Systems (IDSs), system logs (for example, UNIX syslog or Microsoft Windows Event Viewer), traces from user behaviours, etc. In fact, the effectiveness of these systems strongly depends on the quality of the audit data, which is supposed to be real, complete and confident.

Figure 1 shows a SIEM with a centralized architecture monitoring an Intranet. The structure of the Intranet is as follows: firstly, the external traffic is received and distributed by a router; then, the traffic is filtered by a firewall and inspected by a Network IDS (NIDS); finally, a switch organizes the allowed traffic over the different systems connected to the Local Area Network (LAN). As for the monitoring process, all the devices in the Intranet are enabled to collect audit data (firewall alerts, system logs, etc.) and send such data to a central entity in the SIEM. Finally, the central entity in the SIEM aggregates, correlates and analyses the received data and reports an alert in case an anomaly is detected.

System administrators make use of SIEMs to determine if any threatening activity is currently taking place in their systems. The sooner an administrator realizes a malicious activity is happening, the sooner she can take actions to stop it and minimize its impact. As a consequence, if an attacker is able to evade the detection of a system's SIEM, she can stealthily compromise the system and thus, she becomes a serious and risky adversary.

Preventing an attacker from evading a SIEM requires to properly evaluate the SIEM, which is an extremely difficult task due to all the variables involved. In particular, three main steps are important when evaluating a SIEM:

1. The entity or entities aggregating, correlating and analysing the audit data from the monitored system must be evaluated to ensure that the SIEM efficiently detects the major number of attacks by generating the minimal number of false alarms.

2. Each audit data collector must be independently evaluated in order to guarantee that the collected data is correct and real.

3. The communications between the different entities in the SIEM must be secured in order to avoid attacks such as packet injection or packet modification, whose effects can clearly compromise the analyses carried out by the SIEM.

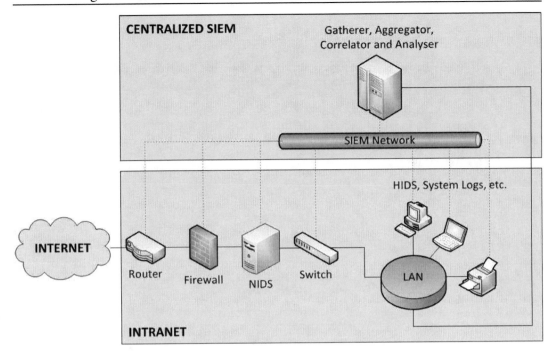

Figure 1. Architecture of a centralized SIEM monitoring an Intranet

This chapter focuses on the second step of SIEMs evaluation. In particular, the chapter presents an overview of the existing methods aimed to evade two of the most important audit data collectors, namely IDSs and firewalls.

The rest of the chapter is organized as follows. Section 2 provides a description of IDSs and firewalls. Section 3 presents the most important techniques used to evade IDSs. Section 4 comments on the current state of firewall evasion. Finally, Section ?? provides some general conclusions about SIEM evasion.

2. Background

In this section, the audit data collectors that will be analysed later in this chapter are described in detail.

2.1. Intrusion Detection System (IDS)

An IDS is a system that analyses data so as to detect malicious activity, reporting an alert if such an activity is found. IDSs are normally formed from several components. In the most classical architecture, IDSs consists of 4 components (see Figure 2), namely the decoder, the preprocessor (or set of preprocessors), the detection engine and the alert module. The way in which these components work is described following:

1. The decoder receives pieces of raw audit data from the audit data collectors and transforms each of these pieces into data that the preprocessor can handle.

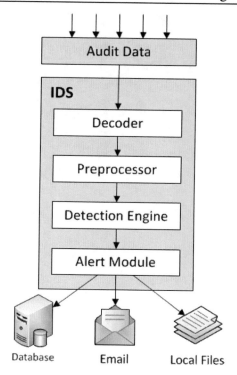

Figure 2. Architecture of a classical IDS

2. The preprocessor receives the pieces of data transformed by the decoder, analyses them to determine which pieces are dependant on each other and treats dependant pieces in such a way that they can be later scrutinized by the detection engine. A typical preprocessor widely used in NIDSs is the TCP preprocessor, whose main task is to compose session flows from a given set of TCP segments (reordering fragments, assembling them, etc). Currently, sophisticated preprocessors are able to perform detection tasks supplementing those performed by the detection engine.

3. The detection engine receives the data treated by the preprocessor and examines it searching for intrusions. If an intrusion is found, the detection engine requests the alert module to raise an alert.

4. The alert module is in charge of raising the alerts requested by the detection engine. Raising an alert can range from logging the alert in a local file to emailing the alert to the system administrator.

As for IDS classification, there exist many different taxonomies. Following, the most important and currently used ones are presented:

1. Regarding the source of the audit data, an IDS can be network-based or host-based:

   (a) Network IDSs (NIDSs): they analyse network traffic. The level of detection may vary from one NIDS to another, but most of them have modules in charge of analysing traffic from the network, transport and application layers in the OSI model. For instance, Snort [1], one of the most used open source IDSs, has a preprocessor specialized in HTTP data, another one for TCP data and the same for the other protocols and layers in the OSI model. NIDSs are normally placed outside the system being monitored but in the same network segment, thus enabling them to monitor a complete LAN (see Figure 1).

(b) Host IDSs (HIDSs): they analyse the data in one particular device. Most of them analyse the sequence of system calls of the programs running in the device perform. Within these sequences, optimal HIDS analyse system call arguments, memory registers, stack states, system logs, user behaviours, etc.

2. Regarding the model used to detect malicious activity, an IDS can be signature-based, anomaly-based or hybrid:

(a) Signature-based IDSs: in this type of IDS, abnormal behaviours are modelled as rules (also known as signatures) and intrusion detection is accomplished by comparing these rules with the behaviours taking place in the monitored system.

(b) Anomaly-based IDSs: in this type of IDS, the normal behaviours of the system are represented in a model and any activity falling out of the model is considered abnormal.

(c) Hybrid IDS: in this type of IDS, both signature and anomaly-based techniques are combined. Normally, the preprocessor performs the anomaly-based detection process and the detection engine performs the signature-based one.

3. Regarding the type of action triggered when a malicious behaviour is detected, an IDS can be active or passive:

(a) Passive IDS: when a malicious behaviour is detected, an alert is raised and no further action is taken.

(b) Active IDS: apart from raising an alert, the IDS tries to neutralize the malicious data, working so as an Intrusion Prevention System (IPS).

Apart from the previous classifications, there are many other possible ones. For example, in [2], a taxonomy based on the following characteristics is presented:

1. Regarding the technology, IDSs may be wired or wireless. Furthermore, wireless IDSs can be further classified as fixed or mobile.

2. Regarding the data processing method and the arrangement of its components, IDSs can be centralized or distributed.

3. Regarding the timing of the detection process, IDSs can be real time or non-real time.

4. Regarding the detection technique, IDSs can be state-based or transition-based.

Table 1. Contingency matrix for binary classification problems: true negatives (TN), false positives (FP), false negatives (FN) and true positives (TP)

		Detection	
		Negative	Positive
Real	Negative	TN	FP
	Positive	FN	TP

In order to evaluate the effectiveness of IDSs, two important measures are mainly used: the hit rate and the false positive rate. The hit rate (denoted H) measures the effectiveness of an IDS by indicating the percentage of intrusions that it detects (see Equation 1). The false positive rate (denoted F) measures the accuracy of an IDS by indicating the percentage of false alarms that it raises (see Equation 2). In order to calculate these two statistics, the following four values are necessary (see contingency matrix in Table 1): the number of real intrusions detected (true positives), the number of real intrusions undetected (false negatives), the number of alarms raised without any real intrusion taking place (false positives) and the number of normal events considered normal (true negatives).

$$H = \frac{TP}{TP + FN} \tag{1}$$

$$F = \frac{FP}{FP + TN} \tag{2}$$

Another important statistic that in the recent years has become relatively popular in the field of IDSs evaluation is the intrusion detection capability index [3] (denoted C_{ID}, see Equation 3). It measures the amount of uncertainty of the input resolved once the IDS output is obtained, and takes into account the prevalence (B in the formula) in the dataset besides the hit rate and the false positive rate. Since not all systems have the same probability of being attacked, the intrusion detection capability index provides a more accurate measure than the hit rate and the false positive rate. Moreover, evaluating an IDS using H and F is ambiguous, as it must be defined an optimal trade-off between the two measures. As the C_{ID} considers the two measures along with the prevalence of attacks, it can be used as a single scalar measure to evaluate the IDS (the higher the C_{ID} is, the better the IDS is).

$$
\begin{aligned}
C_{ID} = &-BH \log \frac{BH}{BH + HF} - \\
&- B(1 - H) \log \frac{B(1 - H)}{B(1 - H) + (1 - B)(1 - F)} - \\
&- (1 - B)(1 - F) \log \frac{(1 - B)(1 - F)}{(1 - B)(1 - F) + B(1 - H)} - \\
&- (1 - B)F \log \frac{(1 - B)F}{(1 - B)F + BH}
\end{aligned}
\tag{3}
$$

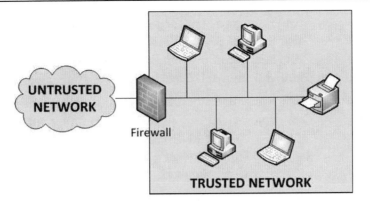

Figure 3. Basic firewall scenario

2.2. Firewall

A firewall is a security component (hardware and/or software) designed to restrict the access between a trusted and an untrusted network (see Figure 3). Note that the term *trusted network* can refer from a single device (e.g., a personal computer) to a complex set of heterogeneous devices (e.g., a company's LAN). As for the term *untrusted network*, it can refer to any type of network; however, it usually refers to the Internet.

The main functions of a firewall are to examine all the packets moving between the trusted and the untrusted network, and to discard all the packets that are not accepted regarding the firewall's security policy. A firewall's security policy consists of a set of filtering rules in which each rule indicates the properties (e.g., source IP address) that packets must have in order to be discarded or accepted. For instance, a typical filtering rule used to prevent the employees of a company from connecting to a particular site is to define a rule indicating that any outgoing packet (a packet going from the trusted to the untrusted network) with a destination IP address equal to the site's IP address must be discarded.

Firewalls can be classified regarding different characteristics:

1. Regarding the type of analysis performed so as to decide whether a packet is discarded or not, firewalls can be classified as follows [4]:

   (a) Static packet filters: in these types of firewalls, the decision of discarding a packet depends only on the value of five of its header fields, namely the source and destination IP addresses, the source and destination port numbers, and the type of transport layer protocol. Consequently, the filtering rules specified in the firewall's security policy use these five header fields to determine which traffic is allowed and which traffic is denied.

   (b) Dynamic packet filters: these types of firewalls are an extension of the static packet filters. They perform the same operations as their predecessors but taking into account connection streams (a connection stream is the set of all the packets with the same source and destination IP addresses, source and destination port numbers, and transport layer protocol). In particular, these firewalls maintain a table of allowed connection streams and use it to check if a particular packet belongs to an existing connection stream. If it does, no further analysis is performed and the packet is allowed to traverse the firewall. If it does not, the packet is analysed according to the firewall's filtering rules and in case the packet is allowed, the table of connection streams is updated.

(c) Connection filters: these firewalls are an extension of the dynamic packet filters. Apart from the operations that any dynamic packet filter would do, they verify that each TCP packet belongs to a valid TCP connection. In order to do that, they check three fields in the packet's TCP header, namely the SYN and the ACK flags, and the sequence number.

(d) Application filters: these firewalls extend the functionality of connection filters. In addition to the operations that their predecessors perform, these firewalls analyse the various fields contained in each packet's application header. For instance, an application filter can be configured to discard all the packets not complying with the HTTP protocol. The problem of these types of firewalls is that they have to manage information regarding different application-layer protocols and therefore, the time and resources consumed in the detection process may be so high that it may result inefficient.

2. Regarding the type of trusted networks that firewalls protect, they can be classified as follows:

(a) First-generation firewalls: traditional firewalls, which are usually deployed as dedicated devices, are in charge of protecting networks from unwanted communication activities.

(b) Web application firewalls (WAFs): a WAF is an enhanced application filter in which the trusted network contains a web server. Apart from the typical operations that any application filter would do, these types of firewalls are specialised in the HTTP protocol and therefore, they analyse the payload of each packet's application layer. With such an enhancement, a WAF can discard, for example, HTTP packets containing harmful HTML code.

(c) Personal firewalls: a personal firewall is a software components that is executed inside a personal computer so as to protect it from harmful communications.

3. Regarding the proxy capabilities of firewalls, they can be classified as follows:

(a) Without proxy capabilities: in these types of firewalls, the packets passing all the firewall's filtering rules are directly sent to their destinations.

(b) With proxy capabilities: in these types of firewalls, the packets passing all the firewall's filtering rules are dropped and new packets with the same intentions are constructed and sent instead.

Depending on the security level that a firewall is meant to provide, firewalls can be deployed in different architectures [5]. Following, the three most usual firewall architectures are described (see Figure 4):

1. Dual-homed host: in this type of architecture, the firewall is deployed inside a dual-homed host, a computer directly connected to the firewall's trusted and untrusted networks. While the dual-homed host offers services to hosts in both networks, the firewall blocks all the IP traffic going from one network to the other one. In case two hosts in different networks were to communicate, the firewall should be provided with proxy capabilities.

2. Screened host: in this type of architecture, the firewall resides in a router that connects the firewall's untrusted network with one particular host in the trusted network, known as the bastion host. In this way, all the traffic between the trusted and the untrusted network must go through two physically separated barriers, the firewall router and the bastion host. For most purposes, this type of architecture provides better security and usability than dual-homed architectures.

3. Screened subnet: in this type of architecture, the firewall functionality is divided into two routers placed in between the firewall's trusted and untrusted networks. The network formed by these routers is called perimeter network and is used as an extra layer of security, holding and isolating the bastion host. Thanks to this isolation, if an attacker evades the firewall router connected to the untrusted network and compromises the bastion host, the access to the trusted network is limited as there is another firewall router in between the bastion host and the trusted network.

As far as the evaluation of firewalls is concerned, the most widely used technique is penetration testing. Penetration testing evaluates the security of a system (in our case, a firewall) by simulating a series of attacks and analysing their effects. In the literature, some methodologies for firewall penetration testing have been proposed [6, 7]. However, the efficacy of penetration testing is rather limited in the firewall domain, as the attacks included in the testing process are usually very general and do not take into consideration the security requirements of the specific firewall being tested. Other type of techniques in which such requirements are considered are also available in the literature [8, 9]. The idea behind such techniques is to construct a formal model of the firewall security policy and verify its correctness using some mechanical approach, such as for example, a CASE tool [8].

3. Evasion of IDSs

In this section, a series of relevant works published in the field of IDS evasion are presented. For clarity purposes, the works are organized chronologically and following the first IDS classification presented in Section 2.1 (Network IDSs and Host IDSs).

3.1. Evasion of Network IDSs

Four different approaches aimed to evade Network IDSs (NIDSs) are presented following. Note that although the objective of all of the approaches is the same, the techniques that they use are not the same, as they try to exploit different parts of the complex architecture of a NIDS.

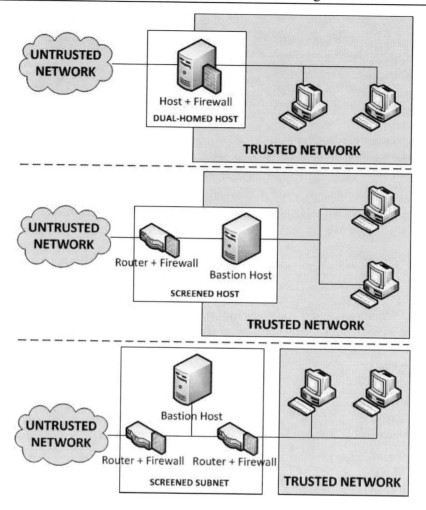

Figure 4. The three most usual firewall architectures

3.1.1.   Ptacek and Newsham 1998

In 1998, Ptacek and Newsham proposed the first methods to evade IDSs, particularly NIDSs [10]. In their seminal paper, the authors highlighted that the ambiguities in the IP and TCP protocols, and the implementation problems present in many NIDS could lead different end systems to interpret the same traffic flow differently. In particular, the authors detected two types of situations in which the data flow processed by the NIDS was different from the one processed by the endpoint:

- Packet insertion: this situation occurs when the preprocessor of the IDS accepts a packet that the preprocessor of the endpoint does not (see Figure 5).

- Packet evasion: this situation occurs when the preprocessor of the IDS drops a packet that the preprocessor of the endpoint accepts.

The main packet characteristics that, according to [10], are prone to be exploited to succeed in evading NIDSs are presented following:

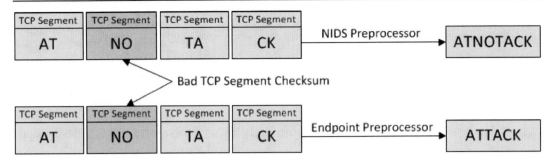

Figure 5. Example of packet insertion

- IP and TCP headers: an attacker can tamper with the IP and TCP headers of packets or make use of the ambiguity of IP and TCP options in order to achieve packet insertions and evasions. A typical example of IP header field that can be used for packet insertion is the TTL (Time To Live) field. Every time an IP packet is forwarded by an intermediate router or hop, the value of its TTL is decreased. Since IP implementations discard packets with a TTL value equal to or lower than 0, if an attacker knows the network architecture (i.e., the location of the NIDS and the location of the victim host), it can set a TTL value big enough to reach the NIDS but small enough not to reach the endpoint. An example of TCP header field which can also lead to packet insertion is the checksum field. A bad checksum value causes the packet to be dropped in most endpoint implementations; however, due to flaws in NIDS implementations, some of them do not verify the correctness of the checksum value. As shown in Figure 5, such a lack of verification enables an invalid packet to reach and deceive the detection engine of a NIDS. In the particular case presented in Figure 5, if the NIDS is signature-based and it is looking for the pattern "ATTACK" to generate an alarm, the insertion of an invalid packet with the payload "NO" prevents the detection engine from generating the alarm, which is obviously a security problem taking into account that the payload arriving at the endpoint is actually "ATTACK".

- TCP connections: maintaining information about open connections is crucial for a NIDS to properly handle packets (e.g., to reassemble IP fragments). Knowing when to record a particular connection state is essential to avoid memory overloads and consequently, DoS (Denial of Service) attacks. However, if the state of a connection is not properly tracked, problems like packet desynchronization can occur (e.g., setting the SYN flag in packets belonging to an already established connection). Another problem that NIDSs have to face is to determine when to stop recording the state of a connection. Normally, the end of a connection is triggered by an RST or FIN packet. However, an attacker may decide not to send such a packet in order to force a connection to remain open forever. An attacker may also manipulate an RST or FIN packet so that it arrives at the NIDS but not at the endpoint, causing the connection to be closed in the NIDS but remain open forever in the endpoint.

- Packet fragmentation, reassembly and overlapping: since IP packets can be fragmented and they can arrive at the destination out of order and duplicated, NIDSs should reorder, reassemble and handle duplicate packets before processing them. Due to efficiency reasons, some NIDSs do not perform any of these operations and therefore, they are vulnerable to multiple types of attacks. Another typical problem arises when the last packet of an IP message (such a packet has the MF (More Fragments) flag unset) never arrives at the NIDS, which is bound to cause a memory flooding unless some special mechanism is implemented. Other more complex problems are related to the need of NIDS to mimic the behaviour of an endpoint. If the NIDS receives a packet with the same sequence number of a previous one, it must know which the policy of the endpoint is in order to substitute the previous or drop the new one. Regarding TCP, a more complicated problem occurs with the window size value, as it have to accept the same size that the endpoint does.

In order to defend NIDS against these evasive methods, several techniques have been proposed so far. Most of these techniques are based on the idea of modifying the traffic arriving at the NIDS so that it fulfils some specific format. In 2000, Handley et al. introduced the concept of traffic normalizers [11]. A traffic normalizer is a tool in charge of removing the possible ambiguities in the traffic arriving at the NIDS. Since some of the evasive techniques are based on packet fragmentation and reassembly, the state of each connection together with some meta-data must be stored and processed by the normalizer. In 2008, Vutukuru et al. proposed a more efficient normalizer using packet hashes and connection tables to provide an overview of the unacknowledged and out-of-order packets in each connection [12]. In 2004, Watson et. al proposed a system for generating well-formed TCP data from any TCP traffic [13]. The goal of such a system was to ensure that NIDSs and endpoints interpreted TCP traffic in the exact same way. The system was based on state machines, which were used to indicate the states that any TCP connection had to step in, modifying or dropping the packets that did not follow a valid state sequence.

Some other solutions that do not modify the traffic arriving at the NIDS have also been proposed. In 2002, Shankar and Paxon proposed a system in charge of informing the NIDS about the network topology and the interpretation policy of the endpoint being monitored [14]. With such information, the NIDS could adapt its configuration so as to mimic the behaviour of the endpoint. For example, Snort [1] adopts this technique in its IP processor (frag3). In 2006, Varguese et al. presented the idea of dividing an entire signature of the NIDS into single smaller pieces [15]. A fast path finds matches with any of these pieces, and if it detects any match of them with the packet being analysed, a slower path inspects it deeper. Finally, In 2009, Antichi et al. proposed the use of Bloom Filters [16] to perform signature matching over a set of unassembled packets [17]. This technique improves the efficiency of NIDSs and allows all intrusions to be detected. However, the number of false positives is also very large.

3.1.2. Vigna et al. 2004

In 2004, Vigna et al. presented a method to evaluate the response of different signature-based NIDSs against evasion attacks [18]. The authors proposed an automated mechanism to generate variations of a given exploit by applying mutant operators to a predefined exploit template. As the modifications could provoke the exploit to become ineffective, they proposed the use of a system (an oracle, according to the authors) to monitor the quality of the exploit.

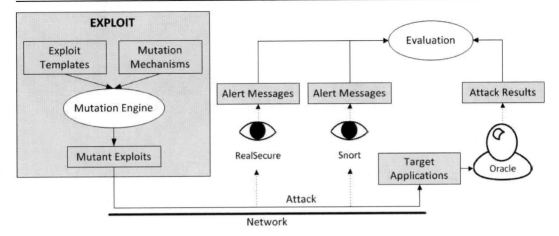

Figure 6. Framework designed to mutate exploits capable of evading Snort and RealSecure

The authors built a framework that, given a series of mutation mechanisms and a set of exploit templates, combined both sets to deterministically generate a set of mutant exploits. Then, these mutant exploits were analysed by the external oracle in order to verify that the changes were valid (such a verification was made by checking that the application of the exploits to the target applications were successful). Finally, the mutant exploits were presented to the analysed NIDSs, Snort and RealSecure, where it was verified whether the mutant exploits could actually evade the detection or not. Figure 6 shows the schema of the proposed framework.

It is important to remark that the set of mutations mechanisms included, amongst others, the mechanisms presented by Ptacek and Newsham in 1998 (see Section 3.1.1): packet fragmentation, protocol flow modifications, etc. They also used polymorphic shellcode and alternate encodings to directly modify the semantics of the exploits.

As for the results, they were quite promising, as 6 out of 10 exploits were evaded in Snort and 9 out of 10 were evaded in RealSecure.

3.1.3.   Fogla et al. 2006

The main characteristic of a worm is the self-replicating capability among different victims. In particular, a polymorphic worm changes its appearance every time it is instantiated. These types of worms can effectively evade the detection of signature-based NIDS, as it is not feasible for a NIDS to manage all the different signatures of all the possible instances of a worm. However, polymorphic worms are not classed as normal behaviour and therefore, they cannot evade anomaly-based NIDS. In 2006, Fogla et al. [19] extended the idea of polymorphic worms and proposed the use of Polymorphic Blending Attacks (PBAs), a technique that allows changing a worm so that it can blend in with the normal behaviour of a network.

A PBA is composed of three parts: the attack vector, used to exploit the desired vulnerability in the target host; the attack body, encrypted with some simple reversible substitution algorithm; and the polymorphic decryptor, in charge of decrypting the malicious code and transferring the control to it. The main steps involved in the generation of a PBA are de-

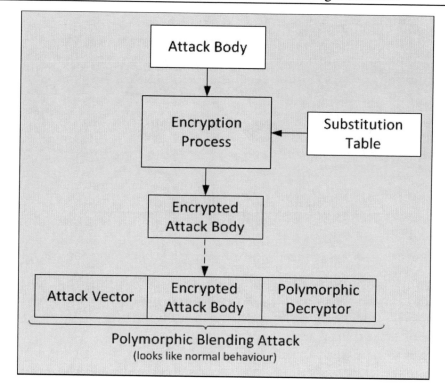

Figure 7. Generation of a Polymorphic Blending Attack (PBA)

scribed following (see Figure 7):

1. Learning the normal profile of the NIDS: the authors assume that the attacker has complete knowledge of the anomaly-based NIDS to be evaded. With such knowledge, the adversary can use the NIDS learning algorithm and a set of normal traffic in order to construct a statistical normal profile similar to the one used by the NIDS.

2. Encrypting the attack body: in order to generate polymorphic instances of an attack vector, the attack body (i.e., the malicious code) is encrypted using a simple reversible substitution algorithm, where each character in the attack body is substituted according to a particular substitution table. The objective of such a substitution is to masquerade the attack body as normal behaviour, guaranteeing that the statistical properties specified in the normal profile are satisfied (note that finding an optimal substitution table is a very complex task, according to [20]).

3. Generating the polymorphic decryptor: when the PBA reaches the victim host, the attack body must be decrypted and executed. In order to do that, a polymorphic decryptor is required. Such a decryptor consists of three parts: the code implementing the decryption algorithm, the substitution table necessary to perform the decryption process and the code in charge of transferring the control to the attack body.

In [20], the authors extended their work and proposed a formal framework to automatically generate PBAs against any statistical anomaly-based NIDS. They stated (and proved) that such NIDSs could be represented as a Finite State Automata (FSA), either deterministic (FSA) or stochastic (sFSA). As a consequence, the problem of finding a PBA for a NIDS became equivalent to finding a PBA for an sFSA. However, finding such a PBA was, as proved by the authors, an NP-complete problem. For this reason, they proposed a method to reduce the NP-complete problem to either a satisfiability (SAT) problem (if the NIDS had been represented as a FSA) or Integer Linear Programming (ILP) problem (if the NIDS had been represented as a sFSA), two types of problems for which polynomial-time algorithms already existed.

3.1.4.   Pastrana et al. 2011

In [21], we presented a new approach to look for flaws and weaknesses in NIDS. As the behaviour of a NIDS is usually very complex (even obscure if its source code is proprietary), our approach tries to model it by means of Genetic Programming (GP). GP is a paradigm that evolves programs (also known as individuals) represented by trees, where intermediate nodes are functions and leafs are terminals. The evolution is performed by crossing and mutating the best individuals of the current population and repeating the process until a certain condition is held.

In the case at stake, the result of the GP evolution is a simple model that behave as similarly as possible to the original NIDS. Since the resulting model is simpler that the original NIDS, it can be used to finding evasions that otherwise would be very difficult to find. In the paper, evasions are performed over a NIDS built specifically for that purpose. Following, an overall description of the methodology used is presented (see Figure 8):

1. A controlled network infrastructure is used to generate system traces, both normal and abnormal ("1" in Figure 8).

2. Raw traffic along with its respective output are combined and processed in order to generate labelled traces that represent the relationships between the inputs and the outputs of the NIDS and therefore, its behaviour. These traces are exposed to data mining procedures in order to extract and select the most relevant features to model the NIDS by means of GP.

3. The labelled traces are inputted to GP so as to generate the models that will classify the network traffic very similarly to the original NIDS. In order to optimize the process, some GP parameters must be correctly defined, namely the mutation and crossover rates, the selection method and the most important one, the fitness function, in charge of deciding which of two individuals is better ("2" in Figure 8).

4. The resulting GP models are used to look for evasions. The way in which this search is performed is not defined. In future works, we will try to automatize the process ("3" in Figure 8).

5. If an evasion over the models is found, it is then tried over the original NIDS, evaluating so if it actually succeeds ("4" in Figure 8).

The main advantage of this methodology is that it can be adapted to any IDS. The only requirement that the IDS must fulfil is having the relationships between its inputs and its

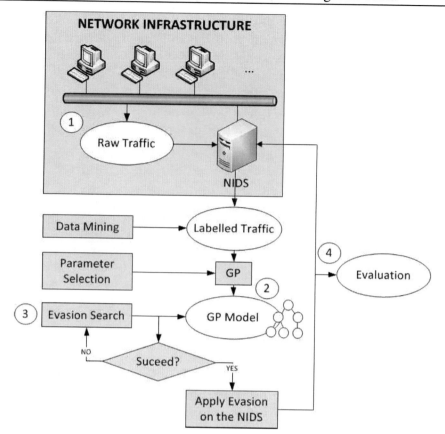

Figure 8. Methodology using Genetic Programming (GP) to search for vulnerabilities in NIDSs

outputs. Note that it is possible to use more than one technique (different from GP) to generate the models.

The paper also presents a proof of concept of the methodology. It uses a simple NIDS built specifically for that purpose and the dataset LBNL[1], which contains both normal traces and traces corresponding to a port scanning attack. Before using the methodology, the NIDS was able to detect most of the port scanning traces, but after using it, we succeeded in evading detection.

3.2. Evasion of Host IDS

Since Host IDSs (HIDSs) look for intrusions inside computer hosts, the evasion techniques applied to them are mainly focused on modifying system calls, memory registers, the stack, etc. The first evasion technique for HIDSs appeared in 2002 and since then, an important evolution process has occurred. Following, four relevant works illustrating such a process are presented.

---

[1]http://www.icir.org/enterprise-tracing/

3.2.1.   Tan et al. 2002

In 2002, Tan et al. presented a novel idea to evade anomaly-based HIDS that do not take into account the arguments of system calls [22]. In particular, they showed how to evade the Stide HIDS [23].

The authors realized that Stide looked for anomalies using a detection window size, i.e., it only detected anomalies if the number of involved system calls was smaller than the window size. For the sake of illustration, the paper presented two attacks against two Linux programs, namely *passwd* and *traceroute*. First of all, the authors showed how Stide detected the attacks when they were executed in a victim host. Then, they explained how to modify the attacks so as to evade detection. Finally, they executed the attacks again and verified that they actually bypassed detection.

Since Stide uses a detection window size, if the attacks are modified so that the abnormal sequence of system calls is larger that the window size, the attacks may succeed and still remain undetected. For instance, in the case of the attack against the *passwd* program, the original attack was to execute the sequence of system calls *setuid-setgid*. The authors realized that the same attack could be accomplished with the sequence *chmod-exit*, whose length is the same. However, as Stide's database of normal behaviour contained the sequence *chmod-utime-close-munmap*, there was a chance to combine such a sequence with the one of the attack (i.e., *chmod-exit*) and succeed with the attack. In particular, the authors realized that Stide did not take into account the argument of system calls and thus, they tried their attack with the sequence *chmod-utime-close-munmap-exit*, making sure that the arguments of the *munmap* call were tuned in such a way that the state of the system was not modified. With such a sequence, if Stide used a detection window size of two, no alarms would be generated as no malicious sequence is equal to or smaller than two.

Finally, the authors proposed to automatically look for all the allowed sequences that, if correctly tuned, do nothing to the system and make malicious sequences larger. They presented some experiments to automatically generate such sequences and exposed how they were inserted into malicious sequences of system calls traces without disrupting the wicked intention.

3.2.2.   Wagner et al. 2002

In 2002, Wagner et al. presented six different ways to evade anomaly-based HIDSs [24] (note that they did not tackle evading signature-based IDSs because they considered such a task a "child's play"). Before describing the six ways to evade anomaly-based HIDSs, two assumptions need to be established:

1. The behaviour of the HIDS is known by the attacker, including the database of normal behaviours. This assumption is straightforward in the case of open source IDS, as one can use the public training algorithm with real data in order to obtain the model of normal behaviour. In the case of proprietary systems, some reverse engineering approach may be used (e.g., the one explained in Section 3.1.4).

2. The attacker can gain the control of an application without being detected. This can be due to flaws in the implementation or by forcing the application to generate wrong results.

Once the assumptions were established, the authors described the six methods to evade detection:

1. Slip under the radar: as anomaly-based IDSs look for intrusion evidences by examining system call sequences, the authors state that an attack can remain undetected if no system calls are made. This type of attack can be achieved by forcing an application to compute incorrect results. However, the damage that such an attack can cause is quite limited.

2. Be patient: the authors stated the limitation that at some point in time a HIDS may accept a malicious sequence of system calls, an attacker can wait this time to launch her attack. However, this scenario poses an important problem: after the malicious sequence is executed, the returned address of the application will produce abnormal trace and thus, an alarm may be generated. To solve such a problem, the authors propose to make the application crash, pretending the abnormal trace to be a bug rather than an attack.

3. Be patient, but make your own luck: this method is an improvement of the previous one. In it, the attacker replaces the entire application with a clone manipulated in such a way that the returned address produces no abnormal trace.

4. Replace system call parameters: changing the parameters of a valid system call may allow an attack to be executed undetected. This situation happened because most of the HIDS in 2002 did not examine these parameters when searching for anomalies.

5. Insert no-ops: the idea behind this method is the same as the one explained in Section 3.2.1. Since some HIDSs take into account the length of anomalous sequences to generate an alarm, detection may be evaded if operations without an action in the system are inserted in the sequences.

6. Generate equivalent attacks: generating variations of a particular attack (e.g., by reordering the system calls or replacing some of them with equivalent ones) may help the attack to bypass detection.

3.2.3. Kruegel et al. 2005

In 2005, anomaly-based HIDSs were improved in such a way that they no longer examined only the sequence of system calls of a program, but also additional information such as the values stored in the stack, the origin of the system calls, the information about the call stack, etc.

In [25], Kruegel et al. showed that if a legitimate program containing malicious code is able to modify some memory segments, it can manage to control the flow of the program and execute pieces of the malicious code at memory locations where detection can be evaded. In particular, the authors claimed that such an operation can be achieved by directly modifying the register, the stack and the heap areas. In order for an attacker to be able to launch the aforementioned attack, she must first find a vulnerability in the code of the program to be infected (e.g., using symbolic execution) and then, find a sequence of system calls that can be executed in the program without raising suspicion. In their research,

Kruegel et al. focused on the Intel X86 architecture and managed to infect a vulnerable program written in C as well to bypass the detection of two different HIDSs.

To conclude, it is important to remark that the technique proposed by Kruegel et al. was innovative because no previous work had previously proposed to analyse and modify binary code so as to evade detection.

3.2.4. Kayacik et al. 2011

In 2011, Kayacik et al. proposed a method to generate exploit mutations with which to evade any anomaly-based HIDS capable of outputting anomaly and delay rates [26]. In order to generate such mutations, Genetic Programming (GP) was used (see Section 3.1.4 for more information about GP). GP individuals were represented by ordered sets of system calls with their arguments (if any) and evolved according to a fitness function with three objectives: increasing the attack success, minimizing the anomaly rate and minimizing the delay.

In order to evaluate the attack success, they studied an attack composed of a sequence of 3 defined system calls and arguments. Concretely, as they wanted to add a new user with root privileges, this sequence was:

1. open('/etc/passwd')

2. write('toor::0:0:root:/root:/bin/bash')

3. close('/etc/passwd')

If this sequence was found in the set of system calls of the individual, its fitness was increased.

In their experiments, the authors selected four vulnerable applications, ran them under normal circumstances, recorded their system calls, selected the twenty most frequent ones and inputted them to the GP algorithm. As for the anomaly and delay rates used in the experiments, they were generated by five different IDSs: the Stide HIDS, the Process Homeostasis (PH), the Process Homeostasis with schema mask (PHsm), a Markov model-based detector and an auto-associative neural network. They compared two approaches, a "black-box" approach, where the attacker only knows the outputs that the IDS produces from a particular set of inputs, and a "white-box" approach, where the attacker has knowledge of the internal behaviour of the IDS. The results of such a comparison show that, although using the white-box approach produces lower anomaly-score, the black-box technique may achieve similar rates if the exploit length is increased, even being a more difficult problem. Therefore, they concluded that in certain cases no internal knowledge of an IDS is necessary to evade it. A complementary study made in this work was to determine the effectiveness of the approach when generating exploit mutations for a particular IDS and using the resulting mutations in another IDS. This could be the case where an attacker possesses a IDS but wants to evade another one.

4.   Evasion of Firewalls

Nowadays, the only general mechanism to attain firewall evasion is tunneling, a technique that allows encapsulating one protocol into another. By means of tunneling, an adversary can bypass a firewall and execute a protocol that the firewall blocks (e.g., the BitTorrent protocol) by wrapping it into a protocol that the firewall accepts (e.g., the HTTP protocol). In order for the firewall to detect such an evasion, it must analyze the payload of the application layer and make sure that its data corresponds to regular data of the specified protocol. Since such an analysis is time-consuming, many firewalls fail to perform it and thus, tunneling becomes an effective mechanism to evade firewalls.

Apart from tunneling, the only way to currently evade a firewall is to find and exploit particular vulnerabilities. Firewall vulnerabilities can be caused by different types of errors, being the most common those listed following [27]:

1. Validation error: this error happens when environmental data (e.g., a source IP address) is used without verifying its correctness.

2. Authorization error: this error occurs when a protected operation is invoked without properly verifying the authority of the invoker.

3. Serialization error: this error happens when system operations with asynchronous behaviours permit an adversary to attack the protected system.

4. Aliasing error: this error occurs when an object that has been already validated is modified unexpectedly and hence, its state can no longer be assumed correct.

5. Boundary checking error: this error happens when some boundary or constraint in the firewall (e.g., the maximum size of a buffer) is not checked.

6. Domain error: this error occurs when there exists a security hole that permits information leakage between two protection environments.

7. Design error: this error happens when the origin of a firewall's vulnerability can be traced back to the design phase of the firewall.

Depending on the vulnerabilities that a particular firewall has, an attacker may achieve different types of effects, being the most common ones summarized next:

1. Execution of code: illegitimate code is executed in the firewall or in some device in the protected network.

2. Change of target resource: some resource in the firewall (e.g., a filtering rule table) or in the protected network (e.g., a host) is illegitimately modified.

3. Access to target resource: an attacker gains illegitimate access to some resource in the firewall or in the protected network.

4. Denial of service: an attacker disrupts some service offered by the firewall (e.g., the packet forwarding service) or by some device in the protected network (e.g., an FTP service).

For the sake of illustration, three vulnerabilities found repeatedly in multiple firewalls are briefly described following (note that each of the three vulnerabilities results in an illegitimate access to some resource in the firewall or in the protected network):

1. Some firewalls fail to discard external packets claiming to come from the internal network. This vulnerability is caused by an origin validation error. For this error to be fixed, firewalls must check the interface through which a packet arrives; otherwise, determining if a packet has a spoofed source IP address becomes impossible.

2. The firewall included in some Windows systems (e.g., Windows 2000 Server) accepts all the incoming traffic targeted at the TCP/UDP port 88 (this port is reserved for Kerberos [28], a security protocol that some Windows systems use to authenticate IPsec sessions). This vulnerability is caused by a design error and its solution requires firewalls not to assume that the traffic passing through well-known ports is legitimate and valid.

3. Some firewalls fail to discard external packets claiming to come from an IANA-reserved or private address (e.g., 127.x.x.x). This vulnerability is also caused by a design error and fixing it requires firewalls not to assume that the IP addresses specified in a packet belong to some specific ranges.

To conclude this section, it is worth to remark that an interesting work describing an attempt to evade the so-called "Great Firewall of China" is presented in [29]. In such a work, the authors try to achieve two goals: gaining access to a Web site blocked by the firewall and provoking a denial of service in the firewall's packet forwarding service.

Conclusion

In this chapter, we have presented and analysed some of the most relevant methods to evade IDSs and firewalls. In the case of IDSs, the analysis shows that since the publication of the first technical report in 1998 showing how to evade NIDSs, there has been a worrying evolution of the techniques and methods aimed to evade these systems. For instance, nowadays attackers can use sophisticated artificial intelligence techniques along with high performance systems to evade detection.

In the case of firewalls, the analysis shows that there exists no general methodology to bypass the different types of firewalls. Despite that, we have presented the most common vulnerabilities that an attacker can exploit so as to evade a firewall. Furthermore, by way of illustration, we have introduced a few real vulnerabilities that can be found in some state-of-the-art firewalls.

It is clear that as technology and security barriers become more complex and sophisticated, the knowledge and techniques used to find security vulnerabilities to bypass detection evolve. Consequently, in line with the improvement of security countermeasures, and in order to have advantage over attackers, it is essential to explore and analyse the different mechanisms that allow these barriers to be evaded. In the particular case of SIEMs, due to its great complexity and heterogeneous architecture, it is crucial to secure each of the countermeasures taking part in the detection process.

Acknowledgments

This work has been partially funded by the Regional Government of Madrid, Spain, under the project EVADIR: A Methodology for Evasion Attacks on Network Intrusion Detection Systems.

References

[1] Martin Roesch. Snort: Lightweight intrusion detection for networks. In Proceedings of the 13th Systems Administration Conference, pages 229–238, Seattle, WA, USA, November 1999. USENIX.

[2] Suhair Hafez Amer and John A. Hamilton. Intrusion detection systems (ids) taxonomy - a short review. *Journal of Software Technology*, 13, 2010.

[3] Guofei Gu, Prahlad Fogla, David Dagon, Wenke Lee, and Boris Skorić. Measuring intrusion detection capability: an information-theoretic approach. In Proceedings of the 2006 ACM Symposium on Information, computer and communications security, pages 90–101, Taipei,Taiwan, March 2006. ACM.

[4] Dhiraj Bhagchandka. Classification of firewalls and proxies. Technical report, University of Texas, Department of Computer Science, Texas, USA, 2003.

[5] Milton Abramowitz and Irene A. Stegun. Firewall design. In Deborah Russel, editor, Building Internet Firewalls. O'Reilly and Associates, Inc., San Francisco, CA, USA, 1995.

[6] Philip R. Moyer and E.Eugene Schultz". A systematic methodology for firewall penetration testing. *Network Security*, 1996(3):11–18, 1996.

[7] Reto E. Haeni. Firewall penetration testing. Technical report, The George Washington University Cyberspace Policy Institute, Washington, DC, USA, 1997.

[8] Jan Jürjens and Guido Wimmel. Specification-based testing of firewalls. In Perspectives of System Informatics, volume 2244 of *Lecture Notes in Computer Science*, pages 308–316. Springer, Novosibirsk, Russia, 2001.

[9] Diana Senn, David Basin, and Germano Caronni. Firewall conformance testing. In Testing of Communicating Systems, volume 3502 of *Lecture Notes in Computer Science*, pages 348–348. Springer, Montreal, Canada, 2005.

[10] Thomas H. Ptacek and Timothy N. Newsham. Insertion, evasion, and denial of service: Eluding network intrusion detection. Technical report, Secure Networks, Inc., Syracuse, NY, USA, 1998.

[11] M. Handley, C. Kreibich, and V. Paxson. Network intrusion detection: Evasion, traffic normalization and end-to-end protocol semantics. In USENIX Security Symposium, pages 115–131, Denver, Colorado, USA, August 2000. USENIX.

[12] Mythili Vutukuru, Hari Balakrishnan, and Vern Paxson. Efficient and robust tcp stream normalization. In IEEE Symposium on Security and Privacy, pages 96–110, Oakland, California, USA, May 2008. IEEE.

[13] David Watson, Matthew Smart, Robert G. Malan, and Farnam Jahanian. Protocol scrubbing: network security through transparent flow modification. *IEEE/ACM Transactions on Networking*, 12(2):261–273, 2004.

[14] Umesh Shankar. Active mapping: Resisting nids evasion without altering traffic. In *Security and Privacy*, pages 44–61, Oakland, California, USA, may 2003. IEEE.

[15] George Varghese, J. Andrew Fingerhut, and Flavio Bonomi. Detecting evasion attacks at high speeds without reassembly. In Proceedings of the 2006 conference on Applications, technologies, architectures, and protocols for computer communications, pages 327–338, Pisa, Italy, September 2006. ACM.

[16] Burton H. Bloom. Space/time trade-offs in hash coding with allowable errors. *Communications of the ACM*, 13(7):422–426, July 1970.

[17] Gianni Antichi, Domenico Ficara, Stefano Giordano, Gregorio Procissi, and Fabio Vitucci. Counting bloom filters for pattern matching and anti- evasion at the wire speed. *IEEE Network: The Magazine of Global Internetworking*, 23:30–35, 2009.

[18] Giovanni Vigna, William Robertson, and Davide Balzarotti. Testing network-based intrusion detection signatures using mutant exploits. In Proceedings of the 11th ACM Conference on Computer and Communications Security, page 21, Washington, DC, USA, October 2004. ACM.

[19] Prahlad Fogla, Monirul Sharif, Roberto Perdisci, Oleg Kolesnikov, and Wenke Lee. Polymorphic blending attacks. In Proceedings of the 15th USENIX Security Symposium, pages 241–256, Vancouver, BC, Canada, August 2006. USENIX.

[20] Prahlad Fogla and Wenke Lee. Evading network anomaly detection systems: Formal reasoning and practical techniques. In Proceedings of the 13th ACM Conference on Computer and Communications Security, pages 59–68, Alexandria, VA, USA, October 2006. ACM.

[21] Sergio Pastrana, Agustin Orfila, and Arturo Ribagorda. A functional framework to evade network ids. In Hawaii International Conference on System Sciences, pages 1–10, Koloa,Hawaii,USA, January 2011. IEEE.

[22] K. Tan, K.S. Killourhy, and R.A. Maxion. Undermining an anomaly-based intrusion detection system using common exploits. In Proceedings of the 5th International Conference on Recent Advances in Intrusion Detection, pages 54–73, Zurich, Switzerland, October 2002. Springer-Verlag.

[23] S. Forrest, S.A. Hofmeyr, A. Somayaji, and T.A. Longstaff. A sense of self for unix processes. In *Proceedings of the IEEE Symposium on Security and Privacy*, pages 120–128, Oakland, CA, USA, May 1996. IEEE.

[24] David Wagner and Paolo Soto. Mimicry attacks on host-based intrusion detection systems. In Proceedings of the 9th ACM Conference on Computer and Communications Security, pages 255–264, Washington, DC, USA, November 2002. ACM.

[25] Christopher Kruegel, Engin Kirda, Darren Mutz, William Robertson, and Giovanni Vigna. Automating mimicry attacks using static binary analysis. In Proceedings of the 14th Conference on USENIX Security Symposium, volume 14, pages 11–11, Baltimore, MD, USA, August 2005. USENIX.

[26] Hilmi Güne Kayacik, a. Nur Zincir-Heywood, and Malcolm I. Heywood. Evolutionary computation as an artificial attacker: Generating evasion attacks for detector vulnerability testing. Evolutionary Intelligence, 4(4):243–266, 2011.

[27] Seny Kamara, Sonia Fahmy, Eugene Schultz, Florian Kerschbaum, and Michael Frantzen. Analysis of vulnerabilities in internet firewalls. *Computers and Security*, 22(3):214–232, 2003.

[28] B.C. Neuman and T. Ts'o. Kerberos: an authentication service for computer networks. *IEEE Communications Magazine*, 32(9):33–38, 1994.

[29] Richard Clayton, Steven J. Murdoch, and Robert N. M. Watson. Ignoring the great firewall of china. In George Danezis and Philippe Golle, editors, Proceedings of the Sixth Workshop on Privacy Enhancing Technologies (PET 2006), pages 20–35, Cambridge, UK, June 2006. Springer.

In: Advances in Security Information Management
Editors: G. Suarez-Tangil and E. Palomar

ISBN: 978-1-62417-204-5
© 2013 Nova Science Publishers, Inc.

Chapter 8

HONEYPOT FORENSICS FOR SYSTEM AND NETWORK SIEM DESIGN

Jeremy Briffaut, Patrice Clemente,[*]
Jean-Francois Lalande[†] *and Jonathan Rouzaud-Cornabas*
Centre-Val de Loire Université,
ENSI de Bourges, LIFO, Bourges, France

Abstract

This chapter presents forensic investigations of cyber attackers' activities on a large scale honeypot and shows how these methodologies can be integrated into an SIEM. The chapter describes our high interaction honeypot and analyzes the illegal activities performed by attackers on the basis of the data collected over two years of attacks: logged sessions, intrusion detection system alerts, mandatory access control system alerts. The empirical study of these illegal activities has allowed us to understand the global motivations of the attackers, their technical skills, the geographical location of the attackers and their targets. A generic method is presented that has enabled us to rebuild the illegal activities using correlation techniques operating on system and network events. Monitoring the network and the operations occurring on each system has provided precise and high level characterization of attacks. Finally, the chapter explains how network and system methods for forensics can be integrated into an SIEM in order to more accurately monitor the security of a pool of hosts.

Keywords: Security Information and Event Management (SIEM), Large Scale Honeypot, Forensic Analysis, Ciber Attacks

1. Introduction

With the increase of networks and the exponential number of connected computers, the risk of cyber attacks has dramatically increased in the last few years. This may eventually lead

---

[*]E-mail address: patrice.clemente@ensi-bourges.fr
[†]E-mail address: jean-francois.lalande@ensi-bourges.fr

to a totally insecure worldwide web network. In addition, anti-viruses and firewalls become all but useless since many viruses, malware programs and attacks appear every day. Security administrators are deploying new sensors and services to monitor cyber attacks, to understand and block them. However, with the growing size of networks, the data returned by these monitoring and security systems have developed from human-readable information to very large databases where millions of alarms and events are stored. Moreover, as data come from heterogeneous sources, alarms related to the same cyber attack are not semantically linked. It is thus very difficult to understand and learn the global steps of attacks when they occur.

Computer science security researchers and companies now face a new security challenge. They have to study and analyze the motives and habits of attackers and cyber criminals in order to be able to set up a global protection response. The collected knowledge can be acquired by manual forensics of a compromised host or on the contrary by using automatic methods to classify and analyze a large number of attack events. That generic knowledge deals with multiple scientific locks, such as activity characterization, heterogeneous data mining (coming from heterogeneous sensors), and combining alerts and reports.

In this chapter, we show how we deal with all these issues, starting from manual collection of the activities of attackers to general classification of these activities and attacks. The activities of cyber attackers were captured using a high-interaction clustered honeypot connected to public IPs on Internet. These welcoming hosts allow the attacker to remotely connect to a real computer and to obtain a remote shell that will let him perform any system command as would a regular user. Using the collected data, we started with a rough analysis of raw data and incrementally reached a fine-grained characterization of attacks. Finally, we present correlation techniques before moving on to the description of their implementation into a new SIEM.

Organization.   Section 2 of this chapter starts with a description of the different types of honeypots and the specificity of our honeypot. Thereafter, the traces collected during the attacks allow a first manual forensic analysis to be produced. This analysis gives a characterization of some attackers' goals and behaviors. Nevertheless, the analysis is hard to generalize and to automate. Section 3 shows how automatic tools can help to correlate attackers' traces of different natures. The results obtained, presented in Section 4, are more precise than those of Section 2. They give a better understanding of the global attackers' profiles. Finally, Section 5 presents the way in which the previous forensic analysis can be integrated into an SIEM and describes the prototype implemented.

2.   Forensic Methodology

To understand the goals of cyber criminals, researchers and security teams use compromised hosts that have been penetrated by attackers. This forensic analysis might give information about the attackers, the way they entered the host and what they did during the time of corruption. Nevertheless, the quantity of information is small, since the host has to be reinstalled to guarantee that it is returned to a safe state. An attacker is no longer able to go back to this host since the way he entered the host has now been secured.

Honeypots are "fake hosts" that overcome this problem: their goal is to welcome attackers and to let them perform illegal activities in order to monitor these. When a honeypot has been deployed for several months, the hosts have to be exploited so as to collect information about the attackers, should this information still be present. The challenge is to collect the maximum amount of information and to be able to conclude what happened. The naive way to proceed is to manually analyze some of the host data: the malware programs brought by attackers, the shell commands they executed and their effect on the host. On large scale honeypots, this work is hard to achieve because each attacker behaves differently for each attack.

2.1. Honeypot-based Collection

2.1.1. High and Low Interaction Honeypots

Two types of honeypots are distinguished in the literature. Low level honeypots emulate a limited part of the services, mainly the network protocols. They allow statistical results to be computed and attack activities to be modeled [Kaaniche et al., 2006]. On the other hand, high-interaction honeypots deploy real operating systems that allow more complete information to be captured.

Honeypots are connected to the Internet by public IP addresses. Low-interaction honeypots merely capture the incoming traffic and emulate responses sent to the attacker [Kaaniche et al., 2006, Leita et al., 2008] whereas high-interaction honeypots send the traffic to the real services, if they exist. The major issue with IP addresses is their availability. With the saturation of the IPv4 ranges of addresses, only large companies or institutions are able to deploy large scale honeypots in the form of hundreds of honeypots hidden in thousands of real hosts. Substantial efforts are made to deploy distributed honeypots based on honeyd [Provos, 2004] or agents redirecting attacks to a central honeypot [Antonatos et al., 2007].

When an attacker has been captured in a high-interaction honeypot, the next challenge is to keep him in the honeypot and to collect information about him. First, the honeypot should behave as would a real production host since attackers can use advanced techniques to determine whether the host is a honeypot [Holz and Raynal, 2005, Innes and Valli, 2005]. If the attacker suspects that he has been captured by an honeypot, he can use some tools [Krawetz, 2004] that helps him to test the host. Then, he can launch attacks against the honeypot like flooding it with false information.

2.1.2. Honeypot Architecture Proposal

The proposed honeypot architecture has been described in detail in [Briffaut et al., 2009]. It proposes a high interaction honeypot where each fake host is installed on a physical machine. To avoid being detected as a honeypot, no virtualized operating systems were used nor any service emulated as is classically the case for low interaction honeypots. Each host was installed with a real operating system and some services. The avoidance of any virtualization environment was intended to help convince the attacker that he had gained access to a production server.

Listing 1: Session of zena

```
zena@debian: w
 17:26:01 up 104 days, 4:30, 2 users, load average: 0.29, 0.39, 0.31
 USER TTY FROM LOGIN@ IDLE JCPU PCPU WHAT
 zena pts/0 X.X.X.X 14:58 0.00s 4.65s 0.11s sshd: zena [priv]

zena@debian: ps aux
 ...
zena@debian: cd /dev/shm
zena@debian: ls -a
total 0
drwxrwxrwt 2 root root 40 mai 4 17:46 .
drwxr-xr-x 14 root root 4,0K mai 27 11:15 ..
```

The global architecture is presented in Figure 1. Four hosts are represented on the figure to show that several Linux distributions were deployed. The distribution marked by "SE" refers to the SELinux mandatory access control mechanism which provides a high security level. Each host was connected to Internet using one public IP. No firewalls were deployed to protect these hosts from the attackers and only a hub replicated the packets that were received to send a copy of these packets to another host that would perform off-line analysis. This architecture enabled the attackers to:

- directly send packets to any port of a single host;

- communicate to any available service of a host;

- potentially exploit any known vulnerabilities on these services;

- send packets from the honeypots to the Internet.

Note that allowing attackers to send packets outside is dangerous. Thus, a honeywall host was added to limit the outgoing network traffic and avoid denial of service attacks emanating from the honeypot.

Moreover, a modified version of SSH servers was installed in order to allow the attackers to remotely connect to the honeypot at random. The attackers obtained a shell account with a home-directory on the host they tried to connect to. For example on the debian host, an attacker that tried to connect with user *zena* using password *zena* would have a probability of 0.01 of being authorized to login the system. If he succeeded, a home-directory */home/zena* would be created on-the-fly giving him a prompt shell. Of course, an attacker may have suspected the host to be honeypot if he had studied how many success he would obtain when trying dictionaries of login/password. Nevertheless, classical tools aiming to brute-force a server stop since the first success. Thus, the success rate is never known.

Listing 1 shows the beginning of the shell session of *zena* that tried four classical commands on the debian honeypot. These sessions were recorded using a large panel of tools: network sensors monitored the network activities; system tools controlled the system calls (which could be allowed or refused); a session replayer (RPLD) recorded all the commands and their outputs. All the data collected were stored outside the local network for further

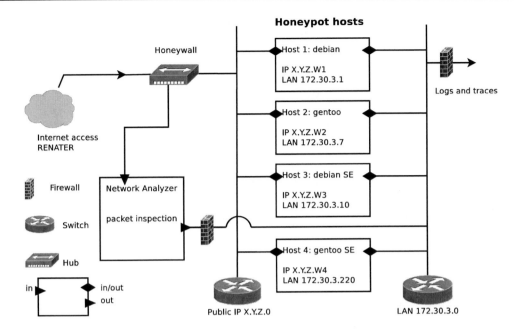

Figure 1. High interaction honeypots architecture

analysis. An attacker may have been able to discover some of the sensors but he should have had the feeling that he had gained access to a very secure server as these tools are classical tools used on production servers.

2.2. Human-supervised Forensics Analysis

2.2.1. Collected Data

The data collected by the different sensors allowed us to compute statistical results about the attackers. Basically, the data collected were: (i) the home-directory of the attacker, (ii) the *.bash_history* file containing all the entered commands, should the file still exist, (iii) the files created or downloaded by the attackers, should they still exist, (iv) the rpld sessions i.e. all the entered commands and their results on *stdout*, (v) the system calls generated by all activities, and (vi) the network packet protocol of all incoming connections.

2.2.2. Overview of Shell Activities

The first basic analysis made was the analysis of the *.bash_history* files. Table 1 shows that a large part of the sessions had empty *.bash_history* files. The main reason is that advanced attackers deleted the history file before leaving the session. Advanced attackers will be discussed later in Section 2.3.3.

Using rpld records, Figure 2 shows that most of the sessions had around 20 commands. The graph omits empty sessions. There were few short sessions and sessions with more than 40 commands. The number of sessions decreased in $\frac{1}{x}$ over time with the departure of

Table 1. Sessions details for each ssh-client

Session type	Number
no history	1627
empty history	7
history < 3 lines	49
history >= 3 lines	173
Sum	1849 / 1856 (total)

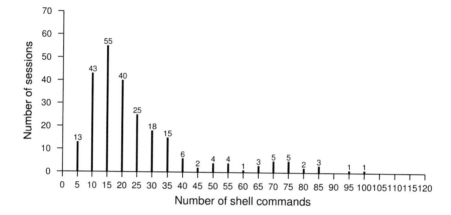

Figure 2. Number of sessions by session size

attackers. Most sessions lasted less than 16 minutes. It is also easy to distinguish automatic sessions (scripts launched by the attacker that have a short time execution, less than one minute) from human sessions.

Statistical results about the most frequent entered shell commands are shown in Table 2. Classical shell commands like *ls* or *cd* appear frequently. Then, the *wget* command indicates that attackers were downloading malware programs in their session. This will be analyzed later. Other classical shell commands indicate that files were being manipulated: *tar, cat, mkdir, mv, nano*. This corresponds to a manipulation of downloaded malware programs. Moreover, others indicate that the attacker was inspecting the host: *ps, cat, id, uname*. Finally, malware programs with classical names were executed: *./start, ./a, ./exploit, ./x*, etc.

2.2.3. Downloaded Malware Programs

We filtered the *wget* commands in the *.bash_history* files in order to study the type of downloaded files. We compared the number of logged downloaded files with the real files on the disk and, if no longer present, we tried to re-download the malware programs. Only a small number of malware programs were able to be re-downloaded, which suggests that the used URLs were only temporarily active.

Table 2. Mostly executed commands

Occurrences	Bash commands
1548	ls
1490	cd
452	wget
200-400	tar cat ps rm perl
100-200	./start ./a passwd mkdir chmod exit nano uname
40-100	ping ./scan mv ftp vi ssh id
10-40	./exploit who pico history ./x ./unix unzip ./v /sbin/ifconfig netstat export uptime info ./muh curl screen ./init ./psynbc ./toto.sh ./s

Table 3. Main types of malware programs (MW)

MW in /home	MW in /tmp	Uncompressed MW from archives (tgz, zip, 7z, …)	Total	Types of MW	MW re-downloads if missing
704	23	3435	4162	ELF 32-bit	150
260	0	389	649	Object file	61
22	0	290	312	Libraries	16
406	1	881	1288	ASCII C program	68
22	3	366	391	ASCII Perl program	10
197	0	366	563	Shell script	37
41	0	177	218	ASCII Pascal program	43
52	0	208	260	C++ program	14
97	3	266	366	Empty file	15
10	0	23	259	Makefile	6

The malware (MW) files are analyzed in Table 3. This is the analysis of all binary executables and source code programs, including a little amount of hidden malwares described later in Table 4. The classification was achieved using the files directly found in home directories but also with the files found in the decompressed archives. A large number of binaries were found, which confirms that attackers download malware programs in order to execute them. Some malware programs were using scripts that launch commands or binaries. Some other files that are not executable were found, mainly text files that were configuration or documentation files provided with the malware programs. The missing files that were re-downloaded have a comparable distribution: we found a lot of binaries, some source codes and a large number of text files.

It is worth noticing in Table 4 that some attackers tried to obfuscate their malware programs by using classical image, text or archive extensions. In this table, a "good" case is a file extension which corresponded to the content of the file. A "bad" case occurs where the extension did not match the content. For example, *jpg* files were mainly gzip files; 7 *tar.gz* files were *tar*, empty or contained other data; 15 *tgz* files were executable binaries or contained other data. Even the half of the *txt* files are archives, binaries, or programs. Nevertheless, most of the malware files presented in Table 3 were not hidden by attackers.

Table 4. Good or bad files containing malware programs

Ext	Total	Good	Bad	.gz	bin	tar	empty	pl	C/C++	others
tar.gz	38	31	7	0	0	2	2	0	0	3
tgz	76	61	15	0	5	0	0	0	0	10
jpg	7	0	7	6	0	0	0	0	0	1
tar	21	5	16	10	6	0	0	0	0	0
txt	121	68	53	0	8	0	8	13	14	10
Total	263	165	98	16	19	2	10	13	14	24

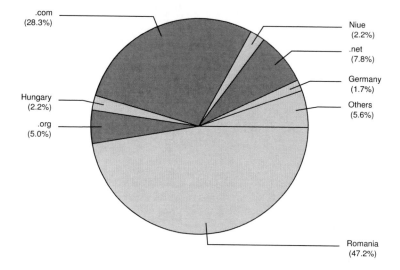

Figure 3. Download countries of malware programs

2.2.4. Geographic Correlation

The study of *.bash_history* files gives information about the possible countries involved in the attack or that provide servers to store malware programs. Figure 3 shows the distribution of URLs involved in a *wget* command. We only used the domain name extension to classify the URLs and did not use geolocalization techniques on IP addresses. Domains like *.com*, *.org*, *.net* hide the origin of the attacks. There could also be international web hosting services. Other countries involved were mainly east-European.

Moreover, the attackers used 27 direct domains (i.e. www.domain.com) and 106 sub-domains (i.e. subdomain.domain.com). The sub-domains were created classically by web hosting providers for their clients. Domains were less frequent because the attackers had to control the domain name and they can be easily identified using the whois databases. This is also observable using TTL requests (Time-To-Live) as opposed to DNS services. TTL requests sends back the amount of time that a domain remains associated with an IP address. We searched the sub-domains and domains TTL that have a small (resp. high) value, less than 10,000s (resp. more than 100,000s). These bounds were chosen arbitrarily

Table 5. Most launched malware programs

Command	Occurrences
./a	117
./start	115
./scan	47
./x	25
./toto.sh	23
./s	22
./unix	20
./psybnc	17
./init	11
./muh	10

as a TTL between 10,000 and 100,000 cannot be safely classified. We obtained 67 URLs that were probably dynamic sub-domains (small TTL), 32 URLs that were domains (high TTL) and 34 URLs that had an unclassifiable TTL.

2.3. Cyber Attackers' Characterization

This subsection gives a basic characterization of the attackers' activities using the analysis of the shell commands entered and investigating the malware programs that were dropped into the home directories (other places where malware programs were dropped are marginal). The first interesting point to investigate is whether the attacker dropped malware files in his home directory. In the absence of a malware program, the session could be said to be an inspection session where the attacker was trying to observe the host he entered to decide what to do next. It is not so difficult to realize that the attacker was inspecting the host but it is almost impossible to guess why the collected information was valuable for him. This inspection could have been extended to the network in order to discover new hosts to attack.

Another characterization is easy to extract from the command line and malware program analysis: we managed to discover the setup of an IRC botnet. A botnet is a distributed network of remotely controlled daemons. An IRC botnet allows the IRC channel owner to remotely control a pool of host [McCarty, 2003]. It is mainly used to launch a denial of service against a targeted server.

2.3.1. Malware Commands Study

Table 5 shows the most frequent commands launched by attackers. This table aggregates the names of commands. There is no guarantee that an attacker launching ./a is executing the same binary as another attacker executing ./a. The similarities between malware programs cannot be analyzed at this level of forensics: this is one of the reasons motivating the correlation of more information on an operating system level, which is performed later in Section 3. Nevertheless, we observe that the attackers tried to hide their activities using neutral binary names (./a, ./x, ./s) but also that some of them directly indicated that they had launched SSH scan (./scan) or IRC bots (./psybnc, ./muh) [McCarty, 2003].

Table 6. Basic classification

Type of session	.bash_history	rpld
Malware	36%	42%
Inspection	9%	17.2%
IRC bot	9%	9%
Local Network Inspection	2.7%	2.7%
Unrecognized sessions	43%	29%

A first classification of attackers' activities has been performed using a simple algorithm that filters the commands found in the *.bash_history* files. This algorithm uses these simple rules:

- If we find *wget*, *tar* and *./* in the same file and in the right order, we consider that it is a malware session.

- If we find at least two of the three commands *cpuinfo*, *ps aux* and *who*, this is considered as an inspection session.

- If we find one of the commands *bot*, *eggdrop*, *bouncer*, or *psybnc*, the session is considered as an IRC bot session.

- If some network commands like *ping*, *netcat*, *telnet* or *ssh* are launched on local IP addresses, the session is considered as a local network inspection session.

Table 6 gives the number of classified sessions and their ratio using the *.bash_history* file or the rpld logs. The inspection sessions were less detected in the bash history (9%) but appeared for about 17% in rpld. This difference suggests that the attackers that inspected our hosts were more human than automatic scripts and that they cleaned the environment before leaving the session, deleting the *.bash_history*. For malware programs and IRC bots this difference was not observed. The last group in this classification is the local network inspection, which is rare and difficult to detect.

2.3.2. Two Case Studio

Finally, we selected the two most frequent scripts used by attackers. We never encountered the same script twice but we manually found two common patterns among all the scripts.

First case study The first pattern corresponds to scans and SSH brute-force attacks. For example, the *pscan2* malware tried to discover IPs that answer on port 22 in order to discover the SSH service. Then, the collected IPs were used by a brute-force malware program that tried to enter these hosts. At the end, the files generated by the first phase of the attack were deleted from the disk, which makes it impossible for a forensic analysis to know what IPs were attacked.

```
echo "*************** PRIVATE SCANNER ! ****************"
echo "*** HACK ATTACKS, ILLEGAL ACTIVITY, SCANS, SPAM. ***"
echo "************ Special pt. Hunter & FLO *************"
echo "
_____"
echo "# incep scanarea frate.."
./pscan2 $1 22

sleep 10
cat $1.pscan.22 |sort |uniq > mfu.txt
oopsnr2=`grep -c . mfu.txt`
echo "# Am gasit $oopsnr2 de servere"
echo "_____"
echo "# Succes frate !"
./ssh-scan 100
rm -rf $1.pscan.22 mfu.txt
echo "Asta a fost tot :)"
```

Second case study   The second script, encountered multiple times, tried to install an IRC bot on the system and to add it to the rc.d scripts to execute automatically at boot time. Moreover, the *rc.sysinit* file was protected in order to guarantee its integrity: the attacker would not be able to add lines at the end of this script in an attempt to hide the IRC bot like the *kswapd* service of the kernel. This type of IRC bots try to join a botnet session in order to launch denial of service attacks.

```
#!/bin/sh
cl=""
cyn=""
wht=""
hcyn=""
echo "${cl}${cyn}|${cl}${hcyn}-- ${cl}${hwht}Installing mech...${cl}${wht}"
./entity-gen >>../install.log
cp -f mech.set /usr/sbin
cp -f mech /usr/sbin/mech
cp -f mech.help /usr/sbin
cp -f host /etc
cp -f kswapd /usr/sbin
echo >>/etc/rc.d/rc.sysinit
echo "Starting kswapd.." >>/etc/rc.d/rc.sysinit
echo "/usr/sbin/kswapd" >>/etc/rc.d/rc.sysinit
echo >>/etc/rc.d/rc.sysinit
/usr/sbin/kswapd
echo "${cl}${cyn}|${cl}${hcyn}-- ${cl}${hwht}Done.${cl}${wht}"
```

2.3.3.   Hidden Activities

As already described, some attackers hide their activities by deleting their *.bash_history* file. We analyzed 93 users logged by rpld. Table 7 shows that 43 sessions had no *.bash_history* file. On these sessions we computed how many times the attacker used the session (each SSH connection creates a rpld log). The first connection was obtained when the SSH brute-force succeeded. Then the attacker connected to our honeypot again to execute malware

Table 7. Rpld Statistics

	Total	Existing .bash_history	No .bash_history
Rpld sessions analyzed	93	50	43
Avg number of connections per user	2.73	2.93	2.56
Avg number of commands	24.6	23	26.5

programs. If some results were generated by the executed malware program, the attacker would probably come back for the third time to recover them. For example, if the malware program was an IRC bot, controlled on an IRC channel, the attacker would just need two connections to setup the bot. That explains the average number of connections of 2.73 on our honeypot. The average is low because the attackers that hid their session by deleting their *.bash_history* files entered more shell commands than the others.

We also observe that attackers used special folders to deploy their malware programs: the attackers used the */dev/shm* folder 19 times, the */var/tmp* folder 74 times, and the */tmp* 64 times. The */dev/shm* folder is a special folder created in the memory and is consequently not persistent if the computer is halted.

This is not the only way for attackers to hide their malware programs. Some of them tried to create special invisible folders that are difficult to detect when inspecting the host. We give an example of one session with the file *jet.tgz*, downloaded in a special sub-folder of */var/tmp*:

```
[xxx@localhost] $ find / | grep jet.tgz
/var/tmp/.. .. /jet.tgz
[xxx@localhost] $
```

Using the folder ".. .." hides it and its content, because folders beginning by a dot are hidden for the *ls* command. Moreover, it is more difficult for a non specialist to enter the folder because one has to type *cd* ".. .." to open the right directory instead of a *cd .. ..* that does not work. Some variants of this kind of directory have been tried by attackers: ".../", "..,", ". /", ".,".

2.3.4.   Discussion

This section has presented the manual forensics of the data collected from the home directories of attackers, the *.bash_history* files, and the *rpld* traces. We obtained a first evaluation of the activities of cyber attackers, geographical information about them and analyzed some scripts they used frequently. This is a mandatory process in our work in order to be able to setup more sophisticated and automatized methods. Manual forensics cannot be employed on large scale computers or distributed honeypot because of the quantity of data. Nevertheless, these investigations helped us to build a correlation methodology presented in the next section of this chapter.

3. Automatic Classification of Attacks

Understanding how attackers behave was an objective that we partially reached in the previous section. However, when dealing with many machines encountering large numbers of attacks, manual forensics become too difficult to apply, especially for the analysis of scripts. Moreover, malware programs are impossible to analyze manually. That is why automated methods are needed. Furthermore, the correlation of multiple sources (IDS, monitoring tools, etc.) remains almost impossible to be performed manually.

In this section, we present how, using self proposed methods or existing tools, we were able to highlight phenomena that were previously not visible, or to statistically confirm or infirm tendencies we obtained through manual analysis. To do this, we used data gathered from particular honeypot hosts having SELinux, in addition to other sensors (e.g. snort). Such SELinux computers log every syscall in accordance to a given policy. Those particular 'SELinux sensors' are a sub-part of the hosts on which we made the analysis of the first section. Thus, some results differ, for example for the geolocalization of sources and targets of attacks. However, it is worth to noting that general trends are the same, in terms of attacker profiles.

In the following, we present the characterization of low level events that occurred during system sessions before moving on to the high level classification of system sessions.

3.1. Characterization of Events

Before explaining the process of characterizing events, it is important to understand what kind of events and alarms are generated by security and monitoring sensors and their differences and interests in the classification of cyber attacks. An event represents an elementary operation on the information system. Those events are divided into two main categories: network and operating system events.

3.1.1. Formatting Events

Events come from heterogeneous sensors, and are not structured in the same way. For example, a pure system event, in most cases, does not contain network information such as an IP address. Sensors can also use different representations for the same information. For example, some sensors encode IP addresses as strings whereas others use integers. To be able to use all the events together, it is critical to structure them using the same format. For this purpose, several frameworks have been developed to provide interfaces to perform a set of preprocessing tasks on each event to fit them to a common format [Ning et al., 2001, Kruegel et al., 2005, Valeur et al., 2004]. This preprocessing task is important in order to optimize event correlation process because even minor changes in the structure of events can greatly improve the performances. For example, changing every IP address from integers to strings reduces the performance of the correlation process because it is more efficient to compare integers than strings.

The IDMEF standard, for example, is a RFC proposal that introduces a common structure to format and store events [Curry and Debar, 2003]. This is used by certain well known sensors (e.g. Snort [Nayyar and Ghorbani, 2006]) and frameworks (e.g. Prelude).

In our work, all sensor logs are formatted to fit the same structure, whenever possible: a *Global ID* in the database, a unique *event* (syscall) *ID*, the *date*, the *source* and *target* SELinux contexts, the *PID* and *PPID* of the event, the *hostname* on which it occurred, *security permissions* and *classes* of the event (only SELinux), the command (*comm*) and its attributes (*name*), the device (*dev*), the inode, the session id (*idsession*), the source and destination IP and ports. Of course, depending on the sensor, some fields may be empty.

3.1.2.   Validation of Events

After formatting each event in the same way, the next step is to validate each event. This validation process checks every field of a formatted event. For example, it checks whether an IP address is in the range 0.0.0.0 to 255.255.255.255. If a piece of information is missing, specialized procedures may try to recover it. For example, if an IP address is missing, it may be possible to recover it from other events in the same network session. In some cases, it is also better to delete a malformed or incorrect event than to keep it because this may lead to false detection and classification that could be used to make inaccurate responses.

3.2.   Correlating Local Attackers' Activity: Building Local Sessions

One of the main aims of establishing attack scenarios and reconstructing cyber attacks is to be able to have a complete view of an attack and not be limited to a single event that describes only a part of it. This is why it is important to have an effective way to reconstruct sessions. We divided the local sessions into two main groups: network sessions and system sessions.

3.2.1.   Network Sessions

Network sessions represent all the events linked to a single session as defined in network communication i.e. all the events linked to a connection on a service from the starting packet (SYN/ACK TCP) to the ending one (UDP packets were not studied). They are easier to harvest because a single sensor can concentrate network logs for thousands of computers. Again, the problem of the amount of data remains. Additionally, in the case of encrypted networks packets (e.g. SSH sessions), investigating network sessions provides poor information.

3.2.2.   System Sessions

System sessions contain all the events linked to a single session as defined previously i.e. all the events linked to a connection to a system from the entry point (the login process, e.g. in SSH sessions) to the disconnection of the user from the system (the logout process, e.g. in SSH sessions). System sessions are harder to harvest because a sensor is required on each computer. Still more difficult and contrary to network sessions, system events do not include a unique number common to all events in a single session. Nevertheless, the data gathered from system sessions gives more precise and decrypted information.

In order to link the events together and identify them with a unique session ID, we propose in [Rouzaud-Cornabas et al., 2009] a methodology to isolate system sessions in the PID tree. Figure 4 shows an example of such a tree. An SSH connection is the beginning

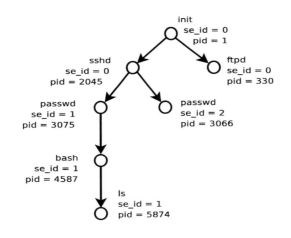

Figure 4. Processus tree

Table 8. SELinux events

scontext	tcontext	name	target name	ppid	pid	host
init_t	ftpd_t	init	ftpd	1	330	www
init_t	sshd_t	init	sshd	1	2045	www
sshd_t	passwd_t	sshd	passwd	2045	3066	www
sshd_t	passwd_t	sshd	passwd	2045	3075	www
passwd_t	bin_t	passwd	bash	3075	4587	www
bin_t	bin_t	bash	ls	4587	5874	www

of a new branch that can be marked as a system session. Also, the fork (the duplication of a process) of the apache (HTTP server) due to a new connection of a user on a web site hosted on the system is the beginning of a new branch that can be marked as a system session. After having chosen which start of a new branch is a new session, it is easy to mark the whole related branch (and the related events) with a unique identification number. This is shown in Figure 4 with the parameter *se_id* that is set to zero for daemons but is automatically increased when the process *passwd* is launched for the incoming attacker. Then, the created *session id* ('se_id') is maintained for all the processes of the created branch.

Other methods of system session reconstruction can be applied based on higher level of information like syslog login and logout information or security labels of Mandatory Access Control (MAC), like the ones used by the SELinux MAC mechanism. When using SELinux, each process and file on the system is marked with a label e.g. *sshd_t* for SSH, *bin_t* for all the files in */bin* directory. Some transitions of a process from one label to another one can be seen as the creation of a new session. For example, when the SSH process goes from *sshd_t* to *user_t*, this represents the connection of a new user. Applying this process to our experimental data, we were able to reconstruct system sessions based on PID trees or SELinux labeling. Our method created a unique session ID for each new branch of the tree. For example, Figure 4 shows the *pid-ppid* tree obtained from the filtered events of Table 8 and the Session IDs added to each (syscall of each) branch.

Table 9. Activity classes of attackers

Class Name	Acronym	Representative event comm attributes
Malevolent execution	ME	`perl|python|sh`(ell) scripts, botnets | malware programs execution
File manipulation	FM	`touch, mkdir, find, mv, cp, ...`
File edition	FE	`vi(m), nano, ...`
File download	FD	`wget, ftp, scp, ...`
Machine administration	MA	`emerge, apt-get, apt, ...`
Machine inspection	MI	`ps, who, cpuinfo, proc, ...`
File unarchiving	FU	`unzip, tar, bzip2, ...`
Source code compilation	SC	`gcc, make, cc, ...`
Brute Forcing	BF	`passwd` (many times)
Local Rebounds	LR	`ssh`

3.3.   Events and Meta–Information

The main issues with our system and network sessions are their size and number. If they are too big and numerous, it is difficult or impossible to group them and classify them with regard to some criteria.

To avoid these issues, meta-events were introduced. Meta-events group a number of events from two to thousands of events into one meta-event that represents them. We divided those meta-events into two main categories depending on the method that created them. The first one is based on similarity between events: for example, we grouped into one meta-event all the events related to the reading of a single file during a given time frame. The second one is based on activity similarities. For example, we linked all the events related to a bash command (like *ls*) into a meta-event.

To group events into meta-events using similarities, we used the commands typed most frequently by attackers that we found using database frequency requests. Below is a short list of such commands:

---

perl, ps, cp, bash, sshd, bzip2, sh, find, tar, sed, cat, rm, mv, ls, wget,
apt–get, sendmail, dd, vi, awk, nmap, chmod, passwd, gcc, make, vim,
ssh, mkdir, tail, nano, ifconfig, head, gzip, scp, ping, dpkg, clear,
cc, uname, chown, uptime, python, who, echo, ftp, . . .

After looking precisely at the effect of those mostly used commands we defined command classes, that we call activity classes. Table 9 presents these classes and sums up the most used/representative commands we considered to define them. Each class is representative of events encountered in sessions. We defined 8 main classes[1] plus 2 particular ones (BF and LR) that were more complicated to isolate. For example, the BF class needs complex computations to be detected, as each `passwd` event has to be repeated more than 50 times.

---

[1]Actually, the ME class includes a network scan subclass that was not explicitly treated in that work.

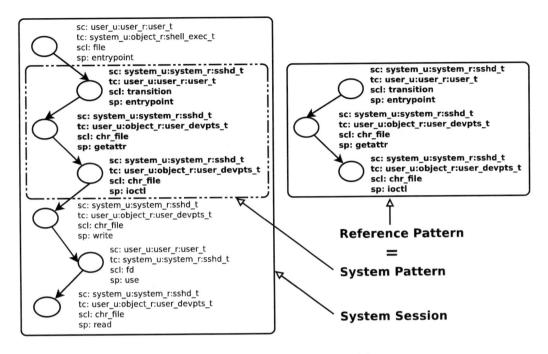

Figure 5. System pattern recognition

3.4.   Session Activity and Session Classification

With the meta-events described above (i.e. small pieces of activity), we were able to create combinations that represent parts of sessions, called system patterns. To work on the data and build these patterns, we stored the logs, and all meta-data for the honeypot in an IBM DB2 Enterprise warehouse database. Using the warehouse allows us to take advantage of *Business Intelligence* software. But, with such large amounts of data (3.10^{11} events), it is impossible to obtain any classification in human time. Thus, we developed our own algorithms and implementations to compute the data using the warehouse [Rouzaud-Cornabas et al., 2009].

First, we used patterns to classify system sessions. These patterns are small combinations of meta-events. Figure 5 shows the recognition of a system pattern (on the right) inside a global system session (on the left). In this example, the 'reference' system pattern represents the connection of a user through *ssh*, i.e. a migration from the *ssh* context (top of figure)) to the user context, then the opening of a virtual console (middle) and finally an interaction between the user and the virtual console (bottom).

Second, by labeling the system patterns with specific activity labels (see Table 9, e.g. file manipulation, file execution, file download, etc.), it was possible for us to link each session to one or more classes. Thus, each session could be seen as a combination of high level activities classified in multiple classes. Using this global classification, it should be possible to provide relevant interpretation of what attackers did. For example, a session having a file download without execution of the file would be classified as a simple download class.

3.5. Experimental Session Results

On the monitored computers we found 71,012 sessions, composed of 306,577,215 events. The average size (number of events) of a session was 1,980, the minimum size 1 and maximum size 4,398,034. The average size sessions were often simple SSH sessions, where attackers succeeded in connecting to the machine but never typed any commands. This often happened because of the number of attackers that tried to brute-force our SSH server and succeeded. The minimal size corresponds to an attacker that tried a password but failed to find the right one. Finally, the maximal size was reached with a session that launched a DOS attack from the honeypot that ran for two days.

Experimental results show that 53% of the sessions were of a size of less than 400. Actually, those sessions correspond to a simple password attempt. The sessions having between 400 and 8,000 events were very small sessions that contained only few command entries. Indeed, with syslog-SELinux, each command generates from 10 to 200 syscalls. Those small sessions represent 46% of the sessions.

The remaining sessions had more than 8,000 events. They represent only 1% of the sessions, i.e. 267 sessions. 30% had more than 32,000 events, that made them long and possibly interesting sessions. We investigate the nature of these sessions more deeply in Section 4.2.4.

4. Attack Profiles Analysis

4.1. Comparison to Manual Investigations

Before going any further into specific attacks analysis, this section presents the benefit of computing syslog-SELinux events rather than *.bash_history* or *rpld* logs.

Firstly, examining the syscalls of binaries execution can help to ensure that the applications launched are not corrupted. For example, in the previous example, the `wget` commands may sometimes have been a malware program downloaded by an attacker. Comparing the syscall generated by the command to a generic signature may help to decide if the application is corrupted or not. For example, in our logs, any `wget` execution that did not contain interaction with the target context *unix_socket* was considered as an execution of a malware program.

Secondly, using the real system events logged, it is almost impossible to miss things that happened on the honeypot. Let us consider the example of the (manual) geographic study presented in the first part of this chapter. Figure 3 presented countries from which malware programs are downloaded. With only the *.bash_history* files or *rpld* information, it was impossible to know if the quantity of data downloaded per country was proportional to the number of downloads per country. By automating a querying procedure searching the database for events having 'wget' as the command (comm) and *unix_socket* (system_:system_r:unix_socket_stream) as the tcontext and read as the security permission (secperm) we can obtain all IPs in the database and their number. By automating geolocalization resolution, we can provide information about download countries that presents a different vision of things. Indeed, the resulting data, shown in Figure 6 show many countries that were not visible in Sect. 2.2.4 and a different distribution. We

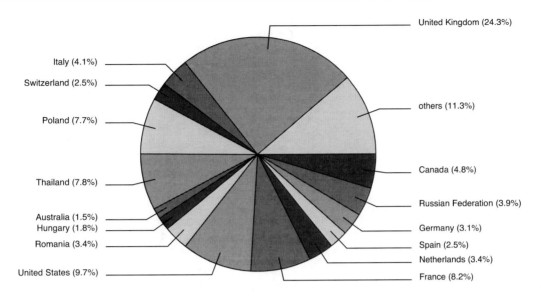

Figure 6. Wget events distribution by country

see that the distribution is much more homogeneous with many countries. The UK, in particular, appeared very often. After this come the USA, France, Thailand and Poland. The 'others' quota is substantial because of the large number of other countries, each having small percents.

By correlating system events and network analysis tools, we were able to answer the download volume question. In fact, by multiplying the number of `wget read` syscalls by the size of packets during each session, we are able to compare in Figure 7 the download quantities with the results given in [McGrew et al., 2006]. The main difference that we observed was a noticeable download volume from Eastern Europe, which McGrew did not. On the other hand, McGrew noticed substantial activity from Asia, which we did not. Some other differences mainly relate to Italy and the USA. It is important to note that except for those differences, the main activities and download sources remain comparable: Europe, the USA, Korea and Canada. The disappearance of some countries and the appearance of others does not imply real changes. It can be the result of the location of our honeypot, in France, whereas McGrew was located in the USA. The USA are traditionally a common target for Asian countries.

Obtained results shows that the use of distinct IPs per country was obviously not proportional to downloading activities per country. It shows that attacks coming from the biggest numbers of distinct IPs were the UK, Switzerland, Poland and France. On the other hand, the most targeted address class by the attackers activities were the UK and Poland. In particular, in one session, a complete scan of all the addresses in the UK was performed, generating millions of events, almost one per IP in UK.

The results show that 98% of the sessions were related to a maximum of four different IPs, whether source or destination IPs. 0.8% of sessions were related to more than 10,000 IPs. The session mentioned above which scanned the UK IPs was one of them. Again, such investigations were not possible during the manual study phase.

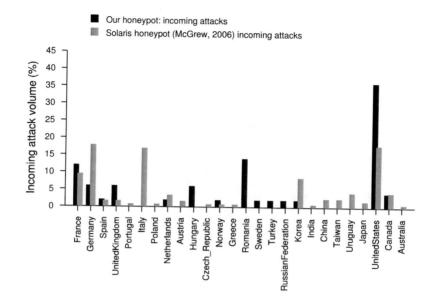

Figure 7. Volume download distribution of attacks between countries compared with [McGrew et al., 2006]

4.2. Attack Profiles

Based on the activity classes of Table 9 we tried to find some high level activities in the sessions. To do this, we searched the database for sessions that comprised events of one given class in a statistically and significantly greater proportion than other sessions. Based on other meta-events, we also defined other high level activities that characterize a wide range of attacks on our honeypot.

Our correlation system was tested among the following most common distributed attack scenarios.

4.2.1. Recognition Attacks

The most commonly distributed type attack is that of recognition processes that scan our network in order to collect information about it. This type of attack rarely causes any damage on the system but helps the following steps of an attack.

4.2.2. Brute–force Attacks

Another common type of attack is that of trying to discover passwords for different services. This method is known as brute-forcing. It uses dictionaries, lists of common passwords or random strings to try to find the password to log into remote services. To detect such profiles, we searched for elements of the BF class in the database. This attack mainly occurred on our SSH servers but, also, on our FTP server and in some cases, on our Samba controller.

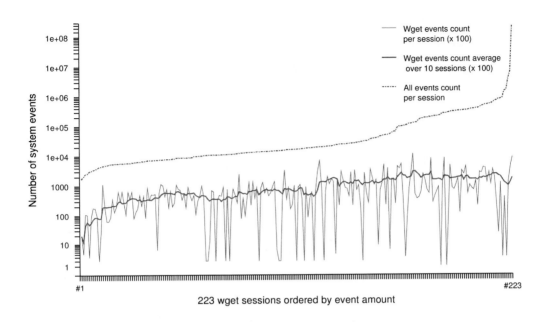

Figure 8. Number of system events in 'wget' sessions

4.2.3. Malware Program Installations

After an intrusion the attacker generally tries different approaches to exploit the system in his interest:

- He may try to use exploit to elevate his privileges;

- He may try to connect to local services to harvest data;

- He may install a root kit or other hidden malware program that periodically reports the state of data and changes related to users and the system;

- He may use the computer as a rebound for other attacks;

- He may install a bot that connects to an outside network, becoming a remotely controlled system.

Let us focus on the 223 download sessions ('wget like') from the 267 long sessions (among our 71,012 total sessions) in order to investigate the activities of the attackers in those sessions. Figure 8 shows that the overall complexity of those sessions in terms of syscall events was more or less proportional to the number of wget events of the sessions (multiplied by 100). This tendency does not hold for the biggest sessions. In those cases, attackers also made some major network scans, generating millions of events.

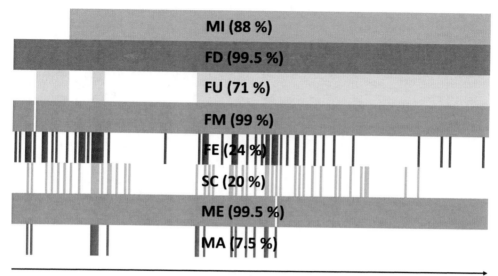

wget sessions

Figure 9. Classification of the 223 'wget like' sessions

4.2.4. Investigating 'wget like' Sessions

To determine what the attackers did exactly during those 'wget like'[2] sessions, we wrote procedures querying the database to search all 'wget like' sessions, i.e. sessions including download commands (wget, ssh/scp, ftp/sftp). We designed programs in order to analyze these data and store meta-data in the database. In particular, we stored any activity class used by each 'wget' session.

We were then able to build a complete characterization of high level activities (or patterns) of 'wget like' sessions, represented in Figure 9. In this figure, each vertical line represents one of the 223 'wget like' sessions we detected in our data.

It appears that in 99.5% of the sessions, a malware program was executed (ME class). It is interesting to observe that all these sessions included file manipulation (FM class). Often multiple file manipulations occurred during a single session, as well as malware program executions. Machine inspection (MI class) and file download (FD class) were also numerous (more than 88%) in 'wget' sessions. Some sessions included edition of configuration file (FE class) or source code that was compiled (SC class) in about 20% of the sessions. Some particular sessions also included machine administration (MA), often *after* having run a malware program, in order to use higher privileges that the malware program was to intended to obtain previously. Those results show that attackers always downloaded their malware programs, and rarely compiled them. Downloaded malware programs are usually compressed, and sometimes, their execution depends on the machine or network inspections the attacker previously performed.

A few sessions, less than 5%, included all activity classes. Those were complex sessions, including multiple commands from each class, and even multiple malware programs

---

[2]By wget like sessions, we mean sessions where some files are downloaded. The distribution of download commands is the following. Wget: 94%, ssh/scp: 5%, ftp: 1%.

used to gain root privileges and to make scans or to install botnets. Many of the malware programs performed scans. Some attackers returned later to gather the results, or their malware programs sent the results outside (ftp, sftp, ...). This part of the complex attacks represents at most 15% of the 'wget' sessions.

The classification revealed that each wget session led to a malware program execution attempt. Sometimes (10%) there was also a scan before or after launching the malware program. Other times, several malware programs were run in the same sessions. Another attackers made multi-step attacks: they entered the honeypot, returned later to analyze the host, returned again to download a malware program, and so on until the excepted results could be gathered. One of the attackers tried to make a strong denial of service against a public IP. His session represented almost 10% of all events for the 71,012 sessions we stored. It was interesting to see that if attackers failed in compiling their malware program, sometimes they tried other ones, such as shell or python scripts, for example. However, only 20% of the sessions included source code compilation which is quite low. Many malware scripts were simple scripts, run by naive attackers, but sometimes, the attackers were able to modify the script, source code, or configuration files in order to adapt them to the local context. Those persons had better attacking skills.

5. SIEM Integration

This section intends to present how the computed security results presented in the previous sections of the chapter can be integrated into an SIEM. A prototype of an SIEM called SYNEMA[3] [Bousquet et al., 2011] was developed to be a lightweight frontend that follows the visual information-seeking "mantra" [Shneiderman, 1996][4]. SYNEMA integrates simple views of the security results of Section 2. It also implements a simplified version of the correlation techniques used in Section 3. Related works are presented in Section 5.1 before moving on to SYNEMA in Sections 5.2 and 5.3.

5.1. Related Works

5.1.1. Network and System SIEMs

Classically, SIEMs aggregate network information from different sensor networks. In [Kolano, 2007, McPherson et al., 2004], the authors try to solve the problem of the amount of the collected data that network SIEMs have to deal with. The issue is even more critical with live analysis [Shabtai et al., 2006, Ball et al., 2004] that requires variations in the amount of collected data to be handled. Such types of SIEM must implement efficient algorithms in order to display valuable information. This could be a difficult task, as for the correlation made in Section 3, since it requires complex analysis.

System SIEMs are very few in the literature. In [Tamassia et al., 2008], more than twenty papers deal with security visualization and most of them only use network sensors.

---

[3]SYstem and NEtwork security tool Monitoring Application, https://traclifo.univ-orleans.fr/SYNEMAhttps://traclifo.univ-orleans.fr/SYNEMA.

[4]In that paper mantra is synonym of paradigm.

In [Francia III, 2008], some system widgets are presented but there is no special correlation algorithm implemented.

5.1.2.   SIEMs and Events Correlation

Many works have contributed to the field of events correlation for intrusion detection. Again, most of them focus on network correlation. Papers about the combination of correlation techniques and visualization are very few.

Important works about detecting intrusions using correlation from multiple sources have been written by Kruegel, Valeur and Vigna [Kruegel et al., 2005]. They propose a general methodology in order to perform correlations for intrusion detection, from data processing to session reconstruction. Other works [Sadoddin and Ghorbani, 2008, Cuppens and Miege, 2002] focus on network session analysis in order to implement a real-time intrusion tool that reduces the number of false positive alerts. A lot of other works propose correlation techniques but the visualization of the results is not their priority.

In [Kolano, 2007], the authors present many tools related to plotting and displaying network alerts from IDS. Their proposal, Savor, tries to give a good visualization of flows of attack between hosts, analyzing and separating legitimate from malicious traffic between IPs.

Few proposals address both the problem of visualizing the security of a set of hosts and integrating correlation capabilities in order to enhance the results displayed. In [Mathew et al., 2006], the authors propose a visualization tool and a correlation methodology that is very similar to our proposal. They define attack categories and define keywords in order to classify events into these categories. The proposed categories are more precise than the classical attack steps: Recognition, Intrusion, Privilege Escalation, and Goal. Then, they propose a correlation methodology that searches for multi-stage attacks, each stage being composed of one or multiple categories. Moreover, the user interface allows the description of categories and stages to be edited and the attacks displayed. The main difference to our work lies in that the visualization is very poor compared to our solution. Moreover, the interface does not attempt to highlight how the correlation has been made and which sensor has been involved at what time.

Another paper [Wu et al., 2009] addresses both visualization and correlation. The authors propose not to use the pattern matching techniques that try to extract valuable information from sensor logs. Instead, they use any valuable data and statistics (CPU usage, router information, ...) as an input for a matrix representation stored in a database that represents the normal behavior of users. Then, new events can be compared to existing events in the database in order to classify them. Afterwards, each identified event is sent to the visualization engine that can display it using curves or geographical maps. Nevertheless, the visualization tool does not display the correlated relation between the events and does not help the user to understand what has been correlated.

5.1.3.   Visualizing System and Networks Events

There are multiple arguments for the visualization of system events. Naturally, in the field of Host Intrusion Detection and Analysis, it is obvious that such an approach can help to react on local hosts. Nowadays, in many cases, attacks can pass through network protection systems, sometimes even without being detected (e.g. using encrypted network packets). Moreover, in large companies, insider threats are likely to occur, including by employees, such as temporary ones. Working on the visualization of system logs can also help for forensics objectives. For this purpose, system events and logs can be monitored and visualized and maybe correlated visually and/or automatically.

This section of the chapter describes an SIEM prototype, called SYNEMA [Bousquet et al., 2011], that aims to visualize and correlate both network and operating system sensors logs, especially in the field of attack detection, analysis and tracking. The main required characteristics to allow the efficient visualization of information and the visual correlation of log data are its conformance to the visual information-seeking mantra [Shneiderman, 1996]:

- Quickly overview the overall high-level activity on the network.

- Zoom on time scales: from 1 year to 1 hour; going forth and back in time and replay logs.

- Filter display on particular nodes or sensors.

- Provide details on demand, such as displaying and coloring the logs that raised the alerts.

- Analyzing correlation results and refining correlation rules.

5.2. Integrating Security Reports

Section 2 of this chapter has described the manual analysis that can be achieved using a set of network and system sensors. Some of the proposed analysis have been implemented in an SIEM prototype, called SYNEMA [Bousquet et al., 2011]. This helps the security administrator to obtain a quick overview of the state of the hosts he is monitoring. The following sections show some examples of the reports that can be achieved with SYNEMA.

5.2.1. Snort Analysis

Figure 10 shows the geographical distribution of the incoming connections, as seen by the snort sensor. This report is less precise than the analysis presented in Section 2.2.4 because Snort generates a lot of false positive alarms whereas our analysis of Section 2.3 is based on wget commands. The right part of the figure shows the distribution of the attacks using the Snort classification.

5.2.2. SELinux Analysis

Figure 11 gives different views of the SELinux alerts on a selected host. The aim of the different graphs is to quantify the number of system alerts and to give proportions by user or type. The bottom right graph shows the number of alerts during one day for two hosts. As SELinux alerts are attempts to violate the access control policy, a safe host should not generate any alerts. Thus, these graphs should reveal a compromised host where an attacker has tried to damage the operating system or to steal protected data.

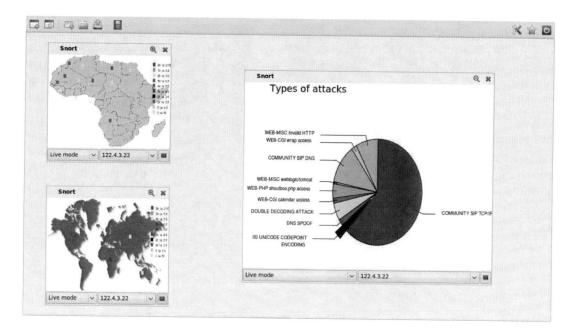

Figure 10. Snort reports

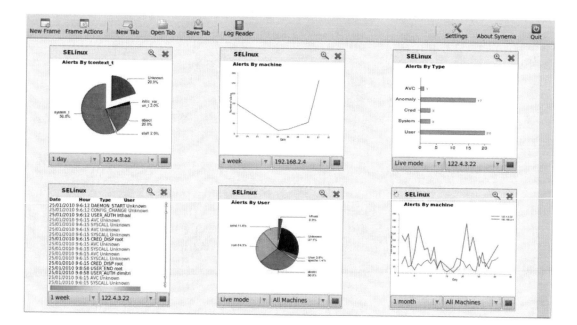

Figure 11. SELinux reports

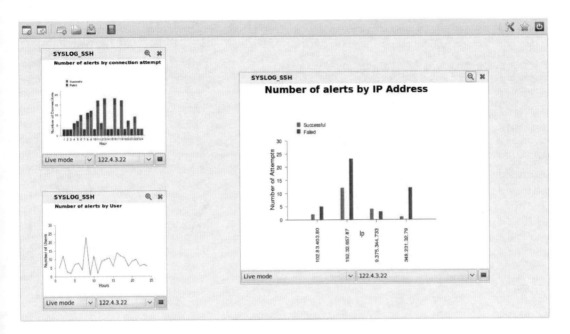

Figure 12. SSH connections seen by syslog

5.2.3. Syslog

Figure 12 shows SSH connection attempts during one day or classified by IP. A large number of failed attempts (red) show that an active attacker tries to brute-force a session. Then, an entered user may generate system alerts, such as those described in the SELinux analysis.

5.3. Integrating Security Correlations

A prototype of a correlation algorithm is implemented in SYNEMA. Our aim is to give a simple example of a correlation algorithm integrated into an SIEM. Thus, it is a simplified version of the methodologies presented in Section 3. Indeed, the methodology presented in Section 3 requires a lot of computing resources to deal with warehouse requests and ad-hoc correlation algorithms. Actually, our correlation was in $\mathcal{O}(n!)$ [Rouzaud-Cornabas et al., 2009] with n the number of events whereas our simplified version can be computed in real-time. In SYNEMA, we show how a lightweight correlation algorithm can be implemented that is usable on a regular desktop environment.

5.3.1. Capturing Events

Each sensor, if well configured, produces a lot of information in its logs. In order to extract valuable security events, a security expert has to define filtering rules using regular expressions. In the rule model shown below, a rule is numbered, associated with a sensor, and two types of match are defined: the *time* keyword indicates that the regular expression defines how to extract the date and time of the event; the *regex* keyword indicates that some data will be extracted from the matching text.

Listing 2: Example of filtering rules for events.

```
1 osiris ::time::compare time: ([a−zA−Z]{3}) ([a−zA−Z]{3})[ ]*([0−9]{1,2}) ([0−9]{2}):([0−9]{2}):([0−9]{2})
    ([0−9]{4})
2 osiris ::regex::[[]mod_ports[]][[]TCP:0:([0−9]*)[]]
3 osiris ::regex::[[]mod_kmods[]][[]kern:([a−zA−Z0−9_]*)[]]
4 selinux ::time::msg=audit\(((0−9]*)
5 selinux ::regex::type=([A−Z_]*).*scontext=([a−zA−Z_]*).*tcontext=([a−zA−Z_]*)
6 selinux ::regex::type=([A−Z_]*)
7 snort ::time::([0−9]{2})/([0−9]{2})−([0−9]{2}):([0−9]{2}):([0−9]{2})
8 snort ::regex::(Priority:) ([0−9])
9 syslog ::time::([a−zA−Z]{3}) *([0−9]{2}) ([0−9]{2}):([0−9]{2}):([0−9]{2})
10 syslog ::regex::Authentication (failure)
11 snort ::regex::[]][.]*[)]* ([^[]*) [[]
```

Listing 3: Example of values for matching events.

	e9 6 APPVC 5
e1 2 80 4	e1 2 80 4
e2 2 22 8	e2 2 22 8
e3 2 8888 0	e3 2 8888 0
e4 2 2265 2	e4 2 2265 2
e5 2 514133	e5 2 514133
e6 3 aes_generic 4	e6 3 aes_generic 4
e7 3 cbc 3	e7 3 cbc 3
e8 5 AVC::system_u::system_u 6	e8 5 AVC::system_u::system_u 6
	e9 6 APPVC 5

filtering_rule# sensor_name ::{time,regex}::regular expression

The Listing 2 shows filtering rules for four sensors: Osiris, SELinux, Snort and Syslog. For example, the first rule extracts from the log a file modification event detected by Osiris. The variable part of the regular expression extracts the date and time of this modification. Rule 5 is a *regex* rule that extracts the SELinux contexts, subject and object having performed a forbidden operation on the system. Note that some rules may include other rules. For example, rule 8 is included in rule 11 which means that two events can be generated from the same line.

The defined rules do not impose any criteria on the flexible parts of the regular expressions. In our methodology we propose to ask the expert to enumerate the flexible part of the regular expression and to quantify the criticality of this event. For example, in some situations, a snort alert may be more important if it concerns the SSH port than the 8080 port. Thus, a second rule file enumerates the possible values of the regular expressions. This second model of rules is shown below:

event_matching_rule# filtering_rule# matching_value criticality

Each rule contains a matching rule number, the reference rule number of Listing 2, the text value that must match the regular expression part between parentheses, and the criticality of this event. The Listing 3 shows examples of matching values. For example, rule e1 specifies that the flexible part of the regular expression of rule 2 of Listing 2 should be 80, which means that the full event is [[]mod_ports[]][[]TCP:0:80[]]. Rule e13 shows the detection of the start of a daemon by SELinux, as the detected line is type=DAEMON_START.

Listing 4: Example of activities.

```
a1 "Network Activity" grey e1:6000 e2:6000 e3:6000 e4:6000 e5:6000 e12:10 e15:6000
a2 "Intrusion Attempt" blue e8:6000 e9:6000 e10:6000 e11:6000
a3 "Changes" red e6:6000 e7:6000 e14:6000
a4 "System activity" green e13:3000 e16:3000
```

Figure 13. Activities and events.   Figure 14. Correlation of activities.

5.3.2. Defining Activities

The number of collected events may be very high and different events from different sensors may correspond to the same activity. For example, an SSH warning reported by SSH and a Syslog login warning corresponds to the same activity: the connection of a user. Thus, we propose to define an activity as a group of events that are linked to the same attacker's activity using the format given below:

activity# "activity_name" color event#1:delta#1 event#2:delta#2 ...

As an event may appear several times over a small amount of time, a delta time (in seconds) is defined to link multiple events of the same type during this delta.

Listing 4 shows four activities. For example, a network activity is created if an event of rule e15 of Listing 3 is found i.e. if the value "ANOM_PROMISCUOUS" is found for the rule 6 of Listing 2. This is an SELinux anomaly detection that is related to a network permission violation. If multiple activities of rule e15 are detected, all the events are grouped in the same activity if their time interval is less than 6000 seconds.

The definition of activities enables us to graphically represent the groups of events as shown in Figure 13.

5.3.3. Correlating Activities

Even if grouping events can be considered as a kind of correlation, we consider that the correlation phase consists in linking different activities and sensors. A correlation is found if some activities are found matching a correlation rule and if:

- for the same activity, different sensors report it in the same correlation time interval;

- for two different activities, one or two sensors report them in the same correlation time interval.

Listing 5: Example of correlation of the same activity.

```
a1 selinux * 60
a1 osiris * 60
a1 snort * 86400
a1 syslog * 60
a2 selinux * 60
a2 osiris * 60
...
a1 syslog snort 10
```

Listing 6: Example of correlation of activities.

```
c1 a1 a2 86400
c2 a2 a3 864000
c3 a3 a2 5
```

Figure 14 shows the three types of correlation that can be represented. The first dotted line (from left to right) shows the activity a_1 correlated between sensor s_1 and s_2. The second dotted line shows two activities $a2$ and $a1$ correlated between sensor s_1 and s_2. The last line shows two activities a_1 and a_2 correlated by the same sensor s_2.

Activities with multiple sensors   The correlation of one activity between multiple sensors is defined by a rule of the form:

activity# sensor#1 sensor#2 delta_time

Listing 5 shows an example of correlation rules. Rule #1 defines a correlation for activity 1 (Network Activity) between SELinux and any other sensor. Note that the rule can be overwritten for two special sensors, for example for the combination $syslog \rightarrow snort$ that has a special time interval of 10 (last line of Listing 5).

The security expert has to describe all the authorized combinations of sensors that might be correlated for the same activity. In this example, 60 seconds are authorized for the correlation of events reported first by SELinux that concerns the "Network Activity" (a1) and then reported by another sensor for the same activity. With this proposed solution, the expert is able to express his knowledge about the attacks: if the first involved sensor is Snort, then 86400s is authorized for the correlation of new events for this activity. Indeed, we consider that the intruder penetrating a system may generate network alerts in Snort and then waste several hours before exploiting the obtained shell and generating new alerts.

Multiple Activities Correlation   Two activities can be correlated if they are declared by the security experts using the following rule:

correlation_rule#1 activity#1 activity#2 delta_time

Listing 6 shows three correlation rules. For example, the first rule c1 expresses that the "Network Activity" (a1) is correlated to the "Intrusion Attempt" activity (a2) if a2 follows a1 in less than one day.

The security expert can model the behavior of an attacker by representing the different steps of the attack. First, events of network activity will be observed before the intrusion itself. The intrusion might be correlated by a change to the system like a file system access, or the loading of a new kernel module. These correlation rules express the link that exists between two activities of an attacker. The choice of the activities that are correlated and the time distance between them is crucial.

Listing 7: Example of sequences of activities.

```
s1 "Connection Attempt" a1:86400:a2 (1)
s2 "Intrusion" a2:86400:a3 (2)
s3 "Intrusion and changes" s1 s2 (3)
```

5.3.4. Attack Sequences

Finally, the security expert might want to describe all the steps in an attack. We call such a correlation a "sequence" as it consists in correlating activities by pairs and describing a path of pairs of activities. Two kinds of rules have to be used to describe a sequence. The first kind is shown below:

```
sequence_rule#1 "Name" activity#aW:delta_time:activity#aX (criticality)
sequence_rule#2 "Name" activity#aX:delta_time:activity#aY (criticality)
sequence_rule#3 "Name" activity#aY:delta_time:activity#aZ (criticality)
```

For example, the sequence_rule#1 means that activity aW and activity aX can be correlated if they occur during delta_time. It is called a simple sequence of two activities. A second kind of rule can be used to refer to those simple sequences:

```
sequence_rule#4 "Name" sequence_rule#1 sequence_rule#2 sequence_rule#3 (criticality)
```

The sequence_rule#4 refers to the simple sequences: sequence_rule#1, sequence_rule#2 and sequence_rule#3. It defines a complex attack sequence of four activities: (activity#aW, activity#aX), (activity#aX, activity#aY), (activity#aY, activity#aZ). In our example of Listing 7, two simple sequences are defined: s1 "Connection Attempt" (activities a1 and a2), and s2 "Intrusion" (activities a2 and a3). Then, the complex sequence s3 is the path constituted by these two simple sequences (activities a1, a2 and a3).

5.3.5. Correlation Visualization Result

Figure 15 shows an example of the resulting output of the correlation plugin of SYNEMA. It is separated into three zones. Zone (1) represents the events detected over time based on four different sensors. Zone (2) gives details for Snort events and zone (3) gives details about SELinux events. Each event is associated with a color for one of the four activities: network activity, intrusion attempt, system change, system activity.

Figure 15-(1) shows in zone a SELinux events of different natures that have correlated timestamps. These events can be grouped into a chain of illegal activities: network activity, intrusion and changes. When such an attack is detected, particular events can be investigated as shown for zone b in (3). In zone c, new network events appear, detected by another sensor (Snort). In this example, this can be due to a new installed service by the attacker, for example, a malicious SIP proxy, as mentioned in (2).

Conclusion

This chapter has presented the manual forensic of a clustered honeypot and the automation of correlation techniques in the aim of studying the attackers in greater depth. A manual forensic analysis of the home directories and commands entered by the attackers gives a

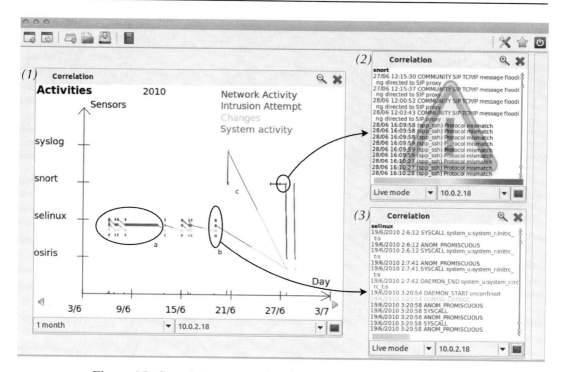

Figure 15. Correlation example of network and system activites

good estimation of the malicious activities captured. The correlation methodology allows us to link operating systems events in order to classify sessions into more complex scenarios.

The different profiles that have been identified are recognition/inspection attacks, brute-force attacks, malware program installations, download sessions. Using correlation techniques, we worked on the entire database of our honeypots that had been running for two years. This represented 1 To of logs to be mined. We chose to work on the longest 267 sessions from the 71,012 sessions in the database. We specifically studied download sessions that represented 223 sessions. In order to classify the activities of attackers, we learned system patterns composed of linked operating system events and we labeled those patterns using a built list of activity classes. The list of activity classes was defined using the commands used by the attackers, such as file download command, malware program execution, etc. The resulting classification gives an overview of the modus operandi of attackers for any case of attack studied. For the download sessions that we studied in more depth, it appeared that some attackers had good skills and were always able to launch at least one malware program execution. Some of them were even able to modify scripts and configuration files in order to adapt malware programs to the local context.

Another important result was the identification of the geographical source of the attacks: we showed that the observation of the operating system events gives a more precise overview than the manual forensic of the penetrated hosts. These attackers generally entered the honeypot for less than 4 times and only a small part of them used the obtained session more than 5 times. The goal of the attackers is the hardest question to answer. With the collected information and the automatic characterization of sessions, we listed the different objectives: to compromise more hosts, to steal data from databases, to hide a malware program that harvest information, to use the compromised hosts as a new starting point to launch new attacks, to install botnets.

Finally, the chapter has presented the integration of the reported analysis into an SIEM. The prototype implemented shows that simple reports, as computed manually, can be easily integrated in the SYNEMA front-end. SYNEMA has also a correlation plugin that demonstrates how the correlation detected between network and system events can be represented to help the administrator to detect complex activities. Even if the prototype requires a large number of correlation rules to be set up manually in order to obtain results, the subsequent output is impressive, compared to the size of the log analyzed.

Perspectives

Information systems are becoming distributed and require several interdependent hosts that need different levels of security. The amount of data generated is increasing with the number of tools and standards. Companies need off-the-shelf solutions to be able to collect information and to take decisions about possible compromise. For the research community, a substantial effort is being made [Vieira et al., 2008] to collect large amounts of data from different experiments in order to be able to compare the data and to produce cross-usage of the collected data. The major difficulty is that the produced and collected information evolves so quickly that previous standards have become outdated [Curry and Debar, 2003]. Finally, the ultimate challenge, when data are correctly collected and interpreted, is to design an efficient rendering tool to visualize them.

This chapter has not covered all the cyber criminal activities targeting servers, as we focused on linux web servers that can be accessed through SSH connections. The honeypot projects have also to be adapted to new environments of attack: web servers and web hosting services, social network technologies, sensor networks, etc. The attacks performed on such networks are of different natures and developing honeypots for these platforms is a great challenge that can be confronted with legal and technical difficulties. The corruption of personal computers also remains to be explored as most of the current studies are interested by the corruption of servers of companies or universities. Technologies such as the Honey@home initiative [Antonatos et al., 2008] install a mixed low/high-interaction honeypot for any host that has available ports and can welcome attackers "at home". With these distributed honeypots, a study of the attackers that target personal computers could be achieved and compared to those that target companies.

Acknowledgments

The initial development of SYNEMA formed the pedagogical support of the algorithm and programming lectures of ENSI de Bourges in 2009. We would like to thank the engineering students of the Security and Computer Science Master's degree, who participated in the development of some SYNEMA plugins. Our special thanks go to Aline Bousquet and Loic Sautreau for their significant help in the manual analysis and the correlation algorithm implementation.

We would also like to thank Janet A. Pinkney for carefully proofreading this chapter. We also appreciated the involvement of Sylvain Lesage who tolerated the deployment of our honeypot despite the large amount of work and the security challenges that were induced.

References

[Antonatos et al., 2007] Antonatos, S., Anagnostakis, K., and Markatos, E. (2007). Honey@home: a new approach to large-scale threat monitoring. In The 2007 ACM workshop on Recurring malcode, pages 38–45, New York, NY, USA. ACM.

[Antonatos et al., 2008] Antonatos, S., Athanatos, M., Kondaxis, G., Velegrakis, J., Hatzibodozis, N., Ioannidis, S., and Markatos, E. (2008). Honey@home: A new approach to large-scale threat monitoring. In WOMBAT Workshop on Information Security Threats Data Collection and Sharing, pages 3–16. *IEEE Computer Society.*

[Ball et al., 2004] Ball, R., Fink, G., and North, C. (2004). Home-centric visualization of network traffic for security administration. In The 2004 ACM Workshop on Visualization and Data Mining for Computer Security, pages 55–64. ACM.

[Bousquet et al., 2011] Bousquet, A., Clemente, P., and Lalande, J.-F. (2011). SYNEMA: visual monitoring of network and system security sensors. In International Conference on Security and Cryptography, pages 375–378, Séville, *Espagne.*

[Briffaut et al., 2009] Briffaut, J., Lalande, J.-F., and Toinard, C. (2009). Security and results of a large-scale high-interaction honeypot. *Journal of Computers, Special Issue on Security and High Performance Computer Systems*, 4:395–404.

[Cuppens and Miege, 2002] Cuppens, F. and Miege, A. (2002). Alert correlation in a cooperative intrusion detection framework. In Symposium on Security and Privacy, pages 202–215, Oakland, USA. *IEEE Computer Society.*

[Curry and Debar, 2003] Curry, D. and Debar, H. (2003). Intrusion detection message exchange format data model and extensible markup language (xml) document type definition. Technical report, IETF Intrusion Detection Working Group.

[Francia III, 2008] Francia III, G. A. (2008). Visual security monitoring gadgets. In The 5th Annual Conference on Information Security Curriculum Development, pages 40–43. ACM.

[Holz and Raynal, 2005] Holz, T. and Raynal, F. (2005). Detecting honeypots and other suspicious environments. In Information Assurance Workshop, pages 29–36, University of Maryland, USA. *IEEE Computer Society.*

[Innes and Valli, 2005] Innes, S. and Valli, C. (2005). Honeypots: How do you know when you are inside one? In Valli, C. and Woodward, A., editors, The 4th Australian Digital Forensics Conference, Perth, Western Australia. School of Computer and Information Science, Edith Cowan University.

[Kaaniche et al., 2006] Kaaniche, M., Deswarte, Y., Alata, E., Dacier, M., and Nicomette, V. (2006). Empirical analysis and statistical modeling of attack processes based on honeypots. In Workshop on Empirical Evaluation of Dependability and Security, pages 119–124, Philadelphia, USA. IEEE/IFIP.

[Kolano, 2007] Kolano, P. Z. (2007). A scalable aural-visual environment for security event monitoring, analysis, and response. In The 3rd international conference on Advances in visual computing, volume 4841, pages 564–575. *Springer.*

[Krawetz, 2004] Krawetz, N. (2004). Anti-honeypot technology. *IEEE Security and Privacy*, 2(1):76–79.

[Kruegel et al., 2005] Kruegel, C., Valeur, F., and Vigna, G. (2005). Intrusion Detection and Correlation: Challenges and Solutions. *Springer.*

[Leita et al., 2008] Leita, C., Pham, V. H., Thonnard, O., Ramirez-Silva, E., Pouget, F., Kirda, E., and Dacier, M. (2008). The leurre.com project: Collecting internet threats information using a worldwide distributed honeynet. In Workshop on Information Security Threats Data Collection and Sharing, pages 40–57, Washington, DC, USA. *IEEE Computer Society.*

[Mathew et al., 2006] Mathew, S., Giomundo, R., Upadhyaya, S., Sudit, M., and Stotz, A. (2006). Understanding multistage attacks by attack-track based visualization of heterogeneous event streams. In The 3rd international workshop on Visualization for computer security, pages 1–6, New York, New York, USA. ACM Press.

[McCarty, 2003] McCarty, B. (2003). Botnets: Big and bigger. *IEEE Security and Privacy*, 1(4):87–90.

[McGrew et al., 2006] McGrew, R., Rayford, B., and Vaughn, J. (2006). Experiences with honeypot systems: Development, deployment, and analysis. In The 39th Annual Hawaii International Conference on System Sciences, page 220, Kauai, Hawaii. *IEEE Computer Society.*

[McPherson et al., 2004] McPherson, J., Ma, K.-L., Krystosk, P., Bartoletti, T., and Christensen, M. (2004). PortVis: a tool for port-based detection of security events. In The 2004 ACM workshop on Visualization and data mining for computer security, pages 73–81, New York, NY, USA. ACM.

[Nayyar and Ghorbani, 2006] Nayyar, H. and Ghorbani, A. A. (2006). Approximate autoregressive modeling for network attack detection. In The 2006 International Conference on Privacy, Security and Trust, pages 1–11, New York, NY, USA. ACM.

[Ning et al., 2001] Ning, P., Reeves, D., and Cui, Y. (2001). Correlating alerts using prerequisites of intrusions. Technical Report TR-2001-13, North Carolina State University, Raleigh, NC, USA.

[Provos, 2004] Provos, N. (2004). A virtual honeypot framework. In The 13th conference on USENIX Security Symposium, pages 1–14, Berkeley, CA, USA. *USENIX Association.*

[Rouzaud-Cornabas et al., 2009] Rouzaud-Cornabas, J., Clemente, P., Toinard, C., and Blanc, M. (2009). Classification of malicious distributed selinux activities. *Journal of Computers, Special Issue on Security and High Performance Computer Systems*, 4:423–432.

[Sadoddin and Ghorbani, 2008] Sadoddin, R. and Ghorbani, A. A. (2008). Real-time alert correlation using stream data mining techniques. In The 20th national conference on Innovative applications of artificial intelligence, volume 3, pages 1731–1737, Fredericton, NB, Canada. AAAI Press.

[Shabtai et al., 2006] Shabtai, A., Klimov, D., Shahar, Y., and Elovici, Y. (2006). An intelligent, interactive tool for exploration and visualization of time-oriented security data. In The 3rd International Workshop on Visualization for Computer Security, pages 15–22. ACM.

[Shneiderman, 1996] Shneiderman, B. (1996). The eyes have it: a task by data type taxonomy for information visualizations. In *IEEE Symposium on Visual Languages*, pages 336–343, Boulder, CO, USA. IEEE Computer Society.

[Tamassia et al., 2008] Tamassia, R., Palazzi, B., and Papamanthou, C. (2008). Graph drawing for security visualization. In Graph Drawing, volume 5417 of *Lecture Notes in Computer Science*, pages 2–13, Heraklion, Crete, Greece. Springer Berlin/Heidelberg.

[Valeur et al., 2004] Valeur, F., Vigna, G., Kruegel, C., and Kemmerer, R. A. (2004). A comprehensive approach to intrusion detection alert correlation. *IEEE Transactions on dependable and secure computing*, 1(3).

[Vieira et al., 2008] Vieira, M., Mendes, N., Durães, J., and Madeira, H. (2008). The amber data repository. In Workshop on Resilience Assessment and Dependability Benchmarking, Anchorage, Alaska. IEEE/IFIP.

[Wu et al., 2009] Wu, Q., Ferebee, D., Lin, Y., and Dasgupta, D. (2009). Visualization of security events using an efficient correlation technique. In IEEE Symposium on Computational Intelligence in Cyber Security, number 978, pages 61–68, Nashville, TN. *IEEE Computer Society*.

In: Advances in Security Information Management
Editors: G. Suarez-Tangil and E. Palomar

ISBN: 978-1-62417-204-5
© 2013 Nova Science Publishers, Inc.

Chapter 9

ADVANCED SIEM TECHNOLOGY FOR CRITICAL INFRASTRUCTURE PROTECTION

*Salvatore D'Antonio, Luigi Coppolino and Luigi Romano**
University of Naples 'Parthenope', Naples, Italy

Abstract

In the last two years an increasing number of coordinated and targeted cyber-attacks, characterized by an unprecedented level of sophistication, has been conducted against critical infrastructures. This cyber-threat generates serious concerns especially when targets of attacks are critical infrastructures, whose failure may result in death of hundreds or thousands of people, as well as in dramatic damages to the environment. The current SCADA technology is not able to cope with cyber-attacks, since it was not designed with security in mind. Protection from cyber-attacks has to be provided by additional technology, which needs to be integrated with the existing SCADA systems in a seamless way. In this chapter we present the approach taken in the MAS-SIF project to enhance current SIEM technology in order to make it suitable for the protection of Critical Infrastructures. In particular, we focus on issues related to data collection and parsing. We propose data gathering techniques and illustrate their implementation in an enhanced SIEM platform. We do this in the context of a challenging case study, namely monitoring and control of a dam.

Keywords: Security Information and Event Management (SIEM), Supervisory Control And Data Acquisition (SCADA), Critical Infrastructure Protection (CIP), security, safety

1. Rationale and Contribution

It was the late 2001 when after a crash between a US spy plane and a Chinese fighter, 1200 US sites, including the White House, the US Air Force, and the Department of Energy, were suffering DDoS attacks or defaced by Chinese hackers.

At the time the concept of cyber-terrorism was rejected by security gurus such as Bruce Schneier who was claiming "The hype is coming from the US government and

---

*E-mail address: {salvatore.dantonio, luigi.coppolino, luigi.romano}@uniparthenope.it

I don't know why. If they want to attack they will do it with bombs like they always have"[Donoghue, 2003]. But a few years later, in 2010, the same Bruce Schneier was considering [Schneier, 2010] as possible the theory supposing that the famous Stuxnet worm was created by a government entity to attack some Critical Infrastructures (CIs). In the last quarter of the same year Symantec produced a report [October-December, 2010] on an evident increase of targeted attacks against CIs and at the beginning of 2011, McAfee declared the cyber-war started as demonstrated by a very sophisticated and carefully planned attack against Energy Providers. The Night Dragon [Services and Labs, 2011], that was the name of the hackers' initiative, had been planned during the previous two years, and demonstrated a level of complexity that was unseen before.

While this aggression to CIs is always dangerous, it can generate dramatic consequences when targets of attacks are safety-critical infrastructures, i.e. those infrastructures whose failure may result in death of hundreds or thousands of people, as well as in serious damages to the environment. Regrettably, most of such infrastructures rely on legacy Supervisory Control And Data Acquisition (SCADA) systems that have been designed without security in mind (mainly because originally they were isolated proprietary systems) and are managed by people with good skills in specific application domains, but with very limited knowledge of security [Baker et al., 2012].

Like in any war, also in cyber-war the capability of gaining and properly managing information is of paramount importance. Logical security is commonly provided by Security Information and Event Management (SIEM) systems. SIEMs are mainly designed to manage and operate in IT-centered applications, i.e. applications where the IT layer plays a crucial role. In Critical Infrastructures, instead, security is mostly threatened by physical actions since the IT layer is typically only functional to the lifeline service provided by the infrastructure.

Traditional SIEM solutions were not designed for the protection of CIs. Indeed, they lack important security features. In particular, they are not capable of collecting events from the physical devices composing the system to be protected, and of correlating physical level events with security-related events generated at the logical level. In order to be effective, current SIEM solutions need to be extended with specific functions, in order to support efficient acquisition and processing of security relevant events which are generated by heterogeneous system layers/components.

Main contribution

In this chapter we:

- Present an enhanced SIEM solution, specifically tailored for protecting Critical Infrastructures, which is being developed within the context of the EU funded project MASSIF [Prieto et al., 2011, Consortium, 2012].

- Discuss the main technical issues, illustrate the design approach, and present the current implementation of the proposed solution. Focus is on the data acquisition layer of the SIEM platform, i.e. the architectural layer which closely interacts with the physical components.

- Demonstrate the capability of the enhanced SIEM platform monitoring the security level of a Critical Infrastructure, specifically a dam. This use case was selected because it represents a very challenging scenario presenting all the main requirements of a SIEM system for CIs protection. Moreover, due to some recent technology trends (which are not likely to change in the future) dams are (and they will be even more so in the future) typically characterized by the coexistence of legacy and new sensor technologies, such as Wireless Sensor Networks (WSNs).

Organization of the Chapter

In the remainder of the chapter, section 2. presents a brief state of the art of current SIEM products. Section 3. introduces the MASSIF project, in particular: subsection 3.1. introduces the project key aspects and challenges; subsection 3.2. presents the layer of MASSIF in charge of gathering data from the field; and subsection 3.3. describes one of the main components of the MASSIF data collection layer, namely "security probes". Section 4. presents the usage of MASSIF in a challenging case study, namely dam management. First an introduction to dams monitoring and control is provided and then the deployment of MASSIF in such a context is discussed. In Section 5. we discuss MASSIF SIEM usage in a complex misuse case related to the selected case study, providing details on the construction of a realistic testbed for the validation of the SIEM system. Finally, Section **??** closes the chapter with final remarks and an overview of future plans.

2.   Related Work

Security Information and Event Management (SIEM) solutions emerged 10 years ago as a solution to the problem of data overload. SIEM solutions are essentially a combination of previously unbundled security management services. A SIEM solution effectively combines elements of security information management with security event management.

This bundling of services has become common across the security products market as vendors look to differentiate themselves by offering "one stop solutions". This allows the end user to provide real-time analysis of security alerts generated by network appliances and applications. One of the main features of these solutions is their advanced log management capabilities. Log management is a process of dealing with large volumes of computer generated log messages. These can be commonly referred to as audit records or event-logs.

In general, log management covers collection, aggregation, retention, analysis, searching and reporting. The key issues with log management tend to be the sheer volume of the log data and the diversity of the logs. SIEM solutions typically correlate, analyse and report information from a variety of data sources such as network devices, identity management devices, access management devices and operating systems. The end result is a holistic view of IT security.

There are a number of leading providers in this area, most notably ArcSight, RSA, and IBM (Q1 Labs). ArcSight [HP, 2012] are viewed by most as the market leader in this area with their Enterprise Threat and Risk Management (ETRM) Platform which functions as an integrated product suite for collecting, analyzing and assessing security and risk information. ArcSight has been positioned in the top right of the Leaders Quadrant in the 2011 Gartner Magic Quadrant for SIEM technologies, highlighting their market leading position and the strength of their technology. Recently ArcSight announced that they will be integrating their SIEM technology with ForeScout in order to boost the efficiency of the technology allowing for a single administrative control to gain full visibility of all aspects of IT infrastructure and security risks [Staff, 2011].

Q1 Labs [IBM, 2012] have experienced a period of rapid growth through their QRadar appliances due to their targeting of large enterprises. Q1 Labs's SIEM appliances provide log management, event management and behavioral analysis for networks and applications. This application behavioral analysis is a distinguishing characteristic of their technology and is facilitated by the collection of NetFlow data. Q1 Labs also has licensing agreements with Juniper Networks and Enterasys, who in turn implement the software on their own applications. Recently Q1 labs released its Risk Manager extension to analyse security and network configuration. QRadar provides the end user with an integrated view of the threat environment and has been rated by customers as having a flexible dashboard, good reporting engine and is easily deployed and maintained [Huston, 2011]. A weakness of the product is its lack of detailed integration with SAP.

RSA's enVision appliance provides a combination of SEM, SIM and log management to its end users. While RSA has one of the largest SIEM installed bases, they are under threat and have become the most frequently displaced SIEM technology due to its reporting performance issues. RSA are attempting to address these shortcomings and are in the middle of trying to integrate enVision with their EMC technology portfolio. enVision is deemed to be highly beneficial for those looking for a single appliance to manage SIM and SEM and who have limited personnel resources to manage their SIEM solution. In addition, enVision is deemed to have a very powerful correlation engine and is quick to install and easy to configure. However in order to boost their market position in relation to Arcsight, RSA need to address all query performance and maintenance issues in order to reduce their current level of customer churn [Grandbois and Huston, 2011].

The most widely used Open Source SIEM is OSSIM, by AlienVault. OSSIM (Open Source Security Information Management) [Karg D., 2008] is released under the GPL license. The main objective of OSSIM is to correlate alerts issued by already available security tools to increase precision and recall of security breaches detection, in fact it does not aim at providing new security detection mechanisms. Nevertheless it may happen that correlation of security information allows to recognize otherwise undetected malicious actions. OSSIM provides integration, management, and visualization of events of more than thirty open source security tools. Also importantly, it allows the integration of new security devices and applications.

3. MAnagement of Security information and events in Service InFrastructures (MASSIF)

3.1. Overview of MASSIF Project

Currently existing SIEM solutions have a number of constraints, e.g. restriction of SIEM to infrastructure and inability to interpret events and incidents from other layers, inability to consider events from multiple organizations.

MAnagement of Security information and events in Service InFrastructures (MASSIF) aims to achieve a significant advance in SIEM by integrating the related events from different system layers and various domains into one more comprehensive view of security aware processes and by increasing the scalability of the underlying event processing technology. On the base of proper multi-level event correlation, MASSIF will provide innovative techniques in order to enable the detection of upcoming security threats and trigger remediation actions even before the occurrence of possible security incidents. MASSIF will be a new generation SIEM framework for service infrastructures, supporting intelligent, scalable and multi-level/multi-domain security event processing and predictive security monitoring.

The MASSIF architecture is divided in four major layers briefly described below.

- Security Information and Event Production: This is the lowest layer in MASSIF architecture and is comprised of devices supplying raw security information and event data. These devices can be of different form depending on the application scenario e.g., physical sensors (water level sensors, tilt sensors etc.), network management and protection systems (firewalls, IDS) or specialized servers (e.g. a mobile payment application).

- Event Collection, Aggregation and Normalization: In this layer, the Event Dispatcher contacts the event sources to receive events. As MASSIF deals with a diverse range of data sources generating various kinds of events, the relevant security information sent by these data sources is needed to be analyzed and converted into MASSIF acceptable format. These different types of events are parsed using Adaptable Parsers which are used to extract relevant information for the event to be inserted in the MASSIF Event Format. Adaptable Parsers receive events from the Event Dispatcher, parse them according to the format specific grammars which contain semantic description of different event formats, and send them to the MASSIF Event Manager, which is responsible for converting the event into the MASSIF Event Format. The MASSIF Event Manager further prepares the event to be sent to the Resilient Event Bus.

- Generic Events Dissemination: This layer is composed of MASSIF Information Switches (MIS) and Resilient Event Bus (REB). MIS is further divided in two types, edge-MIS which is placed on the data collector side and core-MIS which is located on the Core Services side. Edge-MIS receives the information from the lower layer and transfers it to REB. REB is implemented by secure, reliable and real-time communication protocols run by MIS devices. It is a generic event bus which publishes events following a common syntax and semantics. It is a bidirectional, but asymmetric bus. In upstream, it conveys high throughput data sourced by edge-MIS and sinked by core-MIS whereas in downstream, it conveys low throughput commands sourced by core-MIS and sinked by core-MIS and/or edge-MIS.

- Core Services: REB conveys the information collected by the edge-MIS to the core-MIS, and the core-MIS further conveys this information to the Event Processing Engine. This engine processes the information and events, trying to find relationships in the data and to detect anomalies (failures, intrusions). Besides being correlated, data are also archived in a resilient storage system in order to allow forensic analysis. The Engine can process a huge amount of events coming from diverse sources. It sends alerts to the Decision Support System if some anomalies are detected. The Decision Support System sends commands to the REB to countermeasure the detected attacks or anomalous behaviours.

SIEM solutions have become the backbone of the all Service Security systems. They collect data on events from different Security elements, such as sensors, firewalls, routers or servers, analyze the data, and provide a suitable response to threats and attacks based on predefined Security rules and policies. Despite the existence of highly regarded commercial products, their technical capabilities show a number of constraints in terms of scalability, resilience and interoperability.

MASSIF project [Prieto et al., 2011, October-December, 2010] aims at achieving a significant advance in the area of SIEMs by integrating and relating events from different system layers and various domains into one more comprehensive view of security-aware processes and by increasing the scalability of the underlying event processing technology. The main challenge that MASSIF will face is to bring its enhancements and extensions into the business layer with a minimum impact on the end-user operation. In addition to the above objectives, additional goals of the MASSIF project are to integrate these results in two existing Open Source SIEM solutions and to apply them to four industrial scenarios, including the Olympic Games IT infrastructure.

Aligned with the Security needs of these scenarios, MASSIF challenges can be arranged according to the following dimensions:

Collection   The data gathering must have the ability to deal with a large number of highly heterogeneous data feeds. The capabilities of the SIEM will be improved by the integration of new types of security tools/probes. This implies that the parsing/processing logic (and code) should be as much as possible decoupled from the specific characteristics of the data format and related technologies. Additionally, the parsing logic and related languages must allow effective processing of virtually any type of security relevant event. Moreover, the volume of events to be collected and processed per unit of time can occasionally increase resulting in load peaks. The data collection layer should be able to handle such peaks and to propagate relevant events to the SIEM core platform without loss of information. More details about data collection in MASSIF are provided in next section.

Processing   The core of MASSIF is an event processing engine capable of handling high input rate and of optimizing the amount of resources based on the actual load. In other words, the system should monitor both input loads and vital parameters, such as CPU utilization, in order to adjust the amount of resources, i.e., providing more resources during peak load times and decommissioning them during valley load periods. The system must process input data at high rate and provide meaningful results with soft real-time requirements. The engine should be able to aggregate, abstract and correlate heterogeneous events from multiple sources at different levels of the system stack.

Correlation   MASSIF targets at correlation capabilities across layers of security events, from network and security devices as well as from the service infrastructure such as correlation of physical and logical event sources. The engine should be shipped with a set of predefined correlation rules to identify well-known attacks. However, it should also support easy and intuitive creation of user-defined rules.

Resilience   Special emphasis will be placed on providing a highly resilient architecture against attacks, concurrent component failures, and unpredictable network operation conditions. The event flows should be protected, from the collection points through their distribution, processing and storage. The designed mechanisms should offer flexible and incremental solutions for node resilience, providing for seamless deployment of necessary functions and protocols. These mechanisms should take into consideration particular aspects of the infrastructure, such as edge-side and core-side node implementations.

Timeliness   The infrastructure should provide for (near) real-time collection, transmission and processing of events, and ensure the corresponding reliable and timeliness generation of alarms and countermeasures when needed.

Sensitive Information   MASSIF features for forensic support will satisfy the following requirements:

- Data authenticity - Security event data contents, as well as additional/added information related to data origin and destination, must be reliably stored.

- Fault and intrusion-tolerant stable storage - The stable storage system on which data for forensic use will be persisted must be tolerant both to faults and to intrusions.

- Least persistence principle - With respect to sensitive data, only information which is actually needed should be persisted to stable storage (most of the data should be processed in real-time and thrown away).

- Privacy of forensic records - Forensic evidence related to security breaches will be made available only to authorized parties.

3.2.   Data Collection Infrastructure in MASSIF

The role of the data collection infrastructure is crucial for the effectiveness of the overall MASSIF framework. In order that it adequately supports the actions of the MASSIF components responsible for data processing and correlation it is required that the infrastructure for data acquisition be capable of coping with a large number of highly heterogeneous data sources originating from different operational domains, adapting to any new event format by creating a fully functional event parser, handling load peaks in the flow of events generated by the field sensors and propagating the relevant data to the SIEM core platform without causing losses or consistent lags in the processing, and integrating new parsers and collectors in a relatively short time and at a relatively low cost. Furthermore, the parsing/processing logic (and code) should be as much as possible decoupled from the specific characteristics of the data format and related technologies in order to allow the parsing subsystem to run in different environments.

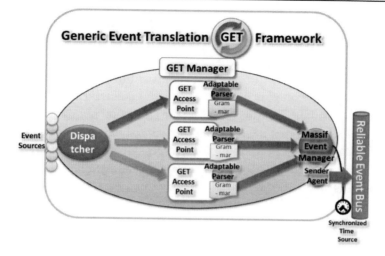

Figure 1. Main components of Generic Event Translator

These requirements have been met by implementing the Generic Event Translation (GET) framework. The main components of the GET framework are represented in Fig. 1. A brief description of each component is provided in the following:

- **Generic Event Translation (GET) Manager:** This component is responsible for the activation of all the modules which belong to the GET framework. In particular, it is in charge of the generation of new Adaptable Parser modules, as new grammars are added to the system.

- **Event Dispatcher:** This component connects each source of sensor events to the appropriate GET Access Point (GAP), in order to provide it with an Adaptable Parser which is capable of processing the specific event format.

- **GET Access Point (GAP):** It is responsible for orchestrating the translation process of the GET. It is in charge of extracting the content of source messages in the source specific format, using the event parsing capabilities of the Adaptable Parsers and requesting the final conversion into the MASSIF Event Format by the MASSIF Event Manager (MEM).

- **Format-specific Grammars:** These contain semantic description of the different event formats that are used for the creation of the Adaptable Parsers.

- **Adaptable Parsers:** These components provide the parsing capabilities for the different types of events used in MASSIF. They allow for extraction of the relevant information for the event to be inserted in the MASSIF Event Format.

- **Massif Event Manager (MEM):** It translates the event content, extracted by the Adaptable Parser to the MASSIF Event Format, thus allowing the event to be sent to the reliable event bus. It also attaches to each MASSIF Event a timestamp, which is made available by the synchronized time source of the Resilient Architecture.

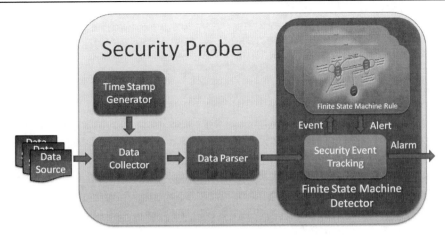

Figure 2. Security Probe architecture

- **Sender Agent:** It is the component that finally sends MASSIF-formatted events to the reliable event bus.

3.3. Security Probes for Service Infrastructures

A Security Probe (SP) for service infrastructures is the MASSIF framework component responsible for monitoring the main activities related to a specific service, classifying them, and detecting any anomalous behaviour of the service usage which may be of interest to the SIEM system. Due to the heterogeneity of the monitored services, different types of data sources provide the security probe with relevant information depending on the selected scenario. Examples of data feeds for a security probe include traffic traces, system logs, firewall logs, etc. In some specific application scenarios, it could be beneficial for a security probe to perform some aggregation of data coming from different sources in order to improve its performance.

Based on these considerations, a security probe is required to interact with heterogeneous data feeds, collect data, and parse it out in order to extract security-relevant information. Furthermore, a key requirement for a security probe is the capability of including new event classification rules and using them in order to improve the accuracy of the detection function. To summarize, an efficient security probe has to be flexible enough in order to: (i) interoperate with different data sources, (ii) support different service scenarios, and (iii) allow for the extension of classification capabilities. In order to meet these requirements we designed a distributed architecture, which is depicted in Fig. 2.

The framework comprises three main components:

- **Data Collector**: the Data Collector is in charge of collecting security-relevant information by directly interacting with data sources.

- **Data Parser**: the Data Parser analyses the data in order to extract valuable information for the identification of service activities.

- **Event Detector**: based on predefined service rules the Event Detector identifies anomalous service events, which need to be reported to the SIEM.

- **Time Stamp Generator**: it is included in the architecture and generates time stamps for the collected events.

Firstly, the Data Collector is the component that collects the information on the status and behavior of the service infrastructure being monitored. Unlike the MASSIF GET platform, its capability to handle different data sources allows the Security Probe to perform a cross-layer data collection. The Data Collector is in charge of starting the communication between the SP and the data sources, managing the collection process, forwarding the data to the proper data parser. Different collection mechanisms —in terms of the type of the collected information, the collection mode (synchronous and asynchronous), and the communication reliability - are needed, to cope with the heterogeneity of data sources. The Data Collector also detects events associated to the arrival at the Security Probe of security-relevant information and activates the proper data parsing process. Other information, like the timestamps of the collected data, the id of the data source, the sequence number of the data collected, is provided by the Data Collector to the other system components. The Time Stamp Generator is the component that generates time stamps for the events collected by the data collector. In the current implementation, it relies on time sources which are made available by the monitoring and/or monitored system.

The information gathered by the Data Collector is analysed by the Data Parser. The main task of this component is to process the data stream and identify valuable information for the monitoring of service infrastructures. The parsing process strictly depends on the format of data to be analyzed. In other terms, since every data source has a specific data format, a different data parsing module should be provided for each of them. This requires for the implementation of flexible data parsing mechanisms in order to be able to process all the data and events arriving at the SP. The requirement for a flexible framework calls for the use of advanced techniques which allow for easily implementing the data parsing functionality. As soon as the information of interest is extracted the Data Parser activates the Event Detector which will be in charge of assessing whether the extrapolated data shows a correct infrastructure operation or not.

Secondly, the Event Detector is the component responsible for the monitoring process. It is in charge of evaluating the information and events collected and extracted by the other system components in order to trace the service infrastructure activities and identify possible anomalous behaviors which can be of interest to the MASSIF SIEM system. In order to achieve such objective a Security Event Tracking is implemented as software module of the Event Detector. It is in charge of identifying specific events occurring in the service infrastructure based on the information extracted by the Data Parser. Since only selected actions are permitted, any service can be easily modeled as a finite state machine, where a single event can modify the status of the service infrastructure. Whenever an unauthorized transition from one service status to another one is detected an alert is generated. The normal infrastructure behaviors are modeled in the Event Detector through Finite State Machine rules. The event extracted by the Security Event Tracking causes a change in the status of the service infrastructure. Anomalous service infrastructure conditions are also described through the use of Finite State Machine rules which generate an alert as soon as the infrastructure moves in those machine states. The requirement for a flexible architecture which allows for easily implementing Finite State Machine rules for different service infrastructures has been met by using innovative state machine generators.

Finally, the Event Detector is also in charge of sending alerts to the MASSIF SIEM system by exporting them in the MASSIF event format. From the implementation point of view two approaches can be used: hard-coding the state machine in source code or generating the state machine source code through automated generator tools. The latter are usually called FSM (Finite State Machine) compilers. The idea of a FSM compiler is to take a formal representation of the state machine graph, then automatically generate the code which implements the FSM to integrate in the software program. State Machine Compiler (SMC) [Rapp, 2011] is a well-known FSM compiler. It allows describing the state diagram in a file by using an easy-to-understand language. According to this file, SMC automatically generates the state pattern classes in several programming languages including C/C++ and Java. The SMC also provides support for coding unexpected event occurring in the state machine. By combining virtual methods with the state pattern, SMC allows to define "Default" transitions, i.e. transitions which allow the generated objects to handle unexpected events, recover from them and continue providing the expected service. The code generated by the SMC is designed to be loosely coupled with the software application.

4.   The Damon Case Study

4.1.   Dams Control and Management

A dam is an infrastructure that can be conceived for a multitude of purposes and its features are strictly related to the aims it is built for: food water supplying, hydroelectric power generation, irrigation, water sports, wildlife habitat granting, flow diversion, navigation are just some examples. Controlling and monitoring activities are influenced by the specific dam functionalities as they depend on components, mechanisms, and operative devices involved in the activities, each one with different requirements in terms of produced data and computational loads.

Dam behaviour monitoring applications use structural and geotechnical instrumentation in combination with Automated Data Acquisition Systems (ADAS) [Myers et al., , Parekh et al., 2010]. An ADAS is typically organized as a Supervisory Control And Data Acquisition (SCADA) system, that is in a hierarchical organization presenting at its lower layer a number of diverse sensors. Moving upward in the hierarchy we can find Remote Terminal Units (RTUs), Master Terminal Units (MTUs), and Master Central Units (MCUs). Further details on SCADA systems organization can be found in [D'Antonio et al., 2012, Baker et al., 2012].

Since dams are complex infrastructures, a huge number of parameters have to be monitored to guarantee their safety and security [Jeon et al., 2009, vaunt, 2010, Dalson et al., 2010]. The type of parameters actually monitored depends on the structure and design (Earthfill, Embankment or rockfill, Gravity, Concrete Arch, Buttress), the purpose (Storage, Diversion, Detention, Overflow), and the function (Hydroelectric power generation, Water supply, Irrigation) of the infrastructure. Table 1 lists some of the most used monitoring sensors together with a brief explanation of their usage.

Indeed, since September 2009 dams are classified as critical infrastructures, and thus monitoring as a tool for detecting malicious faults and cyber attacks has become a critical activity. In a dam scenario, malicious faults present faster dynamics (as compared to non malicious ones) and require continuous monitoring (as opposed to periodic monitoring). In a single dam up to 500 sensors might be deployed for monitoring purposes. Given that dams are typically part of a much larger and more complex water system, security monitoring of such infrastructures requires the ability of timely collecting and processing massive amounts of data. As an example, the considered scenario was inferred from a dam managed by the "Autorita' interregionale di bacino della Basilicata" and that is part of a water system composed of nine reservoirs connected by several rivers and canals, with eight earth dams and one arch gravity dam built at the interconnection points.

Also importantly, due to some recent technology trends (which are not likely to change in the future) dams are (and they will be even more so in the future) typically characterized by the coexistence of legacy and new sensor technologies. This is, as an example, the case of Wireless Sensor Networks (WSNs), that are an effective tool for monitoring existing infrastructures which were not initially planned to be monitored and often span over wide and wild areas. This coexistence of legacy and recent technologies results in a high variety of security related events, formats, and abstraction layers. In our case study, we consider the usage of a Wireless Sensor Network as a way to complement the legacy sensor infrastructure which is already deployed over the instrumented dam. Indeed, the usage of WSNs dramatically reduces costs of deployment, provides the possibility of deploying a proper level of redundancy, and has already been proven to be effective for Critical Infrastructure monitoring [Roman et al., 2007, Poulsen, 2003, Bai et al., 2008].

Another trend in dam control systems is the increase in control automation and especially in remote management of a dam, or even of groups of dams, by a single entity. As an example, the Terni Hydroelectric Complex, managed by E.ON[1] and located about 150 Km in the North of Rome, is composed of 16 hydroelectric power plants, 3 reservoirs (Salto, Turano and Corbara), and 1 pumping plant, all of them supervised by a single Remote Command Post located at Villa Valle. On the other side, the increased automation of systems and remote control, pave the way for a new class of security induced safety issues, because of the possibility that cyber attacks against the IT layer of the dam ultimately result in damage to people and environment [McMillan, 2011, FERC, 2010, Zadereyev, 2009, Poulsen, 2003]. The dam monitoring has the purpose to identify anomalous events related to the infrastructure. Table 2 summarizes a list of possible scenarios motivating the need for monitoring specific parameters.

4.2. Functional and Para-function Attributes Monitoring

DaMon (Dam Monitor) is a flexible application developed by Epsilon R&D department together with the University of Naples Parthenope FITNESS research group, which can be easily configured for monitoring virtually any type of dam. DaMon was designed by keeping in mind the following requirements:

- High density and frequency sampling rates: Dams are being increasingly monitored

---

[1]http://www.eon.com/

Table 1. Dam instrumentation sensors

Sensor	Parameter or physical event
Inclinometer/Tiltmeter	Earth or wall inclination or tilt
Crackmeter	Wall/rock crack enlargement
Jointmeter	Joint shrinkage
Piezometer	Seepage or water pressure
Pressure cell	Concrete or embankment pressure
Turbidimeter	Fluid turbidity
Thermometer	Temperature

against malicious faults. Malicious faults, as compared to non-malicious faults affecting dams, present faster dynamics and require continuous monitoring.

- Scalability and flexibility: Given the need for continuous monitoring, events processing and correlation engines must guarantee high performance. Indeed, while a large dam includes less than 500 sensors deployed, corresponding to less than 1K events per second to be collected and analyzed, often dams are part of a complex water system. This means that the event flow can easily reach rates of Mega events per second. Moreover, DaMon is thought as a general purpose critical infrastructure monitoring and management solution, and as such it has to be easily configurable for new deployments and changing requirements. Besides through a multi-layer design and a modular implementation, a high degree of flexibility was achieved thanks to the use of wireless sensors networks.

- Interoperability with legacy systems: most of dams have already been instrumented for safety related non-malicious fault monitoring. Therefore, it is of paramount importance being able to integrate and to exploit existing monitoring facilities as part of the DaMon solution. This objective has been achieved by using a sensor-independent data gathering infrastructure, supporting industrial standards for sensor data communications, and offering a simple solution for extending supported protocols.

- Remote management: Often the entity in charge of controlling a dam is also responsible for controlling other infrastructures geographically spread over a wide area. This is usually operated by deploying the monitoring facility over the field, but controlling it from a remote management point.

- Friendly and intuitive Human-Machine-Interface (HMI): The system will be typically managed by technicians unaware of the technical aspects related to the communication, sampling, correlation, and processing of the events.

As shown in Fig. 3, DaMon interacts with the field sensors to provide functional services, such as monitoring of water and flow rate levels and thresholds, and thus guarantees the correct operation of the system.

Table 2. Security related scenarios and the respective monitoring

Monitored Event	Impact	Detection
Changes in the flow levels of the seepage channels	Seepages always affect dams (whatever their structure and design are). Seepage Channels are monitored to evaluate the seepage intensity. A sudden change in flow levels could show that the structure is subject to internal erosion or to piping phenomena. This event can be the cause of dam cracks and failures.	By inserting into the channel a weir with a known section the depth of water (monitored by using a water level sensor) behind the weir can be converted to a rate of flow.
Gates opening	Intake gates are opened to release water on a regular basis for water supply, hydroelectricity generation, etc. Moreover Spillways gates(aka overflow channels) release water (during flood period) so that the water does not overtop and damage or even destroy the dam. Gates opening must be operated under controlled conditions since it may result in: i) Flooding of the underlying areas; ii) Increased rate of flow in the downstream that can ultimately result in a catastrophic flooding of down-river areas.	A tiltmeter (angle position sensor) can be applied to the gate to measure its position angle.
Changes in the turbine/infrastructure vibration levels	Increased Vibrations of the infrastructure or of the turbines in a hydro-powerplant can anticipate a failure of the structure. Possible reasons for such event include: i) earthquakes (Fukushima, Japan, a dam failure resulted in a village washed away); ii) unwanted solicitations to the turbines (Sayano-Shushenskaya, Siberia, 75 dead due to a failure of the turbines in a hydro-powerplant).	Vibration sensors can be installed over structures or turbines to measure the stess level they are receiving
Water levels overtake the alert thresholds	Spillway are used to release water when the reservoir water level reaches alert thresholds. If this does not happen the water overtops the dam resulting in possible damage to the crest of the dam (Taum Sauk Hydroelectric Power Station).	Water level sensors can be used to detect unexpected discharges. Moreover water level can be correlated to many other parameter to detect anomalous behaviour (e.g. not revealed gate opening)

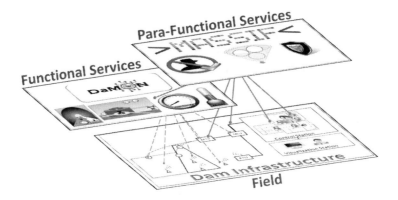

Figure 3. DaMon deployment

a)Main panel   b) Hydro-power station   c) Access Control report

Figure 4. DaMon deployment

The DaMon HMI has been realized by using a powerful web-based, *ajax* enabled framework for SCADA HMI design, named Mango[2]. Figure 4a shows DaMon main panel, where all the alerts related to both the infrastructure and the controlling IT systems are summarized. At the moment the panel offers an overview of the status of: i) the hydro-power station; ii)the seepage and underground tunnels; iii) the basins; iv) the video surveillance system; v) the security applications (IDS, Anti-viruses, Firewall); vi) the Physical Access Control subsystem (RFID-based); vii) the Logical Access Control subsystem (log-ins to the machines in the Control Center).

Each alert can be further investigated by clicking the related icon. As an example Figure 4.b shows a detailed view of the Hydro-power station. In such a view, it is possible to explore the cause of a given alarm by observing the status of individual components.

For each component, the current status is displayed and historical data can be explored. Figure 4.c shows some events collected from the Access Control subsystem. The panel shows events coming from both the RFID-based access control system (i.e. users' accesses to rooms) and the logical access control subsystem (i.e. users accessing PCs into the control room).

Fig. 3 shows the MASSIF SIEM layer that gathers security related information and alerts from both systems deployed in the field and the DaMon system itself. Indeed alerts issued by DaMon, that are related to risky functional conditions, are collected by the MASSIF SIEM and correlated with alerts and events generated by other components, such as IDS, Firewall, RFID gates and so on.

In the following we list some examples of scenarios of interest to DaMon. We remark that this list is far from being exhaustive. It is just a hint for future security evaluations.

Anomalous parameter measurement values   One or more physical sensors report unexpected values: for example the piezometer measures a seepage value out of the predefined range, under a specific environmental condition. The SIEM can correlate this event with other events reported by the networked devices, e.g. any anomalous activity inducing a sensor device tampering, like changes evidenced by the sensor OS fingerprinting, traffic anomalies in the field network, connection attempts to the machine that hosts the WSN Base Station.

Unexpected control commands   A physical sensor reports unforeseen parameter changes due to an action performed by an actuator. The SIEM could verify if the action triggered by

---

[2]http://mango.serotoninsoftware.com/

the SCADA system is a consequence of a predefined behavior, like a scheduled operation, or a change in the device configuration. Attempts of unauthorized accesses to the SCADA control center could be evidence of anomalous activities in the control station.

Missing control commands   Some parameter values reported by a type of sensors mismatch other parameters reported by similar sensors placed in a different site or by sensors measuring other related parameters in the same site. Difference in physical parameter values is unusual. This difference could induce a missing safety operation by the actuator and lead to unpredictable damages to the physical infrastructure. Anomalies or misbehaviors of the sensor network can be symptomatic of suspicious activities.

Control station hacking   The control station sends commands to the actuators or configuration change messages to the SCADA system. The operator can access the control station, but his/her profile does not allow this operation, as stated by an identification procedure. The identification process can be realized by means of devices, such as an RFID, camera identification, or by biometric reconnaissance procedures.

5.   Preliminary Achievements and Experimental Results

5.1.   Experimental test-bed setup

A laboratory testbed was set-up as shown in Fig. 5. The objective of the testbed is to reproduce the main dam-related functional scenarios, such as the ones described in Table 2.

The setup of the testbed required us to visit a number of infrastructures and collect information about features, levels, rates, thresholds, and behaviors characterizing dam installments. Based on such information we have been able to dimension the testbed so that it can reproduce realistic scenarios. The testbed was finally equipped with sensors continuously monitoring the environment and sending events to the MASSIF SIEM. The structure of the testbed includes: two water tanks 1 and 2 representing dam reservoir and river, respectively, whereas the channel labeled as 3 represents both the seepage and the penstock.

Water level sensors are placed inside the penstock and tilt sensor is inclined downward on the penstock. When water flows through the penstock, the tilt sensor shows a tilt which grows with an increase in the amount of water flowing through the penstock. The testbed is also equipped with vibration sensors to measure the vibration of turbine in hydropower station (the water spilling motor in the test-bed), temperature sensors, a tilt sensor to monitor the opening of penstock gate, a weather station to measure the speed and direction of air and amount of rain, an RFID gate and a synchrophasor to monitor the output of the hydro-power station.

The WSN layer is composed of some Libellium waspmote ZigBee devices with digimesh communication protocol. Data collected by the WSN are sent to a base station acting as a wireless RTU. As wired sensors we deployed a piezometer (ATM-N Submersible Depth Sensor), a water current meter (FL530), a turbidimeter (WQ440), and a synchrophasor, all of them sending data to an RTU (based on Datataker DT85G). Both RTUs send data to a server, acting as MTU which provides the DaMon application with the measurement results. Communications between components rely on the Modbus protocol.

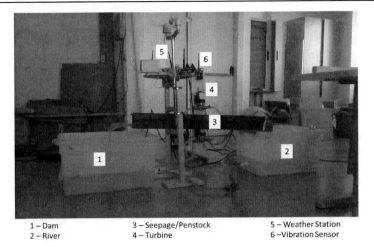

1 – Dam	3 – Seepage/Penstock	5 – Weather Station
2 – River	4 – Turbine	6 –Vibration Sensor

Figure 5. A realistic test-bed of dam equipped with sensors, deployed in lab

5.2.   Misuse case description

This section describes a complex and realistic scenario that could affect the dam infrastructure security. This scenario can be fully re-played in the laboratory test-bed. In the next section we will discuss the possibility to detect and disrupt the attack by using the enhanced MASSIF SIEM.

- Unauthorized access: let us assume that the attacker is an unfaithful employee in charge of cleaning the control station. He has access to the control station through an RFID badge, but he is not authorized to log into the terminal used to operate the gates. Due to his job, he can freely move inside the control station and has physical access to the control machine and flow rate sensor measuring the water flow rate in the penstock. In some way he manages to steal the administrator password of the control machine. As he has physical access to the flow rate sensor, he compromises the sensor so to hide the changes in the water flow rate in the penstock.

- Misuse: The attacker logs into the control machine with stolen administrative credentials. He interrupts the communication between the hydropower station and the control machine, e.g. by installing a software that drops all the packets sent by the hydropower station to the control machine. He opens the dam gate to discharge the reservoir, thus causing an excessive amount of water to the penstock feeding the turbine. The amount of water passing through the turbine exceeds the threshold set for normal turbine operation. Since the flow rate sensor in the penstock has already been compromised by the attacker, it does not report on the increase in the flow rate level to the monitoring station. At the same time, the vibration sensor placed on the hydropower station detects an increased vibration level of turbine and informs the control station. Due to the interruption in the communication between the power station and the control station, the control station does not receive any information related to the increase of vibration level in the turbines and continues to pump water in the penstock.

- Failure: The turbine has a certain limit to bear up the water flow. After that threshold it can exhibit abnormal behaviour or can break down. The excessive amount of water continues to flow through the turbine and the control station takes no action to mitigate this flow, so that the turbine finally breaks down resulting in damages and injuries.

5.3.   Misuse case detection

MASSIF SIEM gathers events from the multiple levels of the system. All these events have different formats. These heterogeneous events are translated into a common format with the help of Generic Event Translator (GET) framework and then used to feed the event processing and correlation engine. In this misuse case, MASSIF SIEM gathers events generated by the sensor nodes, i.e. water level sensors in the reservoir, water flow sensor in the penstock measuring the rate of the water flow going out of the penstock, and other sensors. Figure 6 shows the normalization operated on some sample measurements, specifically on measures taken by field wireless sensors (temperature, angle position, and vibration), and events detected by the presence control sensor (RFID) and by monitoring logins to the machines in the control room.

Once gathered the necessary information, the MASSIF SIEM performs a correlation in order to detect anomalies.

In the presented scenario the following rules are violated:

1.
```
new(what=(event(id='LogonMonitor').user('Admin'))  =>
time_windows(width='1h',navigate='backward',
multiple='false'){
presence(where=sensor(id='RFIDMONITOR'),
what=user('Admin'));
};
```

2.
```
time_windows(width='5sec',navigate='forward',
multiple='false'){
assert(event(id='Hydro_flowrate_out').Flowrate  ==
event(id='Hydro_flowrate_in').Flowrate);
};
```

3.
```
time_windows(width='2sec',navigate='forward',
multiple='false'){
assert((event(id='UP_stream_flowrate').Flowrate-event(
id='Hydro_flowrate_in').Flowrate)  =
event(id='Basin_level').Level;
};
```

Rule 1) asserts that a login event can be recognized by the sensor LogonMonitor, which monitors login access to the computers in the control room, only if the user Admin is in the room (the sensor monitoring the RFID door detects the Admin inside the room). The violation of this rule cannot be considered as a misuse since the door could has been opened by another employee when the administrator entered the room.

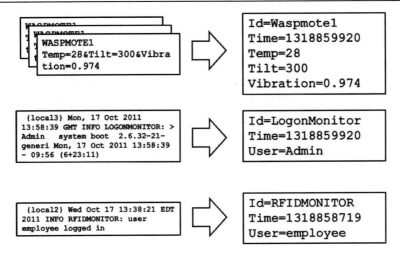

Figure 6. Samples of data normalization operated by the GET framework

Rule 2) asserts that the flow rate measured by the sensor Hydro_flowrate_in (that is the sensor placed in the penstock feeding water to the turbines) must be equal, within a three second long interval, to the flow rate of the water released by the turbine. The violation of this rule is by itself an anomaly, but it could the consequence of non-malicious actions.

Rule 3) asserts that the level of water into the basin of the dam depends on the difference between the incoming water flow and the outgoing flow (the ' =' operator checks that the sign of variations on the first member corresponds to the sign of variations of the second member). Violations of this rule can be caused by multiple conditions (e.g. rain, evaporation).

The violation of each individual rule cannot be considered as a symptom of a misuse, nevertheless the violation of two of them at the same time can increase the level of confidence in detecting an attack. In our simple execution we associated a confidence level of 0.3 (on a range from 0 to 1) to rules 1 and 3, and a confidence level of 0.5 to rule 2. We then used a simple confidence aggregation rule consisting of adding the confidence level of a newly detected violation to the current risk level. By setting an alarm threshold of 0.7 the concurrent occurrence of three violations resulted in an alarm being triggered.

We executed a preliminary experimental campaign of 50 experiments with 10 attack scenarios. We obtained a detection rate of 100%, while only 2 executions wrongly triggered an alarm.

Conclusion

In this chapter we have discussed the main motivations for developing a new class of SIEM solutions specifically aimed at protecting Critical Infrastructures. We have presented the solution proposed by the European Commission funded project MASSIF and described the architecture of this enhanced SIEM system with focus on the layer of the system interacting with the monitored physical infrastructure. We have highlighted the main requirements for such a layer and illustrated the component being developed as part of the SIEM. We have also discussed the usage of the proposed SIEM system to a challenging case study, namely monitoring and control of a dam. A laboratory, fully fledged testbed has been set-up to reproduce features and peculiarities of the case study. We have used it to emulate a complex misuse case affecting the dam infrastructure and to show the way the MASSIF SIEM deals with it. In the future we plan to: i) validate the developed SIEM solution against a complete set of misuse cases reproduced in the testbed laboratory; ii) produce quantitative evidence of the benefits generated by the adoption of the MASSIF SIEM system with respect to traditional solutions; iii) continue the validation campaign by deploying the DaMon application and the MASSIF SIEM on top of a real dam.

Acknowledgments

The research leading to these results has received funding from the European Commission within the context of the Seventh Framework Programme (FP7/2007-2013) under Grant Agreement No. 257475 (MAnagement of Security information and events in Service Infrastructures, MASSIF Project). It has been also supported by the Italian Ministry for Education, University, and Research (MIUR) in the framework of the Project of Na Project of National Research Interest (PRIN) "DOTS-LCCI: Dependable Off-The-Shelf based middleware systems for Large-scale Complex Critical Infrastructures".

References

[Bai et al., 2008] Bai, X., Meng, X., Du, Z., Gong, M., and Hu, Z. (2008). Design of wireless sensor network in scada system for wind power plant. In Automation and Logistics, 2008. ICAL 2008. IEEE International Conference on, pages 3023–3027.

[Baker et al., 2012] Baker, S., Waterman, S., and Ivanov, G. (2012). In the crossfire: Critical infrastructure in the age of cyber war. Technical report, McAffee.

[Consortium, 2012] Consortium, M. (2012). Massif project web site. Technical report, MASSIF.

[Dalson et al., 2010] Dalson, H., Matheu, E. E., Seda-Sanabria, Y., Lopez-Esquerra, A., and Baumgartner, K. M. (2010). Addressing cyber security issues for dams. In 30th Annual USSD Conference Sacramento, California.

[D'Antonio et al., 2012] D'Antonio, S., Coppolino, L., and Romano, L. (2012). Dependability and resilience of computer networks (scada cybersecurity). In CRITICAL INFRASTRUCTURE SECURITY: Assessment, Prevention, Detection, Response. WIT press.

[Donoghue, 2003] Donoghue, A. (2003). Cyberterror: Clear and present danger or phantom menace? Technical report, ZDNet UK.

[FERC, 2010] FERC (2010). Taum sauk pumped storage project (no. p-2277), dam breach incident. Technical report, Federal Energy Regulatory Commission.

[Grandbois and Huston, 2011] Grandbois, N. and Huston, B. (2011). Product review: Rsa security's rsa envision. http://searchsecurity.techtarget.com/magazineContent/Product-Review-RSA-Securitys-RSA-enVision?pageNo=2.

[HP, 2012] HP (2012). Arcsight web site. http://www.arcsight.com/.

[Huston, 2011] Huston, B. (2011). Hot pick: Q1 labs qradar 5.0. http://searchsecurity.techtarget.com/magazineContent/Hot-Pick-Q1-Labs-QRadar-50?pageNo=2.

[IBM, 2012] IBM (2012). Q1 labs web site. http://q1labs.com/.

[Jeon et al., 2009] Jeon, J., Lee, J., Shin, D., and Park, H. (2009). Development of dam safety management system. Advances on Engineering Software, 40.

[Karg D., 2008] Karg D., C. J. (2008). Ossim: Open source security information management. tech. report, ossim. Technical report, AlienVault.

[McMillan, 2011] McMillan, R. (2011). Anonymous hacker claims he broke into wind turbine systems.

[Myers et al.,] Myers, B. K., Dutson, G. C., and Sherman, T. City of salem utilizing automated monitoring for the franzen reservoir dam safety program. Technical report, Engineered Monitoring Solutions.

[October-December, 2010] October-December, S. Q. R. (2010). Targeted attacks on critical infrastructures. Technical report, Symantec.

[Parekh et al., 2010] Parekh, M., Stone, K., and Delborne, J. (2010). Coordinating intelligent and continuous performance monitoring with dam and levee safety management policy. In Association of State Dam Safety Officials,Proceedings of Dam Safety Conference.

[Poulsen, 2003] Poulsen, K. (2003). Slammer worm crashed ohio nuke plant network.

[Prieto et al., 2011] Prieto, E., Diaz, R., Romano, L., Rieke, R., and Achemlal, M. (2011). MASSIF: A promising solution to enhance olympic games IT security. In International Conference on Global Security, Safety and Sustainability.

[Rapp, 2011] Rapp, C. W. (2011). The state machine compiler. SMC: http://smc.sourceforge.net/.

[Roman et al., 2007] Roman, R., Alcaraz, C., and Lopez, J. (2007). The role of wireless sensor networks in the area of critical information infrastructure protection. Inf. Secur. Tech. Rep., 12:24–31.

[Schneier, 2010] Schneier, B. (2010). Schneier on security, stuxnet. Technical report, Schneier.

[Services and Labs, 2011] Services, M. F. P. and Labs, M. (2011). Global energy cyberattacks: "night dragon". Technical report, McAfee.

[Staff, 2011] Staff, C. (2011).   http://www.scmagazineuk.com /forescout-and-arcsight-integrate-security-control-and-siem -technologies/article/211567/.

[vaunt, 2010] vaunt, P. (2010). Long-term monitoring of the vuhred concrete dam, slovenian national building and civil engineering institute. In 30th Annual USSD Conference Sacramento, California.

[Zadereyev, 2009] Zadereyev, Y. (2009). Disaster at the sayano-shushensky power station - a man-made apocalypse.

In: Advances in Security Information Management
Editors: G. Suarez-Tangil and E. Palomar

ISBN: 978-1-62417-204-5
© 2013 Nova Science Publishers, Inc.

Chapter 10

TOWARDS AN INTELLIGENT SECURITY EVENT INFORMATION MANAGEMENT SYSTEM

Guillermo Suarez-Tangil[1], Esther Palomar[1], Arturo Ribagorda[1] and Yan Zhang[2]*

[1]Department of Computer Science
Carlos III University of Madrid, Spain
[2]Simula Research Laboratory, Norway

Abstract

The strategy of combining artificial intelligence (AI) and self–adaptation to optimize different types of computing services is emerging as an automated and efficient approach in computer security. Such a strategy can effectively be used to assist security experts in the protection of organizations. In particular, event correlation poses a promising challenge in providing intuition and cognition to Security Information and Event Management (SIEMs) systems. In this chapter, we enhance the traditional SIEM process as a whole, especially focusing on event correlation, by applying a bio–inspired and adaptive learning system based on Artificial Immune System (AIS). Among the advantages reached, our proposal facilitates an automatic correlation of novel, multi–step attacks.

Keywords: Artificial Immune System, Event Correlation, Security Event Information Management System, Intelligent Rule Generation, Adaptive System

1. Introduction

Security information management is an intriguing dynamic activity that involves different disciplines aimed at proactively protecting, preventing, and swiftly responding to security attacks. The continuous evolution of attacks, specially recent distributed multi–step attacks,

---

*E-mail addresses: guillermo.suarez.tangil@uc3m.es; epalomar, arturo@inf.uc3m.es; yanzhang@simula.no

complicate, even more if possible, this complex task and pose additional challenges to experts and to the entire detection process [Liu et al., 2008]. On one hand, different sources (known as sensors, namely intrusion detection systems (IDSs), firewalls, server logs, to name a few) produce an incessant barrage of security data, generally heterogeneous and difficult to understand. Hence, cooperation among sensors becomes essential. On the other hand, sensors usually work independently of each other and, in general, they are inspected separately, making it difficult the extraction of relevant information of such multi-step attacks.

Security Information and Event Management (SIEM) systems then appear as a holistic solution to gather, organize and correlate security information with the clear objective of reducing the amount of time spent by security administrators and therefore improving the incident response [Aguirre and Alonso, 2012]. However, since current SIEM systems are highly dependent on the configuration of multiple heterogeneous log resources deployed over the network, a common data model to unambiguously and consistently describe the relevant security information is required. For instance, several attempts, from both academia and industry, were made so far to compile and relate the concepts of alerts, events, attacks, sensors, vulnerabilities, software, devices, etc. Hence, there is a pressing need to formalize either a standard method or a formal ground to unequivocally represent knowledge on attacks [Cheung et al., 2003]. Recent work from The MITRE Corporation [Mitre, 2011b] has addressed the necessity of an ontology architecture describing the automatic and semantic interoperability within the SIEM lifecycle [Parmelee, 2010]. In particular, a novel specification has been proposed namely Common Event Expression (CEE) to semi-automate the SIEM process.

On the contrary, several proposals presented so far aim at optimizing the correlation module by the incorporation of some form of advanced logic [Almgren et al., 2008]. Basically, the correlation engine infers extra information from alerts finding out connections between them [Wang et al., 2010]. Principal objectives range from reducing the large number of alerts reported to identify multi–step attack scenarios, and also to identify new attack signatures. Current SIEM systems lack of an efficient mechanism to generate correlation rules and cannot adaptively predict novel attacks either [Anuar et al., 2010]. An efficient correlation should fulfil real–time attack detection through the identification of threat pattern sequences, most in the way of a series of alerts. However, most event correlation solutions currently available still require administrators to a non–negligible configuration effort. The optimization of event correlation becomes therefore essential to realize self-managing SIEM systems.

The main contributions of this chapter are:

- A review of the SIEM approaches which have focused on incorporating any form of AI or self-adaptation is outlined.

- New specifications to the Mitre's ontology architecture —Common Event Expressing— are included for systematically correlate events.

- An enhancement of the traditional correlation process is introduced by using a bio-inspired machine learning technique, namely Artificial Immune System (AIS).

1.1. Overview of our Proposal

Relative to the existing literature on improving SIEM systems by applying AI, our contribution elaborates on the application of AISs to alert correlation. Though it is not the first time this technique is considered in intrusion detection, our approach is novel regarding the way event correlation is formulated. An AIS extracts and applies several interesting properties and concepts of the human immune system to provide solutions to different types of computer processes such as networks' defenses against malicious actions. In fact, phenomena produced within the biological adaptive immune system as a result of protecting the body against the encountered pathogens, can be metaphorically exploited to optimize the attack pattern recognition process.

IDSs along with Intrusion Prevention Systems (IPS) represent traditional strategies which are currently insufficient to protect networks and computers. We introduce a new crosswise component into the SIEM architecture called *Intrusion Learning System* (ILS) as depicted in Figure 1. The main goal of the ILS layer is to bring together intelligent strategies to automatically and dynamically generate correlation rules. ILS is based on widely used AIS–concepts such as the innate immunological memory. The three systems together, namely IDS, IPS and ILS, will define the event correlation framework located at the Intranet which is isolated from the Internet by a perimetric defense, as the skin does in the human body.

Sensors are deployed within the Intranet. Hence, incoming traffic, like a pathogen, has to first trespass that physical barrier which prevents undesired agents to penetrate into the perimeter. Once inside the perimeter, both the IDS and IPS compile traditional strategies to protect network computer systems. Undesired traffic is then redirected to the ILS.

Thus, we position the following statements:

- Generally, the existing SIEM tools present limitations and contextual constraints. In addition, current SIEM frameworks deploy their own architectures. We propose a global framework which integrates the most promising research advances and formalizes an unified architecture design towards an intelligent correlation system.

- Intruder's actions swiftly evolve to become more effective, as well as more sophisticated generations of malware, i.e. polymorphic multi-step malware. In this regard, malware–analysis tools along with a bio-inspired machine learning will integrate our architecture to automatically generate specific correlation fingerprints. We believe that, by providing adaptive intelligence to the correlation engine, time spent in detecting zero-day attacks can be significantly reduced.

- Additionally, we will use advanced sandboxing techniques [Rossow et al., 2011] to automatically extract immunological knowledge by means of dynamic experiments.

1.2. Chapter's Organization

The rest of the chapter is organized as follows. Some preliminaries and foundations of our work are described in Section 2 Next, we present our AIS-based correlation framework in Section 3 In addition, we discuss about the implementation guidelines in Section 4 Finally, we establish the main conclusions as well as the immediate future work in Section 5

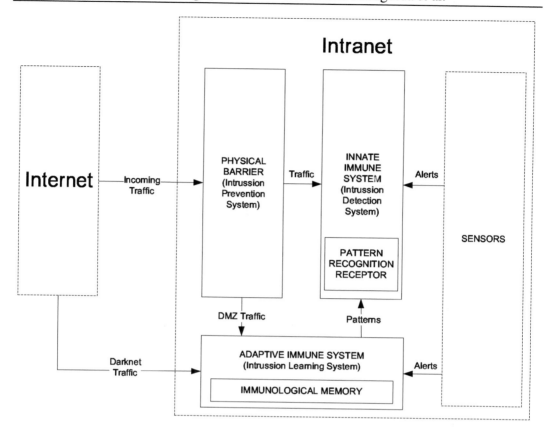

Figure 1. An event correlation framework based on AIS.

2.   Background and Preliminaries

This section gives some background and fundamentals to understand the application of AISs in SIEM systems.

2.1.   AI-based Approaches to Optimize SIEM Frameworks

Several SIEM software products have been recently developed to provide essential intelligence to layered security frameworks, e.g. ArcSight [ESM, 2011], RSA enVision [RSA, 2011], Sensage [SenSage, 2011], Novell IBM [Sentinel, 2011], netForensics [netForensics, 2011], Bitacora [Bitacora, 2011], and OSSIM [AlienVault, 2011], to name a few. Each of the above software products establishes its own architecture and deployment options. We refer the interested reader to [Nicolett and Kavanagh, 2011] for a comprehensive evaluation of current SIEM products.

SIEM frameworks in most cases gather a number of widely–use security and analytical tools to provide automated compliance and real–time threat management. In the literature, such tools have been classified into the following processes, according to their functionality: (i) normalization, (ii) aggregation, and (iii) correlation. Recently frameworks are also incorporating three techniques more, namely (iv) false alarm reduction, (v) attack strategy analysis, and (vi) priorization [Sadoddin and Ghorbani, 2006].

Now, the provision of intelligence and automation to the aforementioned tasks is attracting recent research interest. On the one hand, several works focused on normalization and aggregation have been widely discussed aimed at reaching standards for a common event expression [Mitre, 2011b]. On the other hand, solutions to find out unknown connections between alerts, or to identify the false alerts from those reported, or even to infer potential strategies of attacks do still persist as open issues [Sheyner et al., 2002].

Neural Networks (NN), widely used for optimizing classification problems [Ripley, 1994, Golovko and Kochurko, 2005], have been also applied to partially optimize IDSs, in particular to improve misuse filtering and malicious pattern recognition [Lippmann and Cunningham, 2000, Lei and Ghorbani, 2004, Zhang et al., 2005]. In [Ahmad et al., 2009], readers may find detailed survey on NN–based IDS. Moreover, Evolutionary Computation (EC) is especially suitable for those problems in which a cost–effort trade–off exists such as event correlation [Suarez-Tangil et al., 2009].

By inspiration also in nature, the application of AISs [Farmer et al., 1986] is emerging as a very promising and advantageous solution to optimize and further reason out especially within the domain of computer security. In particular, AISs have been applied to different other domains such as software fault prediction [Catal and Diri, 2009], and musical genre classification [Doraisamy and Golzari, 2010]. An interesting approach for mapping the human immunity entities and process on to the development of computational models is presented in [Dasgupta, 2006]. Furthermore, several works focus on analyzing how immunological concepts may be applied to intrusion detection [Kim et al., 2007], pattern recognition and classification [Carter, 2000], anomaly detection, and distributed detection [Hofmeyr, 1999]. Authors in [Twycross and Aickelin, 2010] introduce a summary of some biological information fusion by means of AIS implementation. More specifically, the work focuses on multi–sensor data fusion for parallel and distributed systems. The objective of this proposal focuses on producing efficient connections between the observed data and thus inferring an optimized decision. In fact, Twycross et al. demonstrate the convenience of applying AIS–based techniques for these purposes. Similarly, the use of Denditric Cell Algorithm (DCA) for information fusion in the context of anomaly detection [Greensmith et al., 2010] becomes a promising solution to the detection of complex attacks as described in the subsection below.

Hence, a supervised learning is possible by using AISs [Watkins et al., 2004], research directions could be headed towards the application of unsupervised learning indeed [De Castro and Timmis, 2002, Timmis and Neal, 2001].

2.2.   On the Utility of Information Fusion Techniques over the Extraction of Relevancy of Events

Works on information fusion have been mainly focused on the enhancement of the analysis task and even on the employment of automatic procedures for real time analysis [Corona et al., 2009]. In particular, the information fusion techniques proposed so far in computer security have been mainly motivated by the fact that the information needed to perform such an analysis is mostly distributed within a multisensor environment. Moreover, these sensing units are typically located at different places, and the information they process is not homogeneous and is represented at different abstraction levels. In fact, information fusion has proven to provide with a very useful support for combining observations coming from different sources, as described in the following.

Current applications of information fusion to computer security range from providing automated classification of events and detection systems to effectively correlating different events which jointly constitute a multi-step attack happening within the monitored environment. For instance, the approach presented in [Giacinto et al., 2003] applies artificial NNs to test specific fusion rules. Each ANN is devoted to classify a different feature set related to the packet under test.

An information fusion framework for intrusion detection is proposed in [Bass, 2000] which prefigures the following levels: Data refinement, Object refinement, Situation refinement, Threat assessment, Resource management, and Knowledge. This conceptual framework serves as a guideline to other models.

Other fusion methods for intrusion classification rely on probability theory such as the DempsterShafer theory and Bayesian probability theory [Siaterlis and Maglaris, 2004].

Currently, information fusion research in computer security points out open issues regarding security data representation, i.e., the context of events, specially when taking a decision about the presence of an intrusion. A context-based representation of events is specially useful for further processing, and the definition of similarity metrics. The overview proposed in [Corona et al., 2009] states that data should be organized considering its context and proposes an uniform way to describe the context of data in terms of: (i) Where data is acquired (ii) When data is acquired, (iii) Which services are available and which data are they related to, (iv) Number of persons who will be able to access each service, (v) Which is the criticality of services, and (vi) Which is the sender and the receiver of each communication. Therefore, data representation should be driven by the knowledge of the relevant features. This sets the basis of other approaches based on predefined attack scenarios which usually apply a common language for formally defining such event patterns like a standardized format such as IDMEF. For example, a fusion model to correlate alerts is proposed in [Feng et al., 2007], which comprises the following stages: source preprocessing, alert data normalization, spacial alert fusion, and temporal alert fusion.

In summary, information fusion is emerging as a practical tool for obtaining more relevant, efficient and qualitatively better information out of the extremely large amount of data produced within a multisensor networking environment.

2.3. Common Correlation Expression. Our Approach

CEE [Mitre, 2011b] standardizes a common language and syntax for security information and events —it defines an event taxonomy for systematically categorizing events. Basically, *event categories* are established to form groups of events based on the categorizations of the events. Common event categories are listed as *CEE Tags* whereas the related events are grouped by *Tag Types*. CEE Dictionary and Event Taxonomy (CDET) helps to identify similar events through an event categorization methodology. CDET defines a collection of *CEE Tags*, which represents common event categories. Each *Tag Type* represents one possible way of grouping related events as part of the event categorization methodology. However, such methodology is conceived to identify only similar events and lacks on com-

Table 1. (a) Application domain concepts, and (b) extension of CEE [Mitre, 2011b] event taxonomy domain for systematically correlate events

	Domain	Concept
(a)	Sensor	Defined as a monitoring device which is focused on detecting events produced under a specific context.
	Event	Event is defined as a phenomenon produced when a particular security pre–condition becomes true. Generally such conditions denote established patterns extracted from previous interactions between two or more networking nodes.
	Event Record	The event's record consists of a set of attributes, which identifies a certain event's properties. CEE terminology refers to this domain as a collection of event fields namely event record. The specification of these attributes depends on the SIEM system.
	Event Category	Group of similar events that represents a possible way of grouping related events (*CEE Tag*). Each categorization is called *Tag Type* and is defined by a catego–rization methodology.
(b)	Event Aggregation	Event aggregation gathers together a collection of events which fulfill particular premises.
	Event Correlation	Event correlation must probabilistically define the relationship between a set of aggregated events.
	Correlation Record	The correlation's record consists of a set of attributes, which identifies a certain correlation's properties.
	Correlation Category	Represents a correlation produced as a response of the successful relationship between a set of attributes (namely *Correlation Tag*).

ponents regarding event correlation concepts. In this section, we propose an extension of the CEE taxonomy to include correlation specifications for categorization. Table 1–(a) depicts the most important concepts within our application domain.

A complete taxonomy should incorporate additional specifications to describe events related to complex multi–step attacks. Thus, we propose new terms to incorporate event correlation specification into the CDET categorization's methodology as defined in Table 1–(b).

Events are aggregated into the same correlation record when they hold the same values for a subset of attributes. A possible correlation record could comprise events with the same values for IP_{src}, IP_{dst}, $Port_{dst}$, $Sensor_{id}$, and $Sensor_{sid}$. Thus, a correlation record can be characterized by its categorization attributes or fields.

We then define the characteristics of a multi–step attack as the relationship between different correlation records. We have identified the following metrics to identify such dependencies:

- *Number of events* for each pair of $Sensor_{id}$, and $Sensor_{sid}$.

- Number of different *correlation categories* per tuple of $Sensor_{id}$, and $Sensor_{sid}$.

- Number of *occurrences* a categorization.

- Total number of different *sources and destinations IP* addresses.

- Total number of *events* and *categories*.

- Maximum and minimum slot of *time* in between events.

Additionally, we have identified several *Correlation Tags* that can be used to systematically categorize correlations between events according to the way events are aggregated. Aggregation of events can be categorized into the following tags: (i) based on the topology described by the interaction between a number C of computers, (ii) based on the nature of the attack, and (iii) on the order of the aggregation, as follows:

I Topological classification: A tuple T of events can describe the aggregation of t events in a $N : M$ topology where N is the number of different sources and M different receivers. According to the topology we can identify the following three kinds of attacks: (i) Unidirectional, (ii) Bidirectional, and (iii) Multi–directional. First, unidirectional attacks are those in which there are only one source and one destination (1:1). Additionally, there are two other interactions that can be categorized in this group, i.e., one source and multiple destinations (1:M), or multiple sources and one destination (N:1) on each tuple. Next, bidirectional attacks are those in which there are two sources (2:2). And multi–directional attacks are those in which there are multiple sources and destinations (N:M).

II Natural classification: According to its nature, an attack is defined to be: (i) insider, or (ii) outsider attack. Insider attacks are launched by any malicious machine which belongs to the network domain being monitored. Hence, passive countermeasures such as blocking connections can be adopted.On the contrary, countermeasures against outsider attacks require an active intervention.

III Ordinal classification: Relative to the importance of the order, an aggregated event can be classified into (i) non-relevant, or (ii) relevant.

For the sake of illustration, consider a correlation extracted from a sandbox in which a `Solaris` server was infected with the `Conficker` worm. Assume that the sandbox has reported several events comprising the following correlation categorization: *insider*, *multi–directional* in $1 : M$ and *non-relevant*. First, we know that the infected machine is located inside the Intranet, and therefore it is compromising other computers within the network. Second, since events generated by `Confiker` are stochastic, the order in which they were reported is not relevant for the correlation. On the other hand, an instantiation of the `Bredavi` Trojan within the same sandbox gives us a *bidirectional* topology, i.e. the attacker tends to contact the compromised system through a *backdoor* (one–direction) and, subsequently, the compromised system sends a reply back (bi–direction). In this case, the order of the events is tagged as *relevant* and the attack is originated by an outsider.

Important Remarks. Classifying multi–step correlations can help security operators to determine the nature of an attack and its impact. Regarding current and also future impact, the malware is actually evolving and so does the wide-spread adoption of automated malware generators. These malware generators facilitate the creation of new pieces of malware by reusing modules of other specimens. Additionally, other utilities and toolkits are used to generate different variants of the same piece of malware with slightly-different packing options or even exhibiting different behavior —both static and dynamic analysis strategies are then obfuscated and therefore concealed. Thus, it is part of our proposal to automate the identification of new encountered malware behavior according to the expected evolution of its ancestors.

2.4.   A Methodology for applying AIS to SIEM

Our goal is to build a complex adaptive system into a SIEM system, which already involves diverse and multiple interconnected elements. In particular, our proposed AIS-based correlation mechanism tends to provide the SIEM system for the capability to change and learn from experience. In this section we further elaborate on the essential concepts which lead to an AIS–based implementation in this domain, as introduced in a previous work [Suarez-Tangil et al., 2011], namely:

1. **Application domain**. We must first define the main assumptions and definitions within this particular application domain and the correlation problem to be solved.

   To this regard, event correlation can be perceived from two different viewpoints, according to its application domain: (i) that automatically learns without human supervision, and (ii) that requires an expert supervision. In our context, the correlation rules which were automatically extracted are then treated as *temporary* rules, until a consolidation process is carried out. On the other hand, expert supervision will guide the process to extract attack-related knowledge and form *permanent* correlation rules.

2. **Immunity–based approach**. As we will describe below, there are different techniques presented so far. To identify the most suitable AIS technique is not trivial in all instances.

   As we mentioned before, several works in the literature address optimization problems by using immunity–based approaches such as *dendric cell algorithm*, *gene libraries*, and *idiotypic networks* [Kim et al., 2007]. Most of the proposals are based on *immune network models* [Jerne, 1974][1], *clonal selection with mutation* [Kim and Bentley, 2001b], and *negative selection* [Kim and Bentley, 2001a]. Basically, immune network models are based on idiotypic networks, and tend to define models in which immune entities, also known as *B cells* [De Castro and Timmis, 2002], are interconnected in accordance with an affinity threshold. On one hand, clonal selection defines the strategy to mitigate an infection, i.e. by cloning the most successful antibodies. In particular, the maturation process introduces random variations over the antibodies cloned and thus increasing the probability to detect unknown behaviors. On the other hand, negative selection is used after the maturation phase, aiming at identifying non–self cells from self–cells, and also at deleting self–reacting cells. This algorithm is used for pattern recognition problems to obtain new patterns from available knowledge.

3. **Representation**. We must establish an interpreted codification for the immune entities and the elements involved in the correlation context.

---

[1]The immune network theory was first introduced by Jerne [Jerne, 1974] as a way to explain the memory and learning capabilities exhibited by the immune system. This theory has inspired a subfield of optimization algorithms as many other fields unrelated to biological immunology.

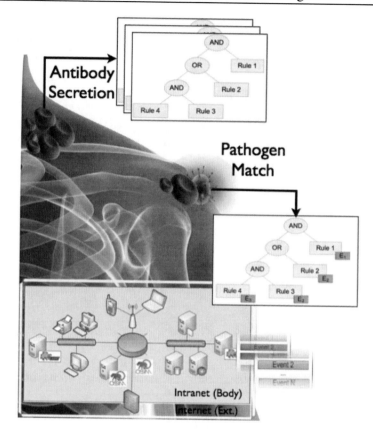

Figure 2. A mapping between the entities of the human immune system and those in our event correlation model.

A representation for an event correlation model in terms of its similarities with the human immune system was previously discussed in [Suarez-Tangil et al., 2011]. In that work, a mapping between the entities of the human immune and those in the correlation model was proposed (see Figure 2 for details). In particular, artificial immune theory defines the concept of secreting proteins (correlation categorizations) as the mechanism used to detect non–self pathogens —malicious activity in the form of events— which in turn are destroyed by antibodies (represented as rule patterns). Proteins constitute the parameters to monitor (as described in Section 2.3) and then allow us to distinguish between self and non–self behaviors.

4. **Adaptive immune algorithm.** Finally, we define the immune algorithm to automatically generate correlation categorizations. We propose an immune algorithm based on the most popular immunological approaches, as described in Section 3 This algorithm elaborates on a novel adaptive component for the proposed ILS module.

3. A Novel Architecture for an Artificial Immunity-based SIEM System

In this section, we introduce a novel approach to extend and enhance traditional SIEM systems based on artificial immune network theory. Our three-layer architecture comprises the following building blocks (separated with solid lines in Fig. 3):

- The physical barrier offers protection against pathogens attacking the system from outside, like some sort of prevention layer.

- The Innate Immune System (present in humans at birth) deploys immune agents which are in charge of protecting the system against invaders as well as providing pattern recognition mechanisms.

- The Adaptive Immune System (included in the ILS) defines the logic of the biological functions and components to learn, adapt and memorize antigens and also to secrete the appropriate anti–body (i.e. which are represented by the correlation rules in our domain).

3.1. The Physical Barrier and the Innate Immune System

Both together, the physical barrier and the innate immune system, already have their equivalences in current SIEM systems.

The physical barrier, placed "in-line", represents a first layer of protection and compiles a number of devices, either hardware or software such as firewalls, VPNs, and IPSs, aimed at protecting the intranet from malicious activity. For instance, unauthorized incoming traffic is not only blocked, but also logged and reported to the SIEM. In other words, these devices prevent pathogens e.g. bacteria and viruses from entering the organism, i.e. the intranet.

A second layer of protection consists then in the innate immune system. The Intranet deploys this layer by monitoring and detecting the encountered malicious activity. To this regard, IDSs are strategically located within intranet (most in the way of network IDS — NIDS, switches and routers) and also on simple hosts or servers (HIDS). These devices must "know" as many attack signatures or patterns as possible. Alerts (the innate responses) from these devices are usually triggered when any monitored packet matches a signature (or an immune pattern).

3.2. The Adaptive Immune System

In our domain, the adaptive immune system is equivalent to the new SIEM component called ILS. Its responsibility ranges from introducing intuition and cognition into the SIEM to allow immunological memory. In particular, ILS will provide (i) more efficient correlation rules, (ii) adaptive immunological memory, and (iii) more effective incident response.

We envision ILS as a three–phase protocol (separated with dashed lines in Fig. 3) which combines traditional IDS concepts, data mining, honeynets and the expert supervision (if strictly needed), as follows:

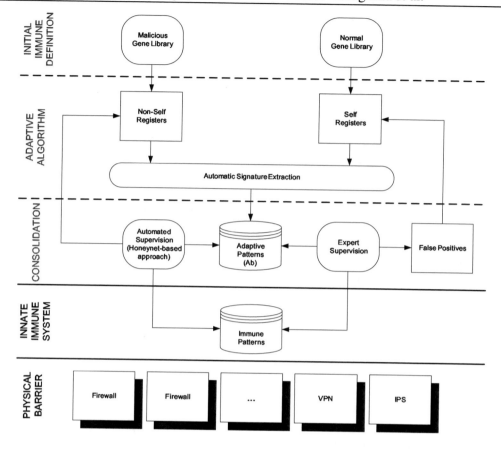

Figure 3. A three–layer architecture which combines traditional IDS concepts, data mining, honeynets and, just when strictly needed, the security expert supervision.

I **Initial innate immune definition**. In this phase, the expert must define a range of values for the collection of correlation categorizations.

II **Adaptive algorithm**. The adaptive algorithm produces a number of correlation categorizations that will be used to learn new correlation rules.

III **Adaptive immunological memory consolidation**. New correlation categorizations are consolidated in this phase.

Sections below further elaborate on these three ILS phases.

3.2.1. Initial Innate Immune Definition

As a SIEM system includes a series of tools and methods to defend an organization from intrusions, so the biological innate immune system receives at birth. In our domain, it is expected that sensors recognize and respond the unauthorized packets at least in a generic way. Thus, a series of correlation categorizations must be defined during the initial phase.

Initial values will act as generic discriminators for both self cells and non-self cells. Now, we must decide how to implement the appropriate value for each correlation categorization. To this regard, existing repositories collect known attacks and their associated correlation rules. Generally, these repositories are also known as *Gene Libraries*, and they are essential for the process below.

Therefore, we define two libraries, namely malicious and normal behavior. The former consists of misuse patterns whereas the latter contains the anomaly–detection data. On one hand, misuse patterns can be extracted from well–known attack rule definition sets, such as Vulnerability Research Team (VRT), Snort rules [Team, 2011] specially suitable for defining network anomaly rules, antivirus signatures [Le Pennec et al., 2005] when looking for host anomaly detection rules, and/or repositories of high-level languages which describe computer–specific attacks like STATL [Eckmann et al., 2002] or CAPEC [Mitre, 2011a]. A knowledge database can be easily extracted to conform with the libraries.

On the other hand, heuristics extracted from an anomaly–based detection can be also defined here [Lee and Stolfo, 2000, Davis and Clark, 2011]. For example, consider an OS-SIM[1] in which misuse patterns are instantiated. Consider that we are using the notation defined in Section 2.3 We could define as a normal activity to log in to a workstation as long as the number of attempts does not exceed a certain threshold t, being $t \in Num.$ *of occurrences–per–categorization*. A categorization here could be established as the number of connections to a telnet, ftp, smtp, or http port. Hence, the appropriate OSSIM's sensor, e.g. OSSIM's *telnet option decoder*, will report an event every time a telnet connection is established. Different values for the threshold —for network probe, scan, flood, DoS, root to local (R2L) and user to root (U2R) rates,— have been extensively analyzed in the literature [Davis and Clark, 2011].

3.2.2. Adaptive Algorithm for an Automatic Signature Extraction

The main objective of the adaptive algorithm is to learn new correlation rules from observing the random adaptations of both normal and malicious gene libraries. Foundations of this algorithm rely on the AIS principles, as follows:

1. **Antibody secretion**. Antibodies are those patterns responsible of identifying a specific sequence of events (i.e. the antigen). Thus, an antibody represents the rule capable of recognizing a certain correlation pattern. In this stage, antibodies are generated by random combinations of the attributes stored in the `Malicious Gene Library` as well as by the mutations occurred to their values.

2. **Negative selection**. Negative selection eliminates inappropriate and immature antibodies. Basically, self-reacting rules are deleted from the set of adaptive candidates, and therefore ensuring that new antibodies will not detect self-cells by mistake. This algorithm applies the knowledge (Normal Gene Library) which was defined during the initial innate immune definition. Additionally, *Danger Theory* can be used here as an intriguing mechanism for reducing the number of false alerts, for example, by

---

[1]OSSIM [AlienVault, 2011] is an open source SIEM implementation which centralizes the detecting and monitoring of the security events within an organization.

responding more aggressively against pathogens based on the correlation of danger signals [Aickelin and Greensmith, 2007].

3. **Pathogen matching**. Pathogens are harmful agents causing disease to their hosts. Pathogen matching is the process in which pathogens are identified by antibodies and is part of the intrusion detection process. Matching event correlation rules has been discussed in [Suarez-Tangil et al., 2009].

4. **Clonal selection**. Clonal selection based on affinity mutation aims at optimizing the pattern recognition algorithm by cloning the most interesting correlation rules and mutating its attributes afterwards.

Note that the above AIS–based techniques will produce a number of randomly generated correlation rules. However, most promising rules will be distinguished during the following consolidation process.

3.2.3.   Adaptive Immunological Memory Consolidation

Correlation rules, obtained automatically, are now consolidated based on two different criteria: (1) by automatic techniques and, just when strictly needed, (2) by using the expertise of security administrators. Consolidation of a rule involves the process of evaluating the convenience of the generated correlations. In case of a rule is likely to detect a certain intrusion, then it will be exported to the immune system as part of the learning process. Otherwise, the rule will continue adapting its definition until consolidation is achieved.

On one hand, we define the automatic consolidation process as follows. Rules generated in the previous phase are automatically evaluated and a likelihood of matching a potential correlation is calculated. Likelihood of matching determines the probability of matching a collection of events as a result of an unknown attack. Only those rules with likelihood above a threshold will be consolidated. To this regard, rules are first deployed in a sandbox which has been exposed to numerous events launched from a network telescope or *darknet* (a number of unused network addresses). In addition, traffic incoming the darknet is, by definition, unrequested and therefore likely to be generated by an intruder. The more similarity between the rule with any of the events produced in the darknet, the more likelihood of the rule. However, if none of the immunological rules matches, then the immunological memory (associated to each correlation) will be decreased.

Furthermore, honeynets appear as the best candidate to assist the automated consolidation process. A honeynet is a group of networking nodes used to trap malware by simulating to be unprotected and vulnerable, so that attackers' activities can be studied. The key idea is to validate the generated categorizations using the non–self activity reported on the darknet as part of a honeynet.

On the other hand, the expert can manually inspect and validate the correlation rules in terms of their accuracy. In any case, correlations that were not consolidated by the expert and/or failed during the automatic consolidation will be discarded.

```
Data: Normal and Malicious Categories
Result: Correlation Rules
// Expert and Automated self/non-self discrimination
GenLibrary ← InitialInnateImmuneDefinition;
while SIEM is learning do
    thread
        MemoryCells ← AutomatedSignatureExtraction(GenLibrary);
        ConsolidatedRules ← AutomatedConsolidation(MemoryCells, Pathogens);
    end
    thread
        // Honeypot--based Sandbox Pathogens ← PathogenGeneration;
        FeatureExtraction(Pathogens);
        Clustering(Pathogens);
    end
    thread
        ExpertSupervision(ConsolidatedRules);
    end
end
```

Algorithm 1: Threefold approach for based on two paradigms: (i) automated and (ii) expert supervision.

4. Discussion

Our implementation efforts focus on integrating the proposed AIS-based framework into an open source SIEM such as OSSIM [AlienVault, 2011]. As mentioned before, implementation can be tackled according to the principles defined on Section , or based on the two criteria above: (i) with an automatic supervision or (ii) requiring the expert supervision, as described in Algorithm 1.

According to the former, the automatic signature extraction principle is based on randomly generating event correlation rules. Source of randomness is seeded not only using elements from the Gene Library [Kim et al., 2007] but also using attributes from the strongest consolidated antibodies. Affinity maturation based on the principles of mutation and selection can be applied here to reach the strongest antibodies.

Secondly, automatic supervision of event correlation rules can be driven by honeypot-based sandboxing. For instance work introduces in [Yegneswaran et al., 2005] presents a system, called Nemean, for automatic generation of intrusion signatures for NIDS from honeynet packet traces. Based on this approach, we define *detectors* as the randomly generated rules. Algorithm 2 describes detector's life cycle as an essential process for correlation rules consolidation. Basically, generated detectors are considered naive until rules are consolidated. If a pathogen matches with a detector, then the latter is incorporated into the immunological memory.

Finally, security experts may optionally supervise the learning process in order to reinforce the consolidation process.

Data: Pathogens, Affinity Mutation, Normal and Malicious Gen Library
Result: Memory Cells

$Detectors \leftarrow RandomGeneration(GenLibraries)$
foreach $NaiveDetector \leftarrow in\ Detectors$ **do**
  if $match(NaiveDetector, Pathogen)$ **then**
    $AddForConsolidation(NaiveDetector);$
    $AddForClonalSelection(NaiveDetector, AffinityMutation);$
  else
    $Dies(NaiveDetector);$
  end
end

Algorithm 2: Automatic signature extraction for event correlation rules.

Conclusion

SIEM technology, focused on developing effective methods and tools to assist network administrators during the whole network security management, is still evolving rapidly. Both, lack of standards and adaptability, hinder even more the analysis of the huge amount of security information collected every day. Similarly, novel multi-step malware is one of the major threats in the Internet today. Several techniques for an automated analysis of malware have been proposed so far. Sandboxing is, in this regard, a powerful tool to accomplish dynamic analysis. However, this and other techniques fail on dynamically establishing cross correlation relationships among traces recorded on multiple affected devices.

In this chapter, we introduce a novel SIEM architecture based on a bio-inspired technique, namely AIS, to adaptively learn new correlation rules and reactively face multi–step attacks. Our SIEM system is designed to learn even from unknown malware. Our proposal comprises various strategies already used in intrusion detection, data mining, honeynets analysis and, when strictly needed, the expert supervision. Our hope is that this new framework will, directly or indirectly, inspire new directions on applying intelligence to security event correlation.

References

[Aguirre and Alonso, 2012] Aguirre, I. and Alonso, S. (2012). Improving the automation of security information management: A collaborative approach. *IEEE Security Privacy*, 10(1):55–59.

[Ahmad et al., 2009] Ahmad, I., Abdullah, A. B., and Alghamdi, A. S. (2009). Artificial neural network approaches to intrusion detection: a review. In Proceedings of the 8th Wseas international conference on telecommunications and informatics, pages 200–205. WSEAS.

[Aickelin and Greensmith, 2007] Aickelin, U. and Greensmith, J. (2007). Sensing danger: Innate immunology for intrusion detection. Information Security Technical Report, 12(4):218–227.

[AlienVault, 2011] AlienVault (Visited November 2011). Open source security information management (ossim). http://www.ossim.net.

[Almgren et al., 2008] Almgren, M., Lindqvist, U., and Jonsson, E. (2008). A multi-sensor model to improve automated attack detection. In Recent Advances in Intrusion Detection, volume 5230, pages 291–310. Springer Berlin / Heidelberg.

[Anuar et al., 2010] Anuar, N., Papadaki, M., Furnell, S., and Clarke, N. (2010). An investigation and survey of response options for Intrusion Response Systems (IRSs). In Information Security for South Africa (ISSA), 2010, pages 1–8. IEEE.

[Bass, 2000] Bass, T. (2000). Intrusion detection systems and multisensor data fusion. Commun. ACM, 43:99–105.

[Bitacora, 2011] Bitacora (Visited November 2011). System of centralization, management and exploitation of a company's events. http://bitacora.s21sec.com/.

[Carter, 2000] Carter, J. H. (2000. The immune system as a model for pattern recognition and classification. *Journal of the American Medical Informatics Association: JAMIA*, 7(1):28–41.

[Catal and Diri, 2009] Catal, C. and Diri, B. (2009). Investigating the effect of dataset size, metrics sets, and feature selection techniques on software fault prediction problem. *Information Sciences*, 179(8):1040–1058.

[Cheung et al., 2003] Cheung, S., Lindqvist, U., and Fong, M. (2003). Modeling multistep cyber attacks for scenario recognition. In Procs. of the DARPA Information Survivability Conference and Exposition, volume 1, pages 284–292.

[Corona et al., 2009] Corona, I., Giacinto, G., Mazzariello, C., Roli, F., and Sansone, C. (2009). Information fusion for computer security: State of the art and open issues. Inf. Fusion, 10:274–284.

[Dasgupta, 2006] Dasgupta, D. (2006. Advances in artificial immune systems. *IEEE Comp. Intelligent Magazine*, 1(4):40–49.

[Davis and Clark, 2011] Davis, J. J. and Clark, A. J. (2011). Data preprocessing for anomaly based network intrusion detection: A review. *Computers & Security*, 30(6-7):353–375.

[De Castro and Timmis, 2002] De Castro, L. and Timmis, J. (2002). Artificial immune systems: a new computational intelligence approach. Springer Verlag.

[Doraisamy and Golzari, 2010] Doraisamy, S. and Golzari, S. (2010). Automatic Musical Genre Classification and Artificial Immune Recognition System. Advances in Music Information Retrieval, page 391.

[Eckmann et al., 2002] Eckmann, S., Vigna, G., and Kemmerer, R. (2002). Statl: An attack language for state-based intrusion detection. *Journal of Computer Security*, 10(1/2):71–104.

[ESM, 2011] ESM, A. (Visited November 2011).   Enterprise security manager. http://www.arcsight.com/products/products-esm/.

[Farmer et al., 1986] Farmer, J. D., Packard, N. H., and Perelson, A. S. (1986). The immune system, adaptation, and machine learning. *Physica D: Nonlinear Phenomena*, 22(1-3):187–204.

[Feng et al., 2007] Feng, C., Peng, J., Qiao, H., and Rozenblit, J. W. (2007). Alert fusion for a computer host based intrusion detection system. In Procs. of the 14th Annual IEEE Int. Conf. and Workshops on the Engineering of Computer-Based Systems, pages 433–440. *IEEE Computer Society.*

[Giacinto et al., 2003] Giacinto, G., Roli, F., and Didaci, L. (2003). Fusion of multiple classifiers for intrusion detection in computer networks. *Pattern Recogn. Lett.*, 24:1795–1803.

[Golovko and Kochurko, 2005] Golovko, V. and Kochurko, P. (2005). Intrusion recognition using neural networks. In IEEE Intelligent Data Acquisition and Advanced Computing Systems: Technology and Applications, pages 108–111. IDAACS.

[Greensmith et al., 2010] Greensmith, J., Aickelin, U., and Tedesco, G. (2010). Information fusion for anomaly detection with the dendritic cell algorithm. *Information Fusion*, 11(1):21–34.

[Hofmeyr, 1999] Hofmeyr, S. (1999). An immunological model of distributed detection and its application to computer security. PhD thesis, University of New Mexico.

[Jerne, 1974] Jerne, N. K. (1974). Towards a network theory of the immune system. *Ann. Immunol.*, 125C:373–389.

[Kim and Bentley, 2001a] Kim, J. and Bentley, P. (2001a). An evaluation of negative selection in an artificial immune system for network intrusion detection. In Proc. of GECCO, pages 1330–1337. Citeseer.

[Kim and Bentley, 2001b] Kim, J. and Bentley, P. (2001b). Towards an artificial immune system for network intrusion detection: An investigation of clonal selection with a negative selection operator. In Proc. of the 2001 Congress on Evolutionary Computation, volume 2, pages 1244–1252. IEEE.

[Kim et al., 2007] Kim, J., Bentley, P., Aickelin, U., Greensmith, J., Tedesco, G., and Twycross, J. (2007). Immune system approaches to intrusion detection–a review. *Natural computing*, 6(4):413–466.

[Le Pennec et al., 2005] Le Pennec, J., Hericourt, O., et al. (2005). Method and system for retrieving an anti-virus signature from one or a plurality of virus-free certificate authorities. US Patent 6,976,271.

[Lee and Stolfo, 2000] Lee, W. and Stolfo, S. (2000). A framework for constructing features and models for intrusion detection systems. ACM Transactions on Information and System, 3(4):227–261.

[Lei and Ghorbani, 2004] Lei, J. Z. and Ghorbani, A. (2004). Network intrusion detection using an improved competitive learning neural network. In Proc. of second annual conf. on communication networks and services research, pages 190–197. IEEE Computer Society.

[Lippmann and Cunningham, 2000] Lippmann, R. P. and Cunningham, R. K. (2000). Improving intrusion detection performance using keyword selection and neural networks. Computer Networks, 34(4):597–603. Recent Advances in Intrusion Detection Systems.

[Liu et al., 2008] Liu, Z., Wang, C., and Chen, S. (2008). Correlating multi-step attack and constructing attack scenarios based on attack pattern modeling. In Procs. of the ISA 2008 Int. Conf. on Information Security and Assurance, pages 214–219.

[Mitre, 2011b] Mitre (2011b). Common event expression. Technical report, The MITRE Corporation. http://cee.mitre.org/docs/CEE_Profile_Specification-v0.6.pdf.

[Mitre, 2011a] Mitre (Visited November 2011a). Common attack pattern enumeration and classification. Technical report, The MITRE Corporation. http://capec.mitre.org/.

[netForensics, 2011] netForensics (Visited November 2011). nfx sim one. http://www.netforensics.com/products/security_information_management/SIM_One/.

[Nicolett and Kavanagh, 2011] Nicolett, M. and Kavanagh, K. M. (2011). Magic quadrant for security information and event management. Gartner RAS Core Research Note G, 21245:1–31.

[Parmelee, 2010] Parmelee, M. C. (2010). Toward the semantic interoperability of the security information and event management lifecycle. In Working Notes for the 2010 AAAI Workshop on Intelligent Security (SecArt), page 18. The MITRE Corporation.

[Ripley, 1994] Ripley, B. (1994). Neural networks and related methods for classification. Journal of the Royal Statistical Society, 56(3):409–456.

[Rossow et al., 2011] Rossow, C., Dietrich, C., Bos, H., and Cavallaro, L. (2011). Sandnet: Network traffic analysis of malicious software. In Proceedings of the First Workshop on Building Analysis Datasets and Gathering Experience Returns for Security, pages 76–86. ACM.

[RSA, 2011] RSA (Visited November 2011). envision. http://www.rsa.com/node.aspx?id=3170.

[Sadoddin and Ghorbani, 2006] Sadoddin, R. and Ghorbani, A. (2006). Alert correlation survey: framework and techniques. In Proceedings of the 2006 International Conference on Privacy, Security and Trust, pages 1–10. ACM.

[SenSage, 2011] SenSage (Visited November 2011). Sensage siem solution. http://www.sensage.com/.

[Sentinel, 2011] Sentinel, N. (Visited November 2011). Sentinel. http://www.novell.com/products/sentinel/.

[Sheyner et al., 2002] Sheyner, O., Haines, J., Jha, S., Lippmann, R., and Wing, J. M. (2002). Automated generation and analysis of attack graphs. In Procs. of the 2002 IEEE Symposium on Security and Privacy, pages 273–. *IEEE Computer Society.*

[Siaterlis and Maglaris, 2004] Siaterlis, C. and Maglaris, B. (2004). Towards multisensor data fusion for dos detection. In Procs. of the 2004 ACM symposium on Applied computing, pages 439–446. ACM.

[Suarez-Tangil et al., 2009] Suarez-Tangil, G., Palomar, E., Fuentes, J. D., Blasco, J., and Ribagorda, A. (2009). Automatic rule generation based on genetic programming for event correlation. In Computational Intelligence in Security for Information, Advances in Soft Computing, pages 127–134, Burgos, Spain. Heidelberg, Springer Berlin.

[Suarez-Tangil et al., 2011] Suarez-Tangil, G., Palomar, E., Pastrana, S., and Ribagorda, A. (2011). Artificial immunity-based correlation system. In Procs. of the Int. Conf. on Security and Cryptography (SECRYPT), page 99.

[Team, 2011] Team, V. R. (Visited November 2011). Vrt certified snort rules. http://www.snort.org/snort-rules.

[Timmis and Neal, 2001] Timmis, J. and Neal, M. (2001). A resource limited artificial immune system for data analysis. *Knowledge-Based Systems*, 14(3–4):121–130.

[Twycross and Aickelin, 2010] Twycross, J. and Aickelin, U. (2010). Information fusion in the immune system. *Information Fusion*, 11(1):35–44.

[Wang et al., 2010] Wang, L., Ghorbani, A., and Li, Y. (2010). Automatic multi-step attack pattern discovering. *International Journal of Network Security*, 10(2):142–152.

[Watkins et al., 2004] Watkins, A., Timmis, J., and Boggess, L. (2004). Artificial Immune Recognition System (AIRS): An Immune-Inspired Supervised Learning Algorithm. Genetic Programming and Evolvable Machines, 5(3):291–317.

[Yegneswaran et al., 2005] Yegneswaran, V., Giffin, J., Barford, P., and Jha, S. (2005). An architecture for generating semantics-aware signatures. In Proceedings of the 14th conference on USENIX Security Symposium-Volume 14, pages 7–7. USENIX Association.

[Zhang et al., 2005] Zhang, C., Jiang, J., and Kamel, M. (2005). Intrusion detection using hierarchical neural networks. *Pattern Recognition Letters*, 26(6):779–791.

INDEX

M

N

O

P

Q

R

S

W

X